THE SYRIAN CONFLICT'S IMPACT ON INTERNATIONAL LAW

Written as the decade-long Syrian conflict nears an end, this is the first book-length treatment of how the Syrian war has changed international law. In *The Syrian Conflict's Impact on International Law*, the authors explain the history of the current conflict in Syria and discuss the principles and process of customary international law formation and the phenomenon of accelerated formation of customary international law known as Grotian moments. They then explore specific examples, including how use of force against ISIS in Syria has changed the law of self-defense against non-state actors, how the allied air strikes in response to Syria's use of chemical weapons have changed the law of humanitarian intervention, and others. This book seeks to contribute both to understanding the concept of accelerated formation of customary international law and the specific ways the Syria conflict has led to development of new norms and principles in several areas of international law.

MICHAEL P. SCHARF is the Dean of the Law School and the Joseph C. Hostetler–BakerHostetler Professor of Law at Case Western Reserve University. He serves as Managing Director of the Public International Law and Policy Group, a Nobel Peace Prize–nominated NGO. He has led USAID-funded transitional justice projects in Uganda, Cote d'Ivoire, Libya, and Turkey (for Syria), and maritime piracy projects in Kenya, Mauritius, and the Seychelles. Scharf is the author of over 100 scholarly articles and nineteen books, four of which have won national book of the year honors. Since 2013, Scharf has been the producer and host of *Talking Foreign Policy*, a radio program broadcast on WCPN 90.3 FM and other NPR affiliates across the country.

MILENA STERIO is the Charles R. Emrick Jr.–Calfee Halter & Griswold Professor of Law at Cleveland-Marshall College of Law. Previously, she was an associate in the New York City firm of Cleary, Gottlieb, Steen & Hamilton, and an adjunct law professor at Cornell, where she taught in the International War Crimes Clinic. She has published numerous law review articles and six books. Professor Sterio is an editor of the prestigious IntLawGrrls blog. In the spring of 2013, Professor Sterio was a Fulbright Scholar in Baku, Azerbaijan, at Baku State University.

DR. PAUL R. WILLIAMS holds the Rebecca I. Grazier Professorship in Law and International Relations at American University where he teaches in the School of International Service and at the Washington College of Law. Dr. Williams is also the co-founder of the Public International Law & Policy Group (PILPG), a *pro bono* law firm providing legal assistance to states and governments involved in peace negotiations, post-conflict constitution drafting, and the prosecution of war criminals. As a world-renowned peace negotiation lawyer, Dr. Williams has assisted over two dozen parties in major international peace negotiations and has advised numerous parties on the drafting and implementation of post-conflict constitutions. Dr. Williams has authored six books on various topics concerning international law, and has published over three dozen scholarly articles on topics of international law and policy.

The Syrian Conflict's Impact on International Law

MICHAEL P. SCHARF

Case Western Reserve University School of Law

MILENA STERIO

Cleveland-Marshall School of Law

PAUL R. WILLIAMS

American University Washington College of Law

CAMBRIDGE UNIVERSITY PRESS

CAMBRIDGE
UNIVERSITY PRESS

University Printing House, Cambridge CB2 8BS, United Kingdom

One Liberty Plaza, 20th Floor, New York, NY 10006, USA

477 Williamstown Road, Port Melbourne, VIC 3207, Australia

314–321, 3rd Floor, Plot 3, Splendor Forum, Jasola District Centre, New Delhi – 110025, India

79 Anson Road, #06–04/06, Singapore 079906

Cambridge University Press is part of the University of Cambridge.

It furthers the University's mission by disseminating knowledge in the pursuit of education, learning, and research at the highest international levels of excellence.

www.cambridge.org
Information on this title: www.cambridge.org/9781108491532
DOI: 10.1017/9781108863650

First published 2020

A catalogue record for this publication is available from the British Library.

Library of Congress Cataloging-in-Publication Data
NAMES: Scharf, Michael P., 1963– author. | Sterio, Milena, author. | Williams, Paul R., 1965– author.
TITLE: The Syrian conflict's impact on international law / Michael P. Scharf, Case Western Reserve University, Ohio; Milena Sterio, Cleveland-Marshall School of Law; Paul R. Williams, American University Washington College of Law.
DESCRIPTION: Cambridge, United Kingdom ; New York, NY, USA Cambridge University Press, 2020. | Includes bibliographical references and index.
IDENTIFIERS: LCCN 2019052946 (print) | LCCN 2019052947 (ebook) | ISBN 9781108491532 (hardback) | ISBN 9781108798440 (paperback) | ISBN 9781108863650 (epub)
SUBJECTS: LCSH: Syria–History–Civil War, 2011–Law and legislation.
CLASSIFICATION: LCC KZ6795.S97 S33 2020 (print) | LCC KZ6795.S97 (ebook) | DDC 341.6–DC23
LC record available at https://lccn.loc.gov/2019052946
LC ebook record available at https://lccn.loc.gov/2019052947

ISBN 978-1-108-49153-2 Hardback
ISBN 978-1-108-79844-0 Paperback

Contents

Authors' Biographies   *page* vii

Acknowledgments   xi

Prologue   xiii

1   Introduction   1

2   Historical Background   4

3   Accelerated Formation of Customary International Law   19

4   Use of Force in Self-Defense against Non-State Actors   29

5   Humanitarian Intervention in Response to Use of
     Chemical Weapons   59

6   Transformation of Accountability Paradigms   90

7   The Syrian Migration Crisis   110

8   International Law and the Syrian Peace Process   133

9   Conclusion   173

Appendix The Chautauqua Blueprint for a Statute for a Syrian
Extraordinary Tribunal to Prosecute Atrocity Crimes   181

Index   213

Authors' Biographies

Michael P. Scharf is the Dean of Case Western Reserve University School of Law, and the Joseph C. Hostetler–BakerHostetler Professor of Law. He is the host of *Talking Foreign Policy*, a radio program broadcast on WCPN 90.3 FM. In addition, Scharf serves as managing director of the Public International Law & Policy Group, a Nobel Peace Prize–nominated NGO. Scharf has led USAID-funded transitional justice missions to the Ivory Coast, Libya, and Uganda; he headed the Blue Ribbon Committee that drafted a statute for a War Crimes Tribunal for Syrian atrocities; he served as Special Assistant to the Prosecutor of the Cambodia Genocide Tribunal; and he served as a member of the international team of experts that provided training to the judges of the Iraqi High Tribunal. During the first Bush and Clinton administrations, Scharf served in the Office of the Legal Adviser of the US Department of State, where he held the positions of Attorney-Adviser for Law Enforcement and Intelligence, Attorney-Adviser for United Nations Affairs, and delegate to the United Nations Human Rights Commission. In 1993, he was awarded the State Department's Meritorious Honor Award "in recognition of superb performance and exemplary leadership" in relation to his role in the establishment of the International Criminal Tribunal for the former Yugoslavia. Scharf graduated from Duke University School of Law, with Order of the Coif and High Honors. He was a judicial clerk to Judge Gerald Bard Tjoflat on the US Court of Appeals for the Eleventh Circuit. He is the author of more than 100 scholarly articles and nineteen books, including *The International Criminal Tribunal for Rwanda*, which was awarded the American Society of International Law's Certificate of Merit for outstanding book, and *Enemy of the State: The Trial and Execution of Saddam Hussein*, which won the International Association of Penal Law's book-of-the-year award. His last five books have been published by Cambridge University Press. Dean Scharf continues to teach international law and was ranked as seventeenth most-cited author in the field since 2010 by the Leiter study.

Milena Sterio is Associate Dean for Faculty Enrichment and the Charles R. Emrick, Jr.–Calfee Halter & Griswold Professor at Cleveland-Marshall College of Law, Cleveland State University. Professor Sterio earned her law degree, *magna cum laude*, from Cornell Law School in 2002. At Cornell, she was Order of the Coif, general editor of the *Cornell International Law Journal* and a member of Phi Beta Kappa. In 2003, she earned a master's degree, *cum laude*, in private international law from the University Paris 1–Pantheon–Sorbonne; in 2002, she earned a *maitrise en droit franco-americain cum laude*, in political science and French literature from Rutgers College, New Brunswick, New Jersey. Before joining the faculty of Cleveland-Marshall, she was an associate in the New York City firm of Cleary, Gottlieb, Steen & Hamilton, and an adjunct law professor at Cornell, where she taught in the International War Crimes Clinic. Her research interests are in the field of international law, international criminal law, international human rights, law of the seas, and in particular maritime piracy, as well as private international law. She has published in the *American University Law Review*, the *Connecticut International Law Journal*, the *Fordham International Law Journal*, the *Cardozo Journal of International and Comparative Law*, the *Denver Journal of International Law and Policy*, the *Florida Journal of International Law*, and the *UC Davis of International Law and Policy*. She is the author of several books, including two that have been published by Cambridge University Press: *Prosecuting Maritime Piracy: Domestic Solutions to International Crimes* (with M. Scharf and M. Newton), and *The Legacy of Ad Hoc Tribunals in International Criminal Law: Assessing the ICTY's and ICTR's Most Significant Legal Accomplishments* (with M. Scharf), which won the Association Internationale de Droit Pénal's 2019 Book of the Year Award for Scholarly Contribution to the Field. Professor Sterio is one of six permanent editors of the prestigious IntLawGrrls blog.

Paul R. Williams holds the Rebecca I. Grazier Professorship in Law and International Relations at American University where he teaches in the School of International Service and at the Washington College of Law. Dr. Williams is also the cofounder and president of the Public International Law & Policy Group (PILPG), a *pro bono* law firm providing legal assistance to states and governments involved in peace negotiations, post-conflict constitution drafting, and the prosecution of war criminals. As a world-renowned peace negotiation lawyer, Dr. Williams has assisted over two dozen parties in major international peace negotiations and has advised numerous parties on the drafting and implementation of post-conflict constitutions. Several of Dr. Williams's *pro bono* government clients throughout the world joined together to nominate him and PILPG for the Nobel Peace Prize. For the past six years Dr. Williams has been advising the Syrian opposition in the Geneva and Astana peace negotiations. During the peace negotiations, Dr. Williams has worked with the opposition on matters of negotiation strategy as well as proposals for a transitional governing body, a constitution-drafting process, power-sharing arrangements, human rights protections, the interpretation of UN Security Council Resolutions, the establishment of ceasefires and de-confliction zones, and the enforcement of OPCW findings. Dr. Williams has also advised them on matters of transitional justice and prosecution of war crimes. Dr. Williams has served as a senior associate with the Carnegie Endowment for International Peace, as well as an Attorney-Adviser for European and Canadian affairs at the US Department of State, Office of the Legal Adviser. He received his JD from Stanford Law School and his PhD from the University of Cambridge. Dr. Williams is a sought-after international law and policy expert. He is frequently interviewed by major print and broadcast media and regularly contributes op-eds to major newspapers. Dr. Williams has authored six books on various topics concerning international law and has published over three dozen scholarly articles on topics of international law and policy. Dr. Williams is a member of the Council of Foreign Relations and has served as a counsellor on the Executive Council of the American Society of International Law.

Acknowledgments

Several people deserve special recognition for the assistance they have furnished us on this book project. First, we wish to thank John Berger, the recently retired acquisitions editor of Cambridge University Press, who supported our vision for this book. We also wish to thank our principal editors at Cambridge University Press, Joshua Penney and Laura Blake who guided us through the publication process. We are also appreciative of the institutional support provided by Case Western Reserve University School of Law, Cleveland-Marshall Law School, and the Public International Law & Policy Group (PILPG). We also wish to thank from Cambridge University Press, Joshua Penney, Martin Barr, and Mathew Rohitt, who improved our text in innumerable ways, and Alexandra Raleigh, who assisted with proofreading. Finally, we offer special thanks to the PILPG Syria Team and the following Cox International Law Center Fellows and members of PILPG who provided us invaluable research assistance: Philip Albers, Christopher Glass, Jessica Levy, Amanda Makhoul, Luke Robert Palmer, Sophie Pearlman, and Taylor Frank.

Prologue

This is an academic book, but the authors are not strictly academics and our relation to the subject matter is not entirely scholarly. The three of us are the directors of the Public International Law and Policy Group, a Nobel Peace Prize–nominated NGO that for the past nine years has been involved in the Syrian peace process and in the effort to establish accountability for atrocities committed during the Syrian conflict.

For two of us (Scharf and Williams), the origins of this book began in June 2013 at an outdoor cafe on what started out as a sunny, languorous afternoon in one of the great cities of the world, Istanbul. We were enjoying Turkish coffee and baklava near Taksim Gezi Park while we prepared for an unusual meeting with two-dozen Syrian jurists who had braved countless governmental and rebel check points to work with us for a week on the blueprint for a Syrian Tribunal to hold regime officials responsible for war crimes and crimes against humanity.[1]

Suddenly, we were surrounded by thousands of college students with cacophonous noise-making devices of every kind, waiving giant red flags emblazoned with the visage of the great Turk secular leader, Ataturk. They were ostensibly protesting Prime Minister Recep Tayyip Erdoğan's urban development plan for one of the last remaining public parks in the city of fourteen million. But the protests were about more – attacks on freedom of expression, encroachments on secularization, and increasing government repression.

The protesters were followed close behind by hundreds of white-helmeted riot police, clad in black body armor and carrying large translucent shields. Moments later, our eyes began to burn as canisters of tear gas landed nearby,

---

[1] The blueprint we came up with is reproduced in the Appendix to this book.

spewing gray mist. Behind us we could hear the rush of cannons firing thousands of gallons of pressurized water into the crowd. And then the screams of the students.

We were instantly caught up in a stampede. Our fight-or-flight response kicked in and we ran with the jostling crowd at our top speed for nearly a mile, trying to gain distance from the riot police. Later we would joke that it was like running with the bulls at Pamplona. But, in that moment, our thoughts turned to one thing – survival. It was frightening, even for two individuals who have had a long history of encounters with dangerous situations in our work around the globe.

The next morning, we awoke to press reports of many injuries from the police clash with the protesters at Taksim. When we met with our Syrian counterparts at the hotel conference room, we asked them if they had witnessed the skirmish between the police and protesters the day before. They said that they had not only seen the confrontation, they joined in to show solidarity with the protesters. "Were you frightened?" we asked. "No," was their emphatic reply. "Compared to being attacked by massive artillery, missiles, barrel bombs, and chemical weapons – this was nothing."

We dedicate this book to these intrepid Syrian jurists and others like them that we have worked with over the years, some of whom have been forced into exile, some gave their lives in the struggle for their people's rights, and some continue to fight for justice in their troubled country.

1

Introduction

Since 2011, Syria has been engulfed in a protracted civil war that began as part of the wave of Arab Spring protests against Middle East tyrants.[1] The Syrian conflict has seen the rise and fall of the ISIS terrorist organization,[2] the largest refugee migration since World War II,[3] and the repeated use of chemical weapons against a civilian population. The situation is complicated by the fact that Russia, Syria's long-time ally, has repeatedly used its veto in the UN Security Council to prevent the Council from taking actions related to the crisis. With all that, Syria has become a dynamic laboratory for the rapid creation of new international law.

Usually, customary international law evolves slowly over many decades.[4] But sometimes world events are such that customary international law

---

[1] For a detailed timeline of events related to Syria's use of chemical weapons and the US–French–UK air strikes, see Associated Press, Timeline of chemical weapons attacks in Syria, Apr. 10, 2018, https://www.yahoo.com/news/timeline-chemical-weapons-attacks-syria-170615069.html

[2] *See* Michael P. Scharf, *How the War on ISIS Changed International Law*, 48 Case W. Res. J. Int'l L. 15–68 (2016).

[3] UN Office for the Coordination of Humanitarian Affairs, *2018 Humanitarian Needs Overview*, Nov. 21, 2017, https://reliefweb.int/report/syrian-arab-republic/2018-humanitarian-needs-overview-syrian-arab-republic-enar

[4] Historically, crystallization of new rules of customary international law was viewed as a protracted process that took many decades, if not centuries, to complete. French jurisprudence generally required the passage of at least forty years for the emergence of an international custom, while German doctrine generally required thirty years. Vincy Fon & Franscesco Parisi, *The Formation of Customary Law* 5 (George Mason Univ. Law, Working Paper No. 02–24, 2000), www.law.gmu.edu/assets/files/publications/working_papers/02-24.pdf (last visited Feb. 22, 2014); G. I. Tunkin, *Remarks on the Judicial Nature of Customary Norms in International Law*, 49 Calif. L. Rev. 419, 420 (1961). The International Law Commission (ILC), at the beginning of its work, demanded state practice "over a considerable period of time" for a customary norm to emerge. Manley O. Hudson, *Special Rapporteur on Article 24 of the Statute of the Int'l Law Comm'n, Ways and Means for Making the Evidence of Customary International Law More Readily Available*, Y.B. Int'l L. Comm'n, U.N. Doc. A/CN.4/16 (Mar. 3, 1950).

develops quite rapidly.[5] Some scholars call these transformative events that accelerate the formation of customary international law or occasion significant interpretive changes of the UN Charter "International Constitutional Moments,"[6] likening them to the revolutionary change in American constitutional law that accompanied the New Deal.[7] Others, including the coauthors of this book, prefer to describe the phenomenon as "Grotian moments," a term named after Hugo Grotius, the fifteenth-century Dutch scholar and diplomat whose masterpiece *De Jure Belli ac Pacis* helped usher in the modern system of international law.[8] This book explores whether the Syria conflict (2011–2020) represents a Grotian moment.

---

[5] North Sea Continental Shelf (Ger. v. Den., Ger. v. Neth.), Merits, 1969 I.C.J. 3, ¶¶ 71, 73–74 (Feb. 20). The Court stated:

> Although the passage of only a short period of time is not necessarily . . . a bar to the formation of a new rule of customary international law . . . an indispensable requirement would be that within the period in question, short though it might be, State practice, including that of States whose interests are specially affected, should have been both extensive and virtually uniform in the sense of the provision invoked; and should moreover have occurred in such a way as to show a general recognition that a rule of law or legal obligation is involved.
>
> *Id.* ¶ 74

While recognizing that some norms can quickly become customary international law, the ICJ held that the equidistance principle contained in Article 6 of the 1958 Convention on the Continental Shelf had not done so as of 1969 because so few states recognized and applied the principle. At the same time, the Court did find that that Articles 1 and 3 of the Convention (concerning the regime of the continental shelf) did have the status of established customary law.

[6] Stanford law professor Jenny Martinez, for example, has written that the drafting of the UN Charter was a "constitutional moment" in the history of international law. Jenny S. Martinez, *Towards an International Judicial System*, 56 STAN. L. REV. 429, 463 (2003). Washington University law professor Leila Sadat has similarly described Nuremberg as a "constitutional moment for law." Leila Nadya Sadat, *Enemy Combatants After Hamdan v. Rumsfeld: Extraordinary Rendition, Torture, and Other Nightmares from the War on Terror*, 75 GEO. WASH. L. REV. 1200, 1206–1207 (2007).

[7] *See* BRUCE ACKERMAN, RECONSTRUCTING AMERICAN LAW 19 (1984); *see also* BRUCE ACKERMAN, WE THE PEOPLE: TRANSFORMATIONS 385, 409 (1991) (coining the phrase "Constitutional moment").

[8] *See generally*, MICHAEL P. SCHARF, CUSTOMARY INTERNATIONAL LAW IN TIMES OF FUNDAMENTAL CHANGE: RECOGNIZING GROTIAN MOMENTS (2014); Milena Sterio, *Humanitarian Intervention Post-Syria: A Grotian Moment*, 20 ILSA J. INT'L L. 344 (2014). The term "Grotian moment" was first coined by Princeton professor Richard Falk. See INTERNATIONAL LAW AND WORLD ORDER 1265–1286 (Burns H. Weston et al. eds., 4th ed. 2006). Grotius (1583–1645) is widely considered to have laid the intellectual architecture for the Peace of Westphalia, which launched the basic rules of modern international law. HEDLEY BULL ET AL., HUGO GROTIUS AND INTERNATIONAL RELATIONS 1, 9 (1992). While the results of Westphalia may have been simplified by the lens of history, and Grotius's role may have been exaggerated, Westphalia has unquestionably emerged as a symbolic marker and Grotius as an emblematic figure of changing historical thought. "Grotian moment" is thus an apt label for transformational events in customary international law.

The book begins by setting forth the history of the current conflict in Syria. Next, it discusses the principles and process of customary international law formation and the phenomenon of accelerated formation of customary international law. This is followed by chapters that examine how use of force against ISIS in Syria has changed the law of self-defense against non-state actors; how the allied air strikes in response to Syria's use of chemical weapons have changed the law of humanitarian intervention; how efforts to prosecute Syrian perpetrators in national courts in Europe have sparked renewed use of novel conceptions of universal jurisdiction after they had largely fallen out of favor; how the mass exodus of Syrians fleeing the war led to transformation in the approach to immigration law and policy across the globe; and how the multilateral peace negotiations developed innovative approaches to post-conflict dispute resolution while ushering in a historic shift in power from the paralyzed UN Security Council to the UN General Assembly.

Written as the nine-year-long Syria conflict nears an end, this is the first book-length treatment of how the Syrian war has changed international law. The situation is analogous to the 1960s and 1970s when the Vietnam War led to transformational changes in international law, inspiring several notable books such as Richard Falk's *The Vietnam War and International Law*; Telford Taylor's *Nuremberg and Vietnam*; and John Norton Moore's *Law and the Indo-China War*. This book in turn seeks to contribute both to understanding the concept of accelerated formation of customary international law and the specific ways the Syria conflict has led to development of new norms and principles in several areas of international law.

Historical Background

To set the stage for the chapters that follow, this chapter traces the historic roots of the strife in Syria as well as the major events during the conflict from 2011 to 2019. It also describes the major actors within and outside of Syria that have played a significant role in the fray. Finally, it discusses the sources of international law applicable to the Syrian conflict.

I ORIGINS OF THE SYRIAN CONFLICT

Ottoman rule of Syria ended in 1918 when Arab troops, supported by British forces, captured Damascus. Syria became a French protectorate in 1920 and remained under French dominion until World War II when Axis powers gained control. After the war, independence protests led to the withdrawal of French forces and establishment of the Arab Socialist Baath Party in 1947. In 1958, Syria joined Egypt to create the United Arab Republic, but a military coup in 1961 dissolved the union. In 1970, Hafez al-Assad, then the Defense Minister, overthrew President Nur al-Din al-Atasi and assumed control; in 1971, Hafez al-Assad was elected to his first seven-year term as president. From 1970 to 2000, Hafez al-Assad ruled Syria by violently suppressing any dissent. During the 1980s, Hafez al-Assad and the Syrian military continually faced and put down various rebellions by the Muslim Brotherhood, culminating in the 1982 massacre in Hama in which the Syrian military killed tens of thousands of civilians.

Born in 1965, Bashar al-Assad, who was trained as an ophthalmologist, took the reins of power in Syria in 2000 after the death of his father, and was initially viewed as a reformist. Immediately after assuming the presidency,

The authors thank Cox Center Fellow Luke Robert Palmer and the staff of PILPG for research assistance for this chapter.

Bashar al-Assad released hundreds of political prisoners and attempted to implement economic reforms. Since 2000, however, al-Assad has failed to continue easing political repression and declined to implement many of the promised economic reforms. Internationally, tensions increased with the United States in 2002 when President George Bush included Syria in a list of states in the so-called axis of evil. In 2005, Syria was implicated in the assassination of Rafiq Hariri, the Prime Minister of Lebanon. In 2007, Israel conducted an air strike in northern Syria, targeting a nuclear facility. In 2009, the International Atomic Energy Agency (IAEA), a UN watchdog group, reported trace amounts of undeclared manmade uranium in Syria. The United States responded in 2010 by renewing sanctions against Syria, citing Syrian connections to terrorist organizations and attempts to obtain weapons of mass destruction.

In 2011, Syria joined the growing uprisings and resistance movements in the Middle East known as the Arab Spring. By 2012, escalating confrontations between the Assad government and the various opposition groups developed into an internal conflict.[1] The Syrian conflict has evolved into a complex international landscape and has been the cause of a massive regional and international refugee crisis. There are over six million internally displaced Syrians and nearly five million seeking refuge abroad. The Syrian conflict has been marked by widespread and brutal atrocities, including a death toll exceeding 470,000.

As the conflict intensified, it attracted foreign actors like moths to a porch light. The United States, Saudi Arabia, Qatar, and Turkey began providing economic and military support to opposition fighters in an attempt to dislodge their long-time regional rival, the Assad government. In the hopes of maintaining a strong regional ally, Iran began providing the Assad government with weapons, money, and support by its own forces and by proxy through Hezbollah militias from Lebanon. Meanwhile, the terrorist group, al-Qaeda, began

---

[1] For documentation concerning the human rights abuses and war crimes committed during the conflict, *see* Amnesty International, *Syria 2017/2018*, https://www.amnesty.org/en/countries/middle-east-and-north-africa/syria/report-syria; Human Rights Watch, *Syria: Events of 2017* (2018), https://www.hrw.org/world-report/2018/country-chapters/syria; Human Rights Watch, *Death by Chemicals: The Syrian Government's Widespread and Systematic Use of Chemical Weapons* (May 1, 2017), https://www.hrw.org/report/2017/05/01/death-chemicals/syrian-governments-widespread-and-systematic-use-chemical-weapons; Ben Taub, *The Assad Files*, NEW YORKER (Apr. 28, 2016), http://www.newyorker.com/magazine/2016/04/18/bashar-al-assads-war-crimes-exposed#; Independent International Commission of Inquiry, *Human Rights Abuses and International Humanitarian Law Violations in the Syrian Arab Republic, 21 July 2016–28 February 2017*, U.N. Doc. A/HRC/34/CRP.3 (Mar. 10, 2017), http://www.ohchr.org/EN/HRBodies/HRC/IICISyria/Pages/IndependentInternationalCommission.aspx

supporting various Islamist opposition groups with weapons and fighters. At the same time, Kurdish groups in northwest Syria, with the support of Iraqi Kurdistan, began operating with increasing independence and autonomy.

A chasm between Russian support for Assad and US insistence that Assad leave power added intransigence to the conflict. Reports of grave breaches of international humanitarian law, such as torture and chemical weapons attacks, and the presence of millions of Syrian refugees in neighboring states prompted international efforts to pursue peace. But several attempts to create a transitional government through peace talks in Geneva from 2012 to the present have failed to yield any positive results for the people of Syria. In response to the rapid rise of Daesh (also known as ISIS/ISIL) starting in 2014, the United States and several allies launched air strikes in both Syria and Iraq to combat the group. The Russians also began conducting their own air strikes in Syria in October 2015, ostensibly to eradicate terrorists from Syria but with the effect of bolstering the Assad regime through suppression of armed opposition groups (AOGs).

After a failed attempt to begin UN-led peace negotiation in Geneva in 2014, the peace process was revived in late 2015 in response to the Syrian refugee crisis. Rounds of Geneva talks have been held intermittently since 2015, but the Assad regime and opposition delegations have yet to engage in face-to-face negotiations or agree on any elements of a resolution to the conflict. Beginning in January 2017, the parallel Astana peace process, led by Russia, Iran, and Turkey as trilateral guarantors, has engaged representatives of the regime and AOGs. The Astana process has focused on ceasefire negotiations and the implementation of de-escalation zones; however, all agreements reached have failed. In January 2018, Russia convened the Sochi Conference, which was intended to be a national dialogue. All major opposition entities boycotted the Sochi Conference. Participants in the Sochi Conference announced that a constitution-drafting committee should be formed with representatives of the regime, opposition, and neutral actors. To date, no constitution-drafting committee has been formed.

The Syrian conflict has created regional instability and resulted in the deaths of over 470,000 people thus far, according to the Syria Center for Policy Research. Additionally, eleven million Syrians have been displaced, there have been over 14,000 documented cases of death by torture, and there has been widespread Syrian government use of internationally prohibited chemical weapons, inherently indiscriminate barrel bombs, cluster munitions, and the indiscriminate use of incendiary weapons in civilian-populated areas.

Syria's war has had a ripple effect throughout not just the Middle East, but also Europe. It sparked the largest humanitarian crisis since the end of World

War II. Millions of refugees poured into Turkey, Jordan, Lebanon, Iraq, and Egypt as well as European countries, where the refugee crisis had an enormous political impact, including being one of the causes of Brexit. Within Syria, more than half of the country's population was displaced and dependent on humanitarian aid for daily subsistence. Destruction of homes, schools, businesses, hospitals, roads, and infrastructure was estimated in the hundreds of billions of dollars.

II PARTIES ENGAGED IN THE SYRIAN CONFLICT

There are so many internal and external actors engaged in the Syrian conflict that the authors thought it would be helpful to provide a scorecard to help the reader keep track of the parties. Below we list first the Syrian parties, followed by the foreign actors involved in the conflict. [2]

A *Syrian Parties*

Government of the Syrian Arab Republic (regime): The current Syrian government, which has been under the executive rule of Bashar al-Assad since July 2000.

Free Syrian Army (FSA): Formed in August of 2011 by defectors from the Syrian regime, the FSA is one of the predominant Syrian AOGs, comprising more than fifty fighting factions.

People's Protection Units (YPG): Kurdish force that has been active in the Syrian conflict. The YPG is considered a terrorist organization by the Turkish government, and has been linked to the long-term insurgency war in Turkey.

Syrian Democratic Forces (SDF): A primarily Kurdish force that also includes local Arab militias, the SDF is comprised in large part of YPG fighters. The SDF are forces particularly active in northern Syria and benefit from US support in anti-Daesh operations.

Al-Qaeda: Al-Qaeda in Syria is comprised largely of non-Syrians, with only limited Syrian membership, and over the course of the conflict has transformed into a range of al-Qaeda "linked" organizations, most famously known as "Jabhat al-Nusra." Most recently, this entity has been renamed "Hayat Tahrir al-Sham," or HTS.

Daesh (also known as "ISIS" or "ISIL"): Highly active, particularly in western Syria. Daesh in Syria is comprised of both Syrian and non-Syrian fighters.

---

[2]   For background on the key actors in the Syrian conflict, *see* Esther Pan, *Syria's Leaders* (July 2, 2012), http://www.cfr.org/syria/syrias-leaders/p9085

B *Third-Party States and Foreign Paramilitary Organizations*

Russia: Since 1971, Russia has operated a major naval base in Syria in the port of Tartus. In 2015, Russia also established a major airbase inside of Syria at the invitation of the Assad regime, where it has deployed bomber and fighter aircraft as well as special forces. Russia regularly attacks the FSA, the SDF, and occasionally Daesh, al-Qaeda, and the al-Qaeda offshoots. Russia is a guarantor of the Astana process along with Iran and Turkey and of the de-escalation zone in southern Syria, along with the United States and Jordan.

Iran: Iran deployed military forces and a significant number of the Iranian Revolutionary Guard Corps (IRGC) al-Quds Force. Iranian forces on the ground in Syria may even outnumber the military forces of Assad. Iranian forces fight on behalf of the regime and engage primarily in operations against the Syrian opposition, including the FSA, and the SDF. In May 2018, Iran launched missiles from Syria into Israeli military positions in the Golan Heights. Iran is a guarantor of the Astana process.

Hezbollah: As of 2016 an estimated 7,000 Hezbollah fighters were based in Syria. Hezbollah largely fights in support of the regime, and primarily engages in operations against the Syrian opposition, including the FSA.

Jordan: Jordan provides support to the FSA. Jordan is also an active participant in overseeing de-escalation zones in Syrian territory, particularly those in the south.

Qatar: Qatar provides funding and weapons to the FSA, and allegedly to al-Qaeda. The majority of Qatar's engagement in the Syrian context is particularly focused on anti-Assad engagement, but not necessarily in cooperation with Saudi Arabia.

Saudi Arabia: Saudi Arabia provides funding and weapons to the FSA, and allegedly to al-Qaeda. As a significant supporter of the Syrian opposition, Saudi Arabia is particularly focused on anti-Assad engagement.

Turkey: Turkey deployed several thousand forces into Syria, both to protect civilians from attack by the Syrian regime and to prevent Kurdish forces from holding contiguous territory along the Turkish border. Turkey also deploys monitors for the de-escalation zones. In 2017, Turkey largely succeeded in securing a swathe of territory in northern Syria known as the "Euphrates Shield" area. In 2018, Turkey gained further territory in northern Syria, including Afrin, under "Operation Olive Branch." Then in October 2019, immediately after the United States announced that it was withdrawing its troops from northeast Syria, Turkey invaded the area to remove Kurdish forces and create a "safe zone." Early in the conflict Turkey downed a Russian MiG fighter, which had crossed into its airspace, but more recently acts in close cooperation with Russia. Turkey is a guarantor of the Astana process.

United States: Provides assistance, including weapons, to both the FSA and the SDF. It has also conducted air strikes against al-Qaeda and Daesh as part of a US-led coalition focused on the elimination of Daesh. Further, the United States has deployed approximately 2,000 special forces and an artillery unit inside Syria. The majority of the US military efforts in the Syrian context are aimed toward the elimination of Daesh. Notably, in April of 2017, the United States launched a substantial cruise missile attack against air assets of the regime, in retaliation for the regime's chemical weapons attack on Khan Sheikhoun. In April of 2018, the United States, this time joined by the UK and France, responded to the regime's chemical weapons attack on Douma with additional targeted strikes against regime military and research assets. The United States is a guarantor of the de-escalation zone in southern Syria.

United Kingdom, France, and other EU states: These states provide assistance to the FSA and have conducted air strikes and deployed special forces against al-Qaeda and Daesh, particularly as part of the US-led coalition. France and the UK participated in the US targeted strikes in response to the regime's alleged use of chemical weapons in Douma.

International al-Qaeda: International al-Qaeda in Syria has been active in the conflict since 2012. At the outset of its participation, al-Qaeda openly claimed the goal of removing Assad and creating an Islamic state. Al-Qaeda has continued to present itself as an anti-Assad force throughout the duration of the conflict.

International Daesh: An offshoot of what was once al-Qaeda in Iraq, International Daesh in Syria became particularly prevalent beginning in 2013, capturing significant portions of Syrian territory and eventually claiming Raqqa as its de facto capital. At the peak of its power, approximately ten million people lived under Daesh control. Daesh engaged in offenses against Syrian opposition armed groups, the regime, SDF forces, members of the US-led coalition, and others. As of late 2017 the US-led coalition seeking to eliminate Daesh claimed that nearly 98 percent of Daesh-held territory has been liberated, and gains against Daesh have continued in 2018.

III CONFLICT TIMELINE

The Syrian conflict can be characterized as consisting of five distinct stages. The first stage was ignited by protests in early 2011.[3] Inspired by the Arab

---

[3] This timeline is based on the following sources: Associated Press, *Timeline of the Syrian Conflict as It Enters 8th Year* (Mar. 15, 2018), https://apnews.com/792a0bd7dd6a4006a78 287f170165408; Aljazeera, *Syria's Civil War Explained from the Beginning* (Apr. 14, 2018),

Spring uprisings across the Middle East, Syrian children in the city of Daraa scrawled anti-regime graffiti on public walls. They were arrested, held for days, and tortured, in turn prompting local demonstrations that called for their release. Protests rapidly spread across Syria. As the expression of dissent gained momentum, the regime unleashed its military firepower to suppress the protests.

The second stage was marked by the outbreak of an armed insurgency and Syria's descent into full-scale civil war. By 2012, an array of poorly organized opposition groups had formed rebel brigades that seized cities in the north, including parts of Aleppo, Syria's largest city. As the government lost territory in 2013, Lebanon's Hezbollah openly deployed its fighters and the IRGC dispatched military advisers to prop up the Assad government.

The third stage saw the rise of ISIS and other hardline Islamist groups that recruited local sympathizers as well as foreign fighters. By 2014, ISIS declared the creation of the Islamic State caliphate, which controlled roughly one-third of Syrian territory, with Raqqa as its capital. This prompted direct US military intervention. Meanwhile, moderate rebel groups fighting the government were increasingly eclipsed by extremist factions.

The fourth stage, from 2015 to 2016, witnessed Russian military intervention, especially airpower, against moderate rebel factions. Russia deployed sophisticated weaponry and air defense systems. During this period, the involvement of Hezbollah and Iran also deepened. During this stage, the tide of the conflict turned overwhelmingly in favor of the Syrian regime. During this stage, the US position on the Syrian civil war shifted from countering ISIS to containing Iran.

During the fifth stage, the Assad regime aggressively reasserted its control over most of the country. By the end of 2016, it had retaken major cities, including Aleppo, as well as areas across Syria's strategic western spine. By mid-2018, it also recaptured strategic suburbs surrounding Damascus for the first time in five years. It then turned its sights further south to Daraa, the birthplace of the uprising. It seized the city as well as most of southwest Syria by the summer of 2018. Finally, aided by Russia, in 2019, the regime began its final seize of Idlib province, the last rebel stronghold and home to three million civilians. As the fighting intensified, the UN warned of the potential for the worst humanitarian catastrophe of the twenty-first century. This is likely to be the final stage of the conflict. In its aftermath, there will no doubt be

https://www.aljazeera.com/news/2016/05/syria-civil-war-explained-160505084119966.html; BBC, *The Story of the Conflict* (Mar. 11, 2016), http://www.bbc.com/news/world-middle-east-26116868; Mona Yacobian, *Syrian Timeline* (July 2, 2019), https://www.usip.org/index.php/publications/2019/07/syria-timeline-uprising-against-assad

continuing acts of resistance, protest, and terrorism pending a negotiated peace. Below is a detailed timeline of the major events in the Syrian conflict from 2011 to 2019.

2011

- **March–May**: Protests in Damascus and the southern city of Daraa demand the release of political prisoners. Security forces shoot a number of people dead in Daraa, triggering days of violent unrest that steadily spread nationwide over the following months. Army tanks enter Daraa, Banyas, Homs, and suburbs of Damascus in an effort to crush anti-regime protests.
- **June**: The IAEA nuclear watchdog decides to report Syria to the UN Security Council over its alleged covert nuclear program. The structure housing the alleged reactor was destroyed in an Israeli air raid in 2007.
- **October**: The newly formed Syrian National Council says it has forged a common front of internal and exiled opposition activists. Russia and China veto a UN Security Council resolution condemning Syrian violence and human rights violations against the civilian population. This is the first of twelve Security Council resolutions relating to the Syrian crisis vetoed by Russia.

2012

- **July:** FSA blows up three security chiefs in Damascus and seizes Aleppo in the north. A government offensive to recapture the city makes only limited headway.
- **August:** The government suffers further setbacks. A UN General Assembly resolution demands that President Assad resign, high-level defections gather pace – most notably Prime Minister Riad Hijab – and US President Obama warns that use of chemical weapons would tilt the United States toward intervention. Additionally, President Obama states that there were no plans for military intervention in Syria, but defines the use of chemical or biological weapons as a "red line" that would significantly alter the decision-making process.
- **November:** Several major opposition forces unite to form the National Coalition for Syrian Revolutionary and opposition forces at a meeting in Qatar, including the Syrian National Council. The Arab League stops short of full recognition. Islamist militias in Aleppo, including the Al-Nusra and Al-Tawhid groups, refuse to join the Coalition, denouncing it as a "conspiracy."

- **December:** The United States joins the UK, France, Turkey, and Gulf States in formally recognizing Syria's opposition National Coalition as "the legitimate representative" of the Syrian people.

2013

- **April:** The United States and UK demand investigation into reports that Syrian government forces used chemical weapons against civilians. Opposition National Coalition chairman Moaz al-Khatib resigns, accusing foreign backers of trying to manipulate the group. His successor is veteran socialist George Sabra, leader of the older opposition Syrian National Council.
- **September:** UN weapons inspectors conclude that chemical weapons were used in an attack on the Ghouta area of Damascus in August that killed about 300 people, but do not explicitly assign responsibility for the attack. The United States and Russia agree on a UN Security Council resolution that demands Syria surrender any chemical weapons, but the resolution does not threaten military force.
- **October:** Assad allows international inspectors to begin destroying Syria's chemical weapons on the basis of a US–Russian agreement.
- **December:** The United States and UK suspend "non-lethal" support for opposition fighters in northern Syria after reports that extremist fighters seized some of the bases of the Western-backed FSA.

2014

- **January–February:** Two rounds of UN-brokered peace talks take place in Geneva involving the Syrian regime and the National Coalition for Syrian Revolutionary and Opposition Forces. Important figures involved in discussions included Lakhdar Brahimi, representing the UN and the Arab League; Walid al-Moallem, the Syrian foreign minister; and Ahmed al-Jarba and Haitham Maleh, representing the Syrian opposition coalition. UN-brokered peace talks in Geneva fail, largely because Syrian authorities refuse to discuss a transitional government.
- **May:** Hundreds of opposition fighters are evacuated from their last stronghold in the central city of Homs. The withdrawal marks the end of three years of resistance in the city.
- **June:** The joint mission between the Organisation for the Prohibition of Chemical Weapons (OPCW) and the UN announces that the removal of Syria's chemical weapons material is complete. It also says Syria has destroyed all declared production, mixing, and filling equipment and

munitions. Daesh militants declare they have established a "caliphate" in the territory they control, stretching from Aleppo in northwestern Syria to the eastern Iraqi province of Diyala.

- **August:** The UN says Daesh militants have committed "mass atrocities" in Syria. Tabqa airbase, near the northern city of Raqqa, falls to Daesh, who now control all of Raqqa province.
- **September:** In a nationally televised speech outlining his strategy to combat Daesh, US President Barack Obama says he will not hesitate to take action against the group in Syria as well as in Iraq. The United States announces that it will begin air strikes against the Daesh and other jihadist groups in Syria, but refrains from any military action against the Assad regime. The United States announces possibility of an imminent threat to Western countries by the Khorsan Group, an al-Qaeda-affiliated group in Syria.
- **October:** Daesh forces push toward Syrian Kurdish town of Kobane on the Turkish border.

2015

- **January:** Kurdish forces push Daesh out of Kobane on Turkish border after four months of fighting.
- **March:** Opposition offensives push back government forces. New Jaish al-Fatah (Army of Conquest) Islamist alliance, backed by Turkey, Saudi Arabia, and Qatar, captures provincial capital of Idlib.
- **May:** Daesh fighters seize the ancient city of Palmyra in central Syria and proceed to destroy many monuments at pre-Islamic World Heritage site. Jaish al-Fatah takes control of Idlib province, putting pressure on the regime's stronghold of Latakia.
- **June:** Kurdish forces take Ain Issa and border town of Tal Abyad, Daesh attacks Kobane ad seizes part of Hassakeh, the main city in northeastern Syria.
- **September:** Russia carries out its first air strikes in Syria, saying they target the Daesh, but the West and Syrian opposition say it overwhelming targets opposition forces.
- **November:** The United States and Russia lead peace talks in Vienna, but remain at odds about the future of Assad.
- **December:** The UK joins US-led bombing raids against Daesh in wake of Paris suicide-bombing attacks. The regime allows opposition forces to evacuate remaining area of Homs, returning Syria's third-largest city to government control after four years.

2016

- **February:** A US–Russian-brokered partial ceasefire between government and major opposition forces comes into effect after a major pro-government drive to capture Aleppo. Daesh is not included.
- **March:** Regime forces retake Palmyra from Daesh, with Russian air assistance.
- **May:** The US–Russian-brokered ceasefire is extended to Aleppo after an upsurge in fighting there.
- **December:** Regime forces, with the help of Russia and Iran, recapture Aleppo and regain complete control of Syria's largest city after four years.

2017

- **January:** Russia, Iran, and Turkey agree to a ceasefire between regime forces and opposition forces via the Astana process.
- **February:** Russia and China veto a Security Council resolution authorizing sanctions against the Syrian government
- **April:** A sarin gas attack in the northern opposition-held town of Khan Shaykhoum kills almost sixty people. President Trump orders targeted missile strikes on Shayrat Airbase, from which the regime allegedly launched the chemical weapons attack.
- **May:** The United States arms YPG Kurdish Popular Protection Units to defeat Daesh.
- **June:** United States shoots down a regime fighter jet near Raqqa after it allegedly dropped bombs near US-backed opposition SDF.
- **July:** Hezbollah and regime forces launch a military operation to dislodge jihadist groups from the Arsal area, near the Lebanese–Syrian border.
- **October:** Daesh is driven from Raqqa, its de facto capital in Syria, by US-led coalition forces.
- **November:** The regime takes full control of Deir al-Zour from Daesh. Regime and Iraqi forces put Daesh under pressure in the dwindling areas still under its control.
- **December:** Russian President Putin visits Syria, declaring mission accomplished for his forces in the battle against Daesh. Regime forces, with Russian support, continue reclaiming areas from opposition in the northwestern Idlib province.

2018

- **January:** Turkey launches "Operation Olive Branch" in northern Syria to oust Kurdish forces controlling the area around Afrin.

- **February**: Regime forces launch a massive operation to drive opposition forces from Eastern Ghouta. The UN Security Council demands thirty-day cessation of hostilities in Syria to enable humanitarian aid delivery, unanimously adopting Resolution 2401 on February 24, 2018. Resolution 2401 is not implemented.
- **March:** Regime forces gain control in Eastern Ghouta as opposition forces withdraw. Approximately 110,000 civilians are evacuated from Eastern Ghouta to areas in northwest Syria, including Idlib.
- **April:** On April 7, the regime allegedly carries out a chemical attack in Douma, using chlorine gas. The World Health Organization reports forty-three civilian deaths. The following week, tensions escalate during multiple UN Security Council meetings. The United States, UK, France, and others call for the reestablishment of an investigatory mechanism that can determine attribution. Russia rejects such a mechanism. On April 14, the United States, joined by the UK and France, conduct targeted strikes on regime chemical research and military assets. The OPCW arrives in Douma to conduct an investigation, but the OPCW is not an attribution mechanism.
- **May:** On May 9, Israeli fighter jets conduct target strikes on Iranian assets in Syria, reporting unusual movements of Iranian forces. The United States announces its withdrawal from the Iran nuclear deal. Early on the morning of May 10, Iran's Quds Force, a special forces unit affiliated with Iran's Revolutionary Guard Corps, had launched twenty missiles at Israeli positions in the Golan Heights. In response, Israel launches strikes against dozens of Iranian targets in Syria. During the strikes, Israeli F-35 fighter jets are engaged by regime air defense systems.
- **July**: Syrian army recaptures almost all of the south of the country, up to the borders with Jordan and Israeli-held territory.
- **September–December**: Following an Israeli air strike on a Syrian weapons facility, Russia delivers the advanced S-300 anti-aircraft missile system to beef up Syria's air defenses. Kurdish-led SDF forces launch offensive that reduces Islamic State territory to a tiny enclave on the Iraqi border. UAE reopens its embassy in Damascus, the first Gulf State to do so.

2019
- **February**: After initially stating that it would withdraw all of its troops from Syria, the United States says that it will leave 400 troops as a peacekeeping force.
- **March–April:** Assad regime and Russian forces intensify air strikes on rebel-held northwest Syria. The offensive broke the de-escalation deal

Russia had reached with Turkey in September 2018. US President Donald Trump signs a declaration recognizing Israeli sovereignty over the Golan Heights, a strategic area Israel has occupied since the 1967 Six Day War.

- **May–June:** Assad regime forces launch northwestern ground offensive, capturing a series of towns in Idlib province.
- **October:** Turkey invades northeast Syria to remove Kurdish forces and create a "safe zone" for the resettlement of refugees. The United States conducts a raid near Idlib resulting in the death of the leader of ISIS, Abu Bakr al-Baghdadi.

IV APPLICABLE LAW

International human rights law, as codified in the International Covenant on Civil and Political Rights, the Convention on the Rights of the Child, the Torture Convention, and other treaties to which Syria is a party, applies both during peacetime and during armed conflict to the extent that it is not supplanted by the *lex specialis* of international humanitarian law (the law of armed conflict).[4]

International humanitarian law is codified in the four Geneva Conventions of 1949, to which Syria is a party.[5] Each of the Geneva Conventions has a provision known as Common Article 3 which applies to "armed conflicts not of an international character occurring in the territory of one of the High Contracting Parties" – in other words in a civil war. Common Article 3 applies where an internal situation reaches an intensity beyond "mere cases of civil unrest."[6]

In July 2012, the International Committee of the Red Cross announced that it had determined that the Syrian conflict had risen to the level of a "non-international armed conflict."[7] The next month, the UN's Independent International Commission of Inquiry on the Syrian Arab Republic similarly concluded "that the intensity and duration of the conflict, combined with the

---

[4] Legal Consequences of the Construction of a Wall in the Occupied Palestinian Territory, Advisory Opinion, 2004 I.C.J. 136, para. 106 (July 9).

[5] Syria signed the Geneva Conventions on Aug. 1, 1949 and ratified them on Nov. 2, 1953. *See* Thilo Marauhn, *Sailing Close to the Wind: Human Rights Council Fact-Finding in Situations of Armed Conflict – The Case of Syria*, 42 CAL. W. INT'L L.J. 401, 429 (2013).

[6] ANTHONY CULLEN, THE CONCEPT OF NON-INTERNATIONAL ARMED CONFLICT IN INTERNATIONAL HUMANITARIAN LAW 156 (2010).

[7] Press Release, ICRC, Syria: ICRC and Syrian Arab Red Crescent Maintain Aid Effort Amid Increasing Fighting (July 17, 2012).

increased organizational capabilities of the Free Syrian Army, do, in fact, meet the legal threshold for a non-international armed conflict."[8] On this basis, the Commission of Inquiry applied not only human rights law, but also the law of armed conflict, "including Common Article 3, in its assessment of the actions of the parties during hostilities."[9]

As the more specific body of law, international humanitarian law governs where there is inconsistency between the provisions of human rights law and international humanitarian law. As such, the application of international humanitarian law to the Syrian conflict is important as there are several differences between the legality of actions under international human rights law and under international humanitarian law. In some ways international humanitarian law is more permissive. For example, human rights law prohibits arbitrary killings of civilians, while the law of armed conflict permits the killing of civilians who are directly participating in hostilities as well as civilians who are deemed lawful collateral damage.[10] Moreover, the principle of proportionality has a different meaning in international human rights law and international humanitarian law. The latter involves a balancing between the damage caused and the military necessity, while the former raises the general question of whether a governmental measure excessively burdens the individual compared to the benefits the measure aims to secure.[11]

On the other hand, there are some ways in which international humanitarian law is more stringent than international human rights law. For example, where many of the provisions of international human rights law are derogable in times of "public emergency threatening the life of the nation," the provisions of international humanitarian law are always non-derogable. Thus, while due process rights of detainees are derogable under international human rights law, in situations of armed conflict civilians may only be arrested for particular reasons, with a minimum of due process standards as well as minimum standards of protection during detention.[12]

The Commission of Inquiry concluded that Syria violated the non-derogable right to life enshrined in human rights law through the widespread

---

[8] *See* Human Rights Council, *Report of the Independent International Commission of Inquiry on the Syrian Arab Republic*, paras. 45–59, Annex IV, U.N. So. A/HRC/21/50 (Aug. 16, 2012).

[9] *Id.* at para. 3.

[10] *See* Jann K. Kleffner, *From Belligerents to Fighters and Civilians Directly Participating in Hostilities – On the Principle of Distinction in Non-International Armed Conflicts Once Hundred Years after the Second Hague Peace Conference*, 54 Netherlands Int'l L. Rev. 315 (2007).

[11] Marauhn, *supra* note 4, 445–446.

[12] *Id.* at 251.

killings of civilians by government-controlled security forces.[13] The Commission also found reasonable fear of persecution triggering civilian rights under the Refugee Convention, widespread torture of detained civilians and combatants in violation of the Torture Convention, the use of chemical weapons in violation of treaties outlawing such weapons, and the deployment of inherently indiscriminate barrel bombs and indiscriminate use of incendiary weapons in civilian-populated areas in violation of international humanitarian law. When such attacks against a civilian population are widespread and systematic, they can also constitute crimes against humanity under customary international law.

This factual and legal background provides the context for appraising how the Syrian conflict has fundamentally altered international law in a number of ways.

---

[13] *See generally* Independent International Commission of Inquiry on the Syrian Arab Republic, *Tenth Report of the Independent International Commission of Inquiry on the Syrian Arab Republic*, U.N. Doc. A/HRC/30/48 (Aug. 13, 2015); Independent International Commission of Inquiry on the Syrian Arab Republic, *Ninth Report of the Independent International Commission of Inquiry on the Syrian Arab Republic*, U.N. Doc. A/HRC/28/69 (Feb. 5, 2015); Independent International Commission of Inquiry on the Syrian Arab Republic, *Eighth Report of the Independent International Commission of Inquiry on the Syrian Arab Republic*, U.N. Doc. A/HRC/27/60 (Aug. 13, 2014); Independent International Commission of Inquiry on the Syrian Arab Republic, *Seventh Report of the Independent International Commission of Inquiry on the Syrian Arab Republic*, U.N. Doc. A/HRC/23/58 (Feb. 12, 2014); Independent International Commission of Inquiry on the Syrian Arab Republic, *Sixth Report of the Independent International Commission of Inquiry on the Syrian Arab Republic*, U.N. Doc. A/HRC/24/46 (Sept. 11, 2013); Independent International Commission of Inquiry on the Syrian Arab Republic, *Fifth Report of the Independent International Commission of Inquiry on the Syrian Arab Republic*, U.N. Doc. A/HRC/23/58 (June 4, 2013); Independent International Commission of Inquiry on the Syrian Arab Republic, *Fourth Report of the Independent International Commission of Inquiry on the Syrian Arab Republic*, U.N. Doc. A/HRC/22/59 (Feb. 5, 2013); Independent International Commission of Inquiry on the Syrian Arab Republic, *Third Report of the Independent International Commission of Inquiry on the Syrian Arab Republic*, U.N. Doc. A/HRC/21/50 (Aug. 15, 2012); Independent International Commission of Inquiry on the Syrian Arab Republic, *Second Report of the Independent International Commission of Inquiry on the Syrian Arab Republic*, U.N. Doc. A/HRC/19/69 (Feb. 22, 2012); Independent International Commission of Inquiry on the Syrian Arab Republic, *First Report of the Independent International Commission of Inquiry on the Syrian Arab Republic*, U.N. Doc. A/HRC/S-17/2/Add.1 (Nov. 23, 2011).

3

Accelerated Formation of Customary International Law

I INTRODUCTION

This book examines the ways the Syrian conflict has served as the genesis of new rules of customary international law. Though it has only been nine years since the conflict began, Syria has already brought about profound changes to international law.

Professor Myers McDougal of Yale Law School famously described the customary international law formation process as one of continuous claim and response.[1] To illustrate this process, consider the question of whether international law permits a state to use force to arrest a terrorist leader in another state without the latter state's consent – a question that recently arose when the United States kidnapped an al-Qaeda leader from Libya in October 2013.[2] The claim may be explicit, such as demanding that its special forces be allowed to enter the territorial state to arrest the terrorist, or implicit, such as sending its special forces into the territorial state without its permission to apprehend the terrorist. The response to the claim may in turn be favorable, such as consenting to the operation or refraining from protesting the extraterritorial apprehension. In such case, the claim and response will begin the process of generating a new rule of customary international law. Some states may imitate the practice and others may passively acquiesce in it.

As the first state to initiate a new practice, a "custom pioneer" has no guarantee that its action will actually lead to the formation of a binding

---

[1] Parts of this chapter appeared originally in MICHAEL P. SCHARF, CUSTOMARY INTERNATIONAL LAW IN TIMES OF FUNDAMENTAL CHANGE: RECOGNIZING GROTIAN MOMENTS (2014). *See generally* M. S. McDougal & N. A. Schlei, *The Hydrogen Bomb Tests in Perspective: Lawful Measures for Security*, 64 YALE L.J. 648 (1955).

[2] Ernesto Londoño, *Capture of Bombing Suspect in Libya Represents Rare "Rendition" by U.S. Military*, WASHINGTON POST (Oct. 6, 2013), http://articles.washingtonpost.com/2013-10-06/world/42771116_1_kerry-terrorism-suspects-libyan-government (last visited Feb. 22, 2014).

custom. Indeed, the response may be a repudiation of the claim, as in the case of Libya's protest of the unconsented apprehension of the al-Qaeda operative.[3] In such case, the repudiation could constitute a reaffirmation of existing law, which is strengthened by the protest. On the other hand, the claim and repudiation could constitute a stalemate, which could decelerate the formation of new customary international law. The reaction of third-party states is also relevant. Out of this process of claim and response, and third-party state support, acquiescence, or repudiation, rules emerge or are superseded. Just "as pearls are produced by the irritant of a piece of grit entering an oyster's shell, so the interactions and mutual accommodations of States produce the pearl – so to speak – of customary law."[4] Usually, this process of customary international law formation takes decades.[5] But sometimes world events are such that customary international law develops quite rapidly.[6]

In domestic law, we know what stages legislation needs to go through and how many votes are needed at each stage for a bill to become a law. Likewise, for international conventions, we know what formalities must be undertaken for a text to become a treaty and the number of ratifications required to bring it into force. In contrast, there exists no agreed-upon formula for identifying with precision how many states are needed and how much time must transpire to generate a rule of customary international law.[7]

Professor Maurice Mendelson, the Chair of the International Law Association's Customary International Law Committee, suggests that such a formula is unnecessary. Using the metaphor of building a house, he points out that it is often difficult or impossible to say exactly when construction has reached the point that we can conclude a house has been created. It is neither when the first foundation stone is laid nor when the last brush of paint has been applied, but somewhere between the two. "Do we have to wait for the roof to go on, for

[3]   *Id.*

[4]   Maurice H. Mendelson, The Formation of Customary International Law 190 (1998).

[5]   *See* Vincy Fon & Franscesco Parisi, *The Formation of Customary Law* 5 (George Mason Univ. Law, Working Paper No. 02-24, 2000), www.law.gmu.edu/assets/files/publications/working_papers/02-24.pdf (last visited Feb. 22, 2014); G. I. Tunkin, *Remarks on the Judicial Nature of Customary Norms in International Law*, 49 Calif. L. Rev. 419, 420 (1961); Manley O. Hudson, *Special Rapporteur on Article 24 of the Statute of the Int'l Law Comm'n, Ways and Means for Making the Evidence of Customary International Law More Readily Available*, Y.B. Int'l L. Comm'n, U.N. Doc. A/CN.4/16 (Mar. 3, 1950).

[6]   North Sea Continental Shelf (Ger. v. Den., Ger. v. Neth.), Merits, 1969 I.C.J. 3, ¶¶ 71, 73–74 (Feb. 20).

[7]   Anthony A. D'Amato, The Concept of Custom in International Law 58 (1971) (noting that there is no consensus as to how much time a practice must be maintained to evidence the existence of a custom); Tunkin, *supra* note 2, at 420 (arguing that the element of time is not dispositive as to whether a customary rule exists).

the windows to be put in, or for all of the utilities to be installed? So it is with customary law."[8] Rarely does a decision maker need to know the exact moment that a practice has crystallized into a binding rule, or as Mendelson puts it "precisely when the fruit became ripe." Instead, he concludes, "we are more interested in knowing, when we bite it, if it is now ripe or still too hard or sour."[9]

Mendelson's metaphor is apt, for example, in examining when the continental shelf concept became customary international law. President Truman proclaimed the continental shelf concept in 1945; the 1958 Geneva Convention on the Continental Shelf recognized this entitlement on the part of coastal states; and in 1969 the ICJ acknowledged that the principle was part of customary international law in *North Sea Continental Shelf*.[10] Somewhere during those twenty-four years between 1945 and 1969, the coastal states' rights over the continental shelf had crystallized into customary international law, but it would be difficult to pinpoint the exact moment that occurred.

But sometimes courts or international organizations need to determine more definitively when an emerging norm has ripened into binding customary international law. The Cambodia Tribunal faced that question in determining whether joint criminal enterprise (JCE) liability existed as a principle of customary international law when the Khmer Rouge atrocities were perpetrated in 1975. The question boiled down to whether the Nuremberg Charter and judgment constituted a Grotian moment.

II NUREMBERG AS A GROTIAN MOMENT

During a sabbatical in the fall of 2008, one of the coauthors (Michael Scharf) had the privilege of serving as Special Assistant to the International Prosecutor of the Extraordinary Chambers in the Courts of Cambodia (EEEC), the tribunal created by the UN and government of Cambodia to prosecute the former leaders of the Khmer Rouge for the atrocities committed during their reign of terror from 1975 to 1979.[11] While in Phnom Penh, Scharf was assigned

---

[8] MENDELSON, supra note 4, at 175.

[9] *Id.* at 176.

[10] *North Sea Continental Shelf*, 1969 I.C.J. at 3; White House News Release, President Truman's Proclamations on U.S. Policy Concerning Natural Resources of Sea Bed and Fisheries on High Seas (Sept. 28, 1945), http://www.ibiblio.org/pha/policy/post-war/1945-09-28a.html (last visited May 12, 2014).

[11] For background on the creation of the ECCC, *see generally* Michael P. Scharf, *Tainted Provenance: When, If Ever, Should Torture Evidence Be Admissible?*, 65 WASH. & LEE L. REV. 129 (2008).

to write the prosecutor's brief[12] in response to the defense motion to exclude JCE liability as a mode of liability from the trial of the five surviving leaders of the Khmer Rouge.[13]

JCE is a form of liability somewhat similar to the Anglo-American felony murder rule,[14] and the *Pinkerton* rule,[15] in which a person who willingly participates in a criminal enterprise can be held criminally responsible for the reasonably foreseeable acts of other members of the criminal enterprise even if those acts were not part of the plan. Although few countries around the world apply principles of co-perpetration similar to the felony murder rule or *Pinkerton* rule, since the decision of the Appeals Chamber of the International Criminal Tribunal for the Former Yugoslavia in the 1998 *Tadić* case,[16] it has been accepted that JCE is a mode of liability applicable to international criminal trials. Dozens of cases before the Yugoslavia Tribunal, the International Criminal Tribunal for Rwanda, the Special Court for Sierra Leone, the Special Panels for the Trial of Serious Crimes in East Timor, and the Special Tribunal for Lebanon have recognized and applied JCE liability during the last ten years.

These modern precedents, however, were not directly relevant to the Cambodia Tribunal because the crimes under its jurisdiction had occurred some twenty years earlier. Under the international law principle of *nulem crimin sine lege* (the equivalent to the US Constitution's *ex post facto* law prohibition), the Cambodia Tribunal could only apply the substantive law and associated modes of liability that existed as part of customary international law

---

[12]   Co-prosecutors' supplementary observations on joint criminal enterprise, Case of Ieng Sary, No. 002/19-09-2007-ECCC/OCIJ, Dec. 31, 2009. A year later, the co-investigating judges ruled in favor of the prosecution that the ECCC could employ JCE liability for the international crimes within its jurisdiction. *See* Order on the Application at the ECCC of the Form of Liability Known as Joint Criminal Enterprise, Case No. 002/19-09-2007-ECCC-OCIJ, Dec. 8, 2009.

[13]   Pursuant to the co-investigating judges' order of September 16, 2008, the co-prosecutors filed the brief to detail why the extended form of JCE liability, "JCE III," is applicable before the ECCC. The defense motion argued in part that JCE III as applied by the *Tadić* decision of the International Criminal Tribunal for the former Yugoslavia (ICTY) Appeals Chamber is a judicial construct that does not exist in customary international law or, alternatively, did not exist in 1975–1979. *Case of Ieng Sary*, Ieng Sary's Motion against the Application at the ECCC of the Form of Responsibility Known as Joint Criminal Enterprise, Case No. 002/19-09-2007-ECCC/OCIJ, July 28, 2008, ERN 00208225-00208240, D97.

[14]   For background about, and cases applying, *see generally* David Crump & Susan Waite Crump, *In Defense of the Felony Murder Doctrine*, 8 HARV. J.L. & PUB. POL'Y 359 (1985).

[15]   For background about, and cases applying the *Pinkerton* rule, *see generally* Matthew A. Pauley, *The Pinkerton Doctrine and Murder*, 4 PIERCE L. REV. 1 (2005).

[16]   Prosecutor v. Tadić, Case No. IT-94-1-I, Judgment (Int'l Crim. Trib. for the Former Yugoslavia July 15, 1999).

in 1975. Therefore, the question at the heart of the prosecution's brief was whether the Nuremberg tribunal precedent and the UN's adoption of the Nuremberg principles were sufficient to establish JCE liability as part of customary international law following World War II.

The attorneys for the Khmer Rouge defendants argued that Nuremberg and its progeny provided too scant a sampling to constitute the widespread state practice and *opinio juris* required to establish JCE as a customary norm as of 1975.[17] In response, the prosecution brief maintained that Nuremberg constituted "a Grotian moment" – an instance in which there is such a fundamental change to the international system that a new principle of customary international law can arise with exceptional velocity. This was the first time in history that the term was used in a proceeding before an international court. Despite the dearth of state practice, the Cambodia Tribunal ultimately found JCE applicable to its trials based on the Nuremberg precedent and UN General Assembly endorsement of the Nuremberg principles.[18]

While the Nuremberg trials were not without criticism, there can be no question that Nuremberg represented a paradigm-shifting development in international law. The International Law Commission (ILC) has recognized that the Nuremberg Charter and judgment gave birth to the entire international paradigm of individual criminal responsibility. Prior to Nuremberg, the only subjects of international law were states, and what a state did to its own citizens within its own borders was its own business. Nuremberg fundamentally altered that conception. "International law now protects individual citizens against abuses of power by their governments [and] imposes individual liability on government officials who commit grave war crimes, genocide, and crimes against humanity."[19] The ILC has described the principle of individual responsibility and punishment for crimes under international law recognized at Nuremberg as the "cornerstone of international criminal law" and the "enduring legacy of the Charter and Judgment of the Nuremberg Tribunal."[20]

---

[17] For the definition of "customary international law," *see North Sea Continental Shelf*, I.C.J. ¶ 77.

[18] In Case 002, the ECCC Pre-Trial Chamber later confirmed that JCE I and JCE II reflected customary international law as of 1976, but questioned whether JCE III was actually applied at Nuremberg, and therefore was not applicable to the ECCC trial. Decision on the Appeals against the Co-investigative Judges' Order on Joint Criminal Enterprise (JCE), Ieng et al. (002/10-09-2007-ECCC/TC), Trial Chamber, June 17, 2011.

[19] Anne-Marie Slaughter & William Burke-White, *An International Constitutional Moment*, 43 HARV. INT'L L.J. 1, 13 (2002).

[20] *See* Rep. of the Int'l Law Comm'n on the Work of Its Forty-Eighth Session, 51st Sess., May 6–July 26, 1996, U.N. Doc. A/51/10; GAOR, 51st Sess., Supp. No. 10 (1996), http://legal.un.org/ilc/documentation/english/A_51_10.pdf (last visited Feb. 22, 2014).

Importantly, on December 11, 1946, in one of the first actions of the newly formed UN, the General Assembly unanimously affirmed the principles from the Nuremberg Charter and judgments in Resolution 95(1).[21] This General Assembly Resolution had all the attributes of a resolution entitled to great weight as a declaration of customary international law: It was labeled an "affirmation" of legal principles; it dealt with inherently legal questions; it was passed by a unanimous vote; and none of the members expressed the position that it was merely a political statement.[22]

Despite the fact that Nuremberg and its Control Council Law #10 progeny consisted of only a dozen separate cases tried by a handful of courts over a period of just three years, the ICJ,[23] the International Criminal Tribunal for the Former Yugoslavia,[24] the European Court of Human

---

[21] Affirmation of the Principles of International Law Recognized by the Charter of the Nürnberg Tribunal, G.A. Res. 95(1), U.N. GAOR, 1st Sess., U.N. Doc A/236, pt. 2, at 1144, (Dec. 11, 1946), http://www.un.org/en/ga/search/view_doc.asp?symbol=A/RES/95(I)&Lang= E&Area= RESOLUTION (last visited Feb. 22, 2014). The Resolution states in whole:

> The General Assembly,
>   Recognizes the obligation laid upon it by Article 13, paragraph 1, sub-paragraph a, of the Charter, to initiate studies and make recommendations for the purpose of encouraging the progressive development of international law and its codification;
>   Takes note of the Agreement for the establishment of an International Military Tribunal for the prosecution and punishment of the major war criminals of the European Axis signed in London on 8 August 1945, and of the Charter annexed thereto, and of the fact that similar principles have been adopted in the Charter of the International Military Tribunal for the trial of the major war criminals in the Far East, proclaimed at Tokyo on 19 January 1946;
>   Therefore,
>   Affirms the principles of international law recognized by the Charter of the Nuremberg Tribunal and the judgment of the Tribunal;
>   Directs the Committee on the codification of international law established by the resolution of the General Assembly of 11 December 1946, to treat as a matter of primary importance plans for the formulation, in the context of a general codification of offenses against the peace and security of mankind, or of an International Criminal Code, of the principles recognized in the Charter of the Nürnberg Tribunal and in the judgment of the Tribunal.

[22] Affirmation of the Principles of International Law Recognized by the Charter of the Nürnberg Tribunal, G.A. Res. 95(1), U.N. GAOR, 1st Sess., U.N. Doc A/236, pt. 2, at 1144, (Dec. 11, 1946), http://www.un.org/en/ga/search/view_doc.asp?symbol=A/RES/95(I)&Lang= E&Area= RESOLUTION (last visited Feb. 22, 2014).

[23] Legal Consequences of the Construction of a Wall in Occupied Palestinian Territory, Advisory Opinion, 2004 I.C.J. 136, 172 (July 9).

[24] Prosecutor v. Tadić, Case No. IT-94-1-I, Opinion and Judgment, Trial Chamber, ¶ 623 (Int'l Crim. Trib. for the Former Yugoslavia May 7, 1997); Prosecutor v. Tadić, Case No. IT-94-1-I, Decision on the Defence Motion for Interlocutory Appeal on Jurisdiction, ¶141 (Int'l Crim. Trib. for the Former Yugoslavia Oct. 2, 1995).

Rights,[25] and several domestic courts[26] have cited the General Assembly Resolution affirming the principles of the Nuremberg Charter and judgments as an authoritative declaration of customary international law.

Nuremberg, then, constitutes a prototypical Grotian moment. The Tribunal's formation was in response to the most heinous atrocity in the history of humankind – the extermination of six million Jews and several million other "undesirables" by the Nazi regime. From a conventional view of customary international law formation, the amount of state practice was quite limited, consisting only of the negotiation of the Nuremberg Charter by four states, its accession by nineteen others, the judgment of the Tribunal, and a General Assembly Resolution endorsing (though not enumerating) its principles. Moreover, the time period from the end of the war to the General Assembly endorsement of the Nuremberg principles was a mere year, a drop in the bucket compared to the amount of time it ordinarily takes to crystallize customary international law. Yet, despite the limited state practice and minimal time, the ICJ, European Court of Human Rights, and four international criminal tribunals have confirmed that the Nuremberg Charter and judgment immediately ripened into customary international law.

The Grotian moment concept rationalizes this outcome. Nuremberg reflected a novel solution to unprecedented atrocity in the context of history's most devastating war. Beyond the Nuremberg trial, there was a great need for universal implementation of the Nuremberg principles. Yet, on the eve of the Cold War, it was clear that a widely ratified multilateral convention would not be a practicable near-term solution. In fact, it would take half a century before

---

[25] The European Court of Human Rights recognized the "universal validity" of the Nuremberg principles in *Kolk and Kislyiy v. Estonia*, which stated:

> Although the Nuremberg Tribunal was established for trying the major war criminals of the European Axis countries for the offences they had committed before or during the Second World War, the Court notes that the universal validity of the principles concerning crimes against humanity was subsequently confirmed by, *inter alia*, resolution 95 of the United Nations General Assembly (11 December 1946) and later by the International Law Commission.

> > *Kolk and Kislyiy v. Estonia*, App. No. 23052/04, 24018/04, Decision on Admissibility, Eur. Ct. H.R. (Jan. 17, 2006)

[26] The General Assembly resolution affirming the Nuremberg principles has been cited as evidence of customary international law in cases in Canada, Bosnia, France, and Israel. *See R. v. Finta*, [1994], 1 S.C.C. 701 (Can.); *Prosecutor v. Ivica Vrdoljak*, Court of Bosnia and Herzegovina, July 10, 2008; *see generally* Leila Sadat Wexler, *The Interpretation of the Nuremberg Principles by the French Court of Cassation: From Touvier to Barbie and Back Again*, 32 COLUM. J. TRANSNAT'L L. 289 (1994) (summarizing the *Touvier* and *Barbie* cases in French courts).

the international community was able to conclude a widely ratified treaty transforming the Nuremberg model into a permanent international criminal court. It is this context of fundamental change and great need for a timely response that explains how Nuremberg could so quickly and universally be accepted as customary international law.

III OTHER EXAMPLES OF GROTIAN MOMENTS SINCE WORLD WAR II

As the *Max Planck Encyclopedia of Public International Law* has observed, "recent developments show that customary rules may come into existence rapidly."[27] The venerable publication goes on to explain:

> This can be due to the urgency of coping with new developments of technology, such as, for instance, drilling technology as regards the rules on the continental shelf, or space technology as regards the rule on the freedom of extra-atmospheric space. Or it may be due to the urgency of coping with widespread sentiments of moral outrage regarding crimes committed in conflicts such as those in Rwanda and Yugoslavia that brought about the rapid formation of a set of customary rules concerning crimes committed in internal conflicts.[28]

Let us examine each of these examples in turn, beginning with the rapid formation of the law of the continental shelf. In 1945, US President Truman issued a proclamation that the resources on the continental shelf off the coast of the United States belonged to the United States.[29] This represented a major departure from the existing customary international law of the sea, under which the seabed outside of 12 nautical miles was considered free for exploitation by any state.[30] The Proclamation was driven by technological developments enabling exploitation of offshore oil and gas supplies and the intense postwar demand for such resources for a rebuilding world.[31] Though the United States recognized that it was acting as a custom pioneer,[32] it was

---

[27] Tullio Treves, *Customary International Law*, MAX PLANCK ENCYCLOPEDIA OF PUBLIC INTERNATIONAL LAW (2012), at para. 24; Report of the International Law Association, Committee on Formation of Customary (General) International Law, London Conference (2000), at 20.

[28] Treves, *supra* note 27, at para. 24.

[29] Proclamation 2667 of September 28, 1945, Policy of the United States with Respect to the Natural Resources of the Subsoil and Sea Bed of the Continental Shelf, 10 Fed. Reg. 12,305 (1945).

[30] BARRY BUZAN, SEABED POLITICS 8 (1976).

[31] JAMES B. MORELL, THE LAW OF THE SEA: AN HISTORICAL ANALYSIS OF THE 1982 TREATY AND ITS REJECTION BY THE UNITED STATES 4 (1992); BARRY BUZAN, SEABED POLITICS 7 (1976).

[32] ANN L. HOLLICK, U.S. FOREIGN POLICY AND THE LAW OF THE SEA 30 (1981) (citing Unpublished, National Archives Record Group 48).

careful to couch its justification in legal terms that would render the action easier to accept and replicate by other states. Despite the far-reaching change it represented, the Truman Proclamation was met with no protest;[33] rather, within five years, half of the world's coastal states had made similar claims to the resources of their continental shelves,[34] leading commentators to declare that the continental shelf concept had become virtually instant customary international law.[35] By 1969, the ICJ had confirmed that the Truman Declaration quickly generated customary international law binding on states that had not ratified the 1958 Law of the Sea Convention.[36]

Next, let us examine the formation of outer space law, which rapidly emerged from the great leaps in rocket technology in the 1960s, led by the Soviet Union and the United States, inaugurating the era of space flight. Rather than treat outer space like the high seas (open to unregulated exploitation), the international community embraced a unique set of rules to govern this new area as codified in the General Assembly Declaration on Outer Space, which was unanimously approved in 1963.[37] Though the amount of state practice was limited to a few dozen space flights launched by two states and the lack of protest by the states over which these rockets passed, states and scholars have concluded that the 1963 Declaration represented an authoritative statement of customary international law that rapidly formed in response to new technologies requiring a new international law paradigm.[38]

Finally, let us turn to the customary international humanitarian law that rapidly emerged from the Yugoslavia Tribunal in the 1990s. The establishment of the Yugoslavia Tribunal was made possible because of a unique constellation of events at the end of the Cold War, which included the break-up of the Soviet Union, Russia's assumption of the Soviet seat in the Security Council, and the return of genocide to Europe for the first time since Nazi Germany. In its inaugural case, the Appeals Chamber of the Yugoslavia Tribunal rendered a revolutionary decision that for the first time held that

---

[33] BUZAN, *supra* note 30, at 8.

[34] MORELL, *supra* note 31, at 2.

[35] Hersch Lauterpacht, *Sovereignty over Submarine Areas* 27 BRITISH YEARBOOK OF INTERNATIONAL LAW 377 (1950).

[36] *North Sea Continental Shelf (Federal Republic of Germany v. Denmark; Federal Republic of Germany v. Netherlands)*, Merits, Feb. 20, 1969, ICJ Rep. 3, North Sea Continental Shelf Case, I.C.J. Reports (1969), 33–34, para. 47.

[37] United Nations General Assembly Resolution 1962 (XVIII), Declaration of Legal Principles Governing the Activities of States in the Exploration and Use of Outer Space, Dec. 13, 1963, http://www.oosa.unvienna.org/oosa/en/SpaceLaw/gares/html/gares_18_1962.html

[38] MANFRED LACHS, THE LAW OF OUTER SPACE: AN EXPERIENCE IN CONTEMPORARY LAW-MAKING 138 (1972).

individuals could be held criminally liable for violations of Common Article 3 and Additional Protocol II of the Geneva Conventions for war crimes committed in internal conflict.[39] This decision closed a gaping gap in the coverage of international humanitarian law and was soon thereafter affirmed by the Rwanda Tribunal[40] and Special Court for Sierra Leone.[41] It was codified in the 1998 Statute of the International Criminal Court, which has been ratified by 123 states.[42]

These case studies suggest that the Grotian moment concept has several practical applications. It can explain the rapid formation of customary rules in times of rapid flux, thereby imbuing those rules with greater repute. It can counsel governments when to seek the path of a UN General Assembly resolution as a means of facilitating the formation of customary international law, and how to craft such a resolution to ensure that it is viewed as a capstone in the formation of such customary rules. It can in apt circumstances strengthen the case for litigants arguing the existence of a new customary international rule. It can also furnish international courts with the confidence to recognize new rules of customary international law in appropriate cases despite a relative paucity and short duration of state practice.

At the same time, one must approach the Grotian moment concept with caution. As one author warns, "[i]t is always easy, at times of great international turmoil, to spot a turning point that is not there."[43] With this admonition in mind, the following chapters examine whether the Syrian situation constituted a Grotian moment, spawning rapid formation of new norms and principles in a variety of areas of international law.

In the pages that follow, the authors examine six areas of international law that we believe have been transformed by the Syrian conflict.

---

[39] Prosecutor v. Tadić, Appeals Chamber, Decision on the Defense Motion for Interlocutory Appeal on Jurisdiction, Case No. IT-94-1-AR72 (Oct. 2, 1995), reprinted in 35 I.L.M. 32 (1996), at para. 89.

[40] Report of the Secretary General Pursuant to Paragraph 5 of Security Council Resolution 955, February 13, 1995, UN Doc. S/1995/134, at para. 12.

[41] Statute of the Special Court for Sierra Leone, art. 3 (January 16, 2002), http://www.sc-sl.org/LinkClick.aspx?fileticket=uClnd1MJeEw%3d&tabid=176

[42] Rome Statute of the International Criminal Court, art. 8, July 17, 1998, 2187 U.N.T.S. 90 (distinguishing between "international armed conflict" in paragraph 2(b) and "armed conflict not of an international character" in paragraphs 2(c)–(f)).

[43] Ibrahim J. Gassama, *International Law at a Grotian Moment: The Invasion of Iraq in Context*, 18 EMORY INT'L L. REV. 1, 30 (2004).

4

Use of Force in Self-Defense against Non-State Actors

I INTRODUCTION

In 2014, a militant group calling itself the Islamic State (ISIS)[1] rapidly took over more than 30 percent of the territory of Syria and Iraq. In the process, it captured billions of dollars (US) worth of oil fields and refineries, bank assets and antiquities, tanks, and armaments, and became one of the greatest threats to peace and security in the Middle East. In an effort to "degrade and defeat" ISIS, the United States, assisted by a handful of other Western and Arab countries, launched thousands of bombing sorties and cruise missile attacks against ISIS targets in Iraq and Syria since August 2014.[2] While the Iraqi government had consented to foreign military action against ISIS within Iraq, the Syrian government did not.[3] Rather, Syria protested that the air strikes in Syrian territory were an unjustifiable violation of international law.[4]

The United States claimed that the air strikes in Syria are lawful acts of collective self-defense on behalf of the government of Iraq.[5] Use of force in self-defense has traditionally not been viewed as lawful against non-state actors in a third state unless they are under the effective control of that state,[6] but the

---

[1] Parts of this chapter originally appeared as Michael P. Scharf, *How the War against ISIS Changed International Law*, 48 CASE W. RES. J. INT'L L. 15–67 (2016). ISIS is also known as ISIL and Daesh.

[2] Claire Mills & Louisa Brooke-Holland, *House of Commons Briefing Paper No. 06995, ISIS/ Daesh: The Military Response in Iraq and Syria*, July 7, 2015, at 4–7.

[3] House of Commons Library, *ISIS and the Sectarian Conflict in the Middle East, Research Paper 15/16*, Mar. 19, 2015, at 55. The United States did warn the Assad regime about the imminent launch of airstrikes in September 2014 but did not request the regime's permission. *Id.*

[4] *Id.*

[5] Samantha J. Power, Representative of the United States of America to the United Nations, Note to Ban Ki-moon, Secretary-General of the United Nations, Sept. 23, 2014.

[6] Military and Paramilitary Activities in and against Nicaragua (Nicaragua v. United States) (merits), para. 195, 1986 I.C.J. 14, 195 (June 26); Oil Platforms (Iran v. United States) 2003

29

United States argued that since the 9/11 attacks, such force can be justified where a government is unable or unwilling to suppress the threat posed by the non-state actors operating within its borders.[7]

Article 51 of the UN Charter provides for protection of a State's "inherent right" of self-defense.[8] Reference to an "inherent right" means the question is not one of treaty interpretation but rather discerning whether the evolving customary international law principles support the US position. This chapter begins with background about the nature of the ISIS threat and the US decision to launch air strikes against ISIS in Syria. Next, it explores the US effort as a norm pioneer in the aftermath of 9/11 to establish a right to use force in self-defense against non-state actors who are not under the effective control of the state where they are located. Finally, it examines how the international community's response to the US air strikes against ISIS in Syria may have crystalized a new conception of self-defense against non-state actors.

II BACKGROUND ON THE WAR ON ISIS

ISIS has its roots in the Sunni/Baathist-dominated Iraqi army of Saddam Hussein, which was one of the largest armies in the world before the US-led invasion of Iraq in 2003. After the defeat of the Baathist regime, members of the Baathist party were banned from participating in the army or other government positions. Dispossessed, marginalized, and subjugated under the US occupation and subsequent Shi'ite-dominated Iraqi government of Iraqi Prime Minister Nouri al-Maliki, the former Sunni army personnel launched a protracted rebellion, with the insurgents taking on the name al-Qaeda in Iraq and later changing it to the Islamic State of Iraq (ISI).[9]

Meanwhile, the chaos in Syria, which began as protests against the Assad regime in 2011 and escalated to full-out civil war by 2014, presented ISI with an opportunity to seize territory across the border. In 2014, ISI established its "capital" in the captured Syrian town of al-Raqqah and changed the group's name yet again to the Islamic State of Iraq and Syria (ISIS).[10] Soon thereafter,

---

I.C.J. 161, 195 (Nov. 6); The Construction of a Wall in the Occupied Palestinian Territory, Advisory Opinion, 2003 I.C.J. 136, 139 (July 9); Armed Activities on the Territory of the Congo (Democratic Republic of the Congo v. Uganda) 2005 I.C.J. 168 (Dec. 19).

[7] Ashley S. Deeks, *Unwilling or Unable: Toward a Normative Framework for Extraterritorial Self-Defense*, 52 VA. J. INT'L L. 483, 497 (2012).

[8] U.N. Charter, art. 51.

[9] House of Commons Library, *supra* note 3, at 1.

[10] *Id.*

ISIS seized nearby Syrian oil wells and refineries, providing it with vast financial resources.

ISIS then turned its sights on Mosul, the second-largest city in Iraq, which fell to ISIS in 2014. By this point, ISIS had access to hundreds of millions of dollars from banks, as well as tanks and armaments that it had captured from the Iraqi army when the army fled Mosul with almost no fight.[11] With these vast financial and military resources, ISIS began to capture city after city in Iraq and Syria with ease. Meanwhile, the resentment toward the Maliki government due to its continued suppression of the Iraqi Sunnis enabled ISIS to sweep through Sunni areas in Iraq without much resistance because of resentment toward the ruling regime.[12]

Experts believe the majority of top ISIS decision makers are former members of Saddam Hussein's army, intelligence, and security forces.[13] But during 2014, the ranks of ISIS swelled with as many as 10,000 foreign fighters from across the Arab world and Western Europe who were attracted to its fundamentalist ideology and string of military successes.[14]

The name Islamic State reflects the group's avowed goal to establish an Islamic caliphate across the Eastern Mediterranean. In the lands it controls, ISIS has imposed repressive rules and conditions on the inhabitants, similar to the Taliban's former rule in Afghanistan. ISIS has beheaded thousands of Christians, Kurds, and Shi'ites and destroyed Shi'ite shrines and archeological sites in areas under its dominion in Syria and Iraq.[15]

ISIS's strategy of seizing and controlling territory in Iraq and Syria distinguishes it from the al-Qaeda network, which has mainly focused on attacks on Western interests.[16] Due to ISIS's divergent aims, tactics, and its ongoing conflict with the al-Nusra group (which was seen as the primary representative of al-Qaeda in Syria), in 2013 central al-Qaeda leadership disowned ISIS.[17] The United States thus found itself with three adversaries in the Syrian conflict: The Assad government, the al-Nusra (al-Qaeda) group, and ISIS.

The first US air strikes against ISIS were taken in response to a humanitarian catastrophe unfolding in northern Iraq in August 2014. After capturing nearby Mosul, ISIS forces attacked a number of towns in the Sinjar area populated by a Kurdish minority known as the Yazidis, killing thousands of

---

[11] *Id.* at 16.
[12] *Id.* at 24.
[13] *Id.* at 9.
[14] *Id.* at 6.
[15] *Id.* at 11.
[16] *Id.* at 12.
[17] *Id.* at 14.

men and capturing hundreds of women and children as slaves. When some 40,000 Yazidis took refuge on 4,800-foot Mount Sinjar, the ISIS forces cut off their means of egress from the mountain. With the Yazidis' water and food supplies dwindling, President Obama authorized air strikes on the ISIS forces in order to save their lives, saying, "When we have the unique capacity to avert a massacre, the United States cannot turn a blind eye."[18]

Meanwhile, under US pressure, Iraqi Prime Minister Maliki stepped down a few days after the Yazidi operation, and was replaced by Haidar al-Abadi, who was seen as more moderate and more able to begin a reconciliation process with Sunnis.[19] At the request of al-Abadi, the United States launched operation "Inherent Resolve," consisting of widespread air strikes on ISIS targets in Iraq in August 2014. On September 19, 2014, France joined the United States in bombing ISIS in Iraq, and two weeks later the UK joined its two NATO allies in engaging in air strikes in Iraq.[20]

Under international law, a state can use military force in another state's territory in three situations: (1) with the latter's consent, or (2) with Security Council authorization, or (3) when acting in self-defense against an armed attack. Unlike Iraq, Syria did not consent to the use of force against ISIS by Western countries in Syrian territory, and the US State Department spokesperson stated "We're not looking for the approval of the Syrian regime."[21] At the same time, with its Permanent Member veto, Russia blocked Security Council authorization to use force in Syria. Russia is a historic ally of the Assad regime, in no small part because the regime allows Russia to keep its only naval base outside the former Soviet Union at the Syrian Mediterranean port of Tartus.[22] Russia also seems motivated by the goal of frustrating US policy in the Middle East.[23] The Russian Foreign Ministry has said that without a Security Council resolution, any strike against Syria would constitute an unlawful act of aggression.[24]

---

[18] Helene Cooper & Michael D. Schear, *Militants Seize of Mountain in Iraq Is Over, Pentagon Says*, N.Y. TIMES, Aug. 14, 2014, http://www.nytimes.com/2014/08/14/world/middleeast/iraq-yazidi-refugees.html?_r=0; Helene Cooper et al., *Obama Allows Limited Airstrikes on ISIS*, N.Y. TIMES, Aug. 7, 2014, http://www.nytimes.com/2014.08/08/world/middleeast/obama-weighs-military-strikes-to-aid-trapped-iraqis-officials-say.html

[19] House of Commons Library, *supra* note 3, at 24.

[20] *Id.* at 51–52.

[21] *Id.* at 55.

[22] *Id.* at 42.

[23] *Id.* at 14.

[24] Somini Sengupta, *A Host of Possible Objections to Expanded Airstrikes in Syria*, N.Y. TIMES, Sept. 17, 2014.

Nevertheless, without Syrian consent or Security Council authorization, on September 23, 2014, the United States began air strikes on ISIS targets in Syria, supported by Bahrain, Jordan, Saudi Arabia, and the UAE. Later, in February 2015 and April 2015, respectively, Jordan and Canada, joined the air strikes against ISIS in Syria.[25] US aircraft participating in the strikes included F-15, F-16, F/A-18, F-22 fighter aircraft, and B-1 bombers, as well as Tomahawk missiles deployed from US naval vessels in the Red Sea and North Arabian Gulf.[26]

From August 2014 through August 2015, the US-led coalition had conducted more than 5,500 air strikes on ISIS targets in Iraq and Syria, resulting in the deaths of over 15,000 ISIS fighters.[27] American and British commanders have said that the daily air command has weakened ISIS: "The tide of momentum has begun to creep against them," said British Brig. Gen. Jams Learmont.[28] By 2016, the air strikes enabled anti-ISIS forces to retake 45 percent of the territory it controlled at its peak in 2014.[29]

III THE CHANGING LAW OF SELF-DEFENSE AGAINST NON-STATE ACTORS

The US legal rationale for its military actions in Syria is encapsulated in the September 23, 2014 letter to the United Nations from the Permanent Representative of the United States. The letter states:

> Iraq has made clear that it is facing a serious threat of continuing attacks from ISIL coming out of safe havens in Syria. These safe havens are used by ISIL for training, planning, financing, and carrying out attacks across Iraqi borders and against Iraq's people. For these reasons, the Government of Iraq has asked that the United States lead international efforts to strike ISIL sites and military strongholds in Syria in order to end the continuing attacks on Iraq, to protect Iraqi citizens, and ultimately to enable and arm Iraqi forces to perform their task of regaining control of the Iraqi borders.

> ISIL and other terrorist groups in Syria are a threat not only to Iraq, but also to many other countries, including the United States and our partners in the

---

25 House of Commons Library, *ISIS/Daesh: The Military Response in Iraq and Syria, Research Paper 06995*, July 7, 2015, at 9–10.

26 House of Commons Library, *supra* note 3, at 53.

27 Jim Michaels, *15,000 Killed, But ISIS Persists*, USA Today, July 30, 2015, A1.

28 *Id.*

29 Sarah Almukhtar et al., *ISIS Has Lost Many of the Places It Once Controlled*, N.Y. Times, Oct. 13, 2016, https://www.nytimes.com/interactive/2016/06/18/world/middleeast/isis-control-places-cities.html

region and beyond. States must be able to defend themselves, in accordance with the inherent right of individual and collective self-defense, as reflected in Article 51 of the UN Charter, when, as is the case here, the government of the State where the threat is located is unwilling or unable to prevent the use of its territory for such attacks. The Syrian regime has shown that it cannot and will not confront these safe-havens effectively itself. Accordingly, the United States has initiated necessary and proportionate military actions in Syria in order to eliminate the ongoing ISIL threat to Iraq, including by protecting Iraqi citizens from further attacks and by enabling Iraqi forces to regain control of Iraq's borders. In addition, the United States has initiated military actions in Syria against al-Qaida elements in Syria known as the Khorasan Group to address terrorist threats that they pose to the United States and our partners and allies.[30]

As outlined in this communication, the United States has argued that it can attack ISIS targets in Syria without Syria's consent because (1) ISIS threatens Iraq, (2) Iraq has requested the United States' assistance, (3) ISIS has obtained safe havens in Syria, and (4) the government of Syria has been unable to confront ISIS effectively. In addition, the United States has argued that it can attack Khorasan group targets in Syria because (1) that group poses a threat to the United States and its partners and allies and (2) the government of Syria has been unable to eliminate this threat.

Notably, the United States has not argued that Syria effectively controls ISIS or Khorasan, and as such its argument is a departure from the traditional view proclaimed by the International Court of Justice (ICJ) in the 1986 *Nicaragua* case that victim states may not resort to force in response to attacks by non-state actors unless those actors were effectively controlled by the territorial state.[31] This chapter examines whether the US actions against the al-Qaeda and ISIS terrorist organizations, and the international community's political and tactical reactions to those attacks, generated a Grotian moment, leading to new rules of customary international law concerning use of force against non-state actors.

A *Use of Force against Non-State Actors Prior to 9/11*

The customary international law right to use force in self-defense under international law is codified in Article 51 of the UN Charter. The Charter recognizes an important limit to that right, permitting use of force in

---

[30] Power, *supra* note 5.
[31] Nicaragua v. United States (merits), para. 195, 103–104.

self-defense only "if an armed attack occurs."[32] The UN Charter does not define "armed attack" but the ICJ in the *Nicaragua* case held that only the "most grave forms of the use of force" constitute an armed attack.[33] According to the ICJ, to qualify as an armed attack triggering the right of self-defense, the assault must reach a certain significant scale of violence above "mere frontier incidents."[34] However, the ICJ has also suggested that a string of small-scale attacks can in aggregate constitute an armed attack.[35] Assuming that the attack threshold is reached either by a particularly serious terrorist attack or by a series of attacks, two questions arise: First, whether the armed attack must be attributable to the state against whom the force will be used; and, second, whether targeting terrorists before they launch a new attack is lawful.

1 State Attribution

The ICJ has repeatedly held that unless the acts of non-state actors are attributable to the territorial state, use of force against non-state actors in that state is unlawful. This is because when a rebel group or terrorist organization is physically located within the territory of another state which is not in effective control of its operations, the right of self-defense collides with two other fundamental principles of international law, the sovereign equality of states and the renunciation of force in international relations.[36] The rationale behind the attribution requirement is that a state cannot be held responsible for the acts of all whose activities originate in its territory. "If it were otherwise, Columbia, for example, might be liable for the acts of international drug traffickers working from Colombia, or Russia might be held responsible for the international activities of the Russian Mafia."[37] Thus, under the ICJ's holdings in *Nicaragua*,[38] *Oil Platforms*,[39] the *Wall Advisory Opinion*,[40] and the *Congo* case[41] using force against a terrorist organization whose conduct is not

---

[32] U.N. Charter, art. 51.

[33] Nicaragua v. United States (merits), para. 195, 103–104.

[34] *Id.* 93.

[35] *Id.*; Dem. Rep. Congo v. Uganda, para. 146 ("even if this series of deplorable attacks could be regarded as cumulative in character, they still remained non-attributable to the DRC").

[36] U.N. Charter, arts. 2(1) and 2(4).

[37] Greg Travalio & John Altenburg, *Terrorism, State Responsibility, and the Use of Military Force*, 4 CHI. J. INT'L L. 97 (2003).

[38] Military and Paramilitary Activities in and against Nicaragua (Nicaragua v. United States) (merits), para. 195, 1986 I.C.J. 14, 195 (June 26).

[39] Iran v. United States 2003 I.C.J. 161, 195 (Nov. 6).

[40] The Construction of a Wall in the Occupied Palestinian Territory, Advisory Opinion, 2003 I.C.J. 136, 139 (July 9).

[41] Dem. Rep. Congo v. Uganda.

imputable to the territorial state would itself constitute an unlawful armed attack, warranting justified use of force in response by the territorial state.

Under the ICJ's jurisprudence, attribution requires that the territorial state have "effective control" of the non-state actors. This standard comes from the *Nicaragua* case, where the Court was presented with the question of whether the actions of Nicaragua in providing weapons to rebels in El Salvador was sufficient to justify military action by the United States in collective self-defense with El Salvador. The Court stated that sending "armed bands" into the territory of another State would be sufficient to constitute an armed attack, but "the supply of arms and other support to such bands cannot be equated with an armed attack."[42] In the same case, the ICJ found that the acts of the US-assisted Nicaraguan rebel group called the Contras could not be attributed to the United States because there was no clear evidence that the United States had "exercised such a degree of control in all fields as to justify treating the Contras as acting on its behalf."[43] It is important to note here that the *Nicaragua* attribution requirement was not designed to answer the question of whether an attack by an independent non-state actor could trigger the right of self-defense against that non-state actor; rather, it spoke to the question of whether an attack by the non-state actor could be considered an armed attack by the state that sent the armed groups and therefore justify force in self-defense against that state in response.

2 Anticipatory Self-Defense under Customary International Law

Anticipatory self-defense is the use of force to stop an attack that has not actually commenced but which is reasonably believed to be imminent. The concept recognizes that "no State can be expected to await an initial attack which, in the present state of armaments, may well destroy the State's capacity for further resistance and so jeopardize its very existence."[44] Anticipatory self-defense has its customary international law origins in the notorious *Caroline* incident of 1837.

During the *Caroline* incident, Canada (then part of the United Kingdom) faced an armed insurrection mounted from US territory led by non-state actors. The United Kingdom responded to the armed insurrection by attacking the insurgent's supply ship, the *Caroline*, while it was docked on the US side of the Niagara River. In an exchange of diplomatic notes between

---

[42] Nicaragua v. United States (merits), paras. 119–120, 126–127.
[43] *Id.* 62.
[44] D. W. Bowett, Self-Defense in International Law 191 (1958).

the US Secretary of State, Daniel Webster, and the British Foreign Minister, Lord Ashburton, the two sides agreed that a state would be justified in using force against non-state actors in another state where the "necessity for self-defense" was "instant, overwhelming, leaving no choice of means, and no moment for deliberation."[45] While courts and commentators often substitute the term "imminent" for the longer formulation, the *Caroline* definition is widely recognized as reflecting customary international law.

B *Did 9/11 Alter the Paradigm?*

When the rules governing use of force in self-defense were promulgated, most international conflicts were conducted by states utilizing large movements of military personnel and munitions.[46] In the past, non-state actors (pirates, guerrillas, drug traffickers, and terrorists) appeared less threatening to state security than the well-funded, well-organized, and potent armed forces of an enemy state. To the extent that terrorists were a concern, it was because they were financed by state supporters, such as Iraq, Syria, Libya, Iran, Cuba, and North Korea.[47] The terrorist attacks of September 11, 2001, changed that perception, by starkly illustrating that small groups of non-state actors, acting from failed states without direct government support, can exploit relatively inexpensive and commercially available technology to conduct very destructive attacks over great distance.[48]

1 A Different Kind of Threat

In August 1996, Osama bin Laden, the multimillionaire leader of a then little-known group called al-Qaeda, issued a statement titled "Ladenese Epistle:

---

[45] Letter from Daniel Webster, US Secretary of State, to Mr. Fox (Apr. 24, 1841), reprinted in 29 British and Foreign State Papers 1129, 1138 (1857).

[46] At the time of the adoption of the UN Charter, there had been only a handful of instances in which states pursued ongoing military operations against non-state actors in the territory of other states. A survey of such actions would include the American military expedition into Mexico in 1916, which was provoked by attacks on American territory by the armed bands of Francisco (Poncho) Villa; the American military attack on pirates using Spanish-held Amelia Island off the Florida coast as a base of operations in 1817; and the 1838 *Caroline* incident, in which Britain attacked a steamer in order to prevent an attack by non-state actors on Canada. *See* Roy S. Schondorf, *Extra-State Armed Conflicts: Is There a Need for a New Legal Regime*, 37 N.Y.U. J. INT'L L. & POL. 1, 2 n.6 (2004).

[47] *See* list of state supporters of terrorism, maintained by the US Department of State, http://www .state.gov/j/ct/list/c14151.htm

[48] Olumide K. Obayemi, *Legal Standards Governing Pre-Emptive Strikes and Forcible Measures of Anticipatory Self-Defense under the U.N. Charter and General International Law*, 12 ANN. SURV. INT'L & COMP. L. 19, 23–24 (2006).

Declaration of War," in which he called for all Muslims to make holy war (jihad) against American forces in Saudi Arabia, specifically advocated the use of terrorist attacks with the goal of "great losses induced on the enemy side (that would shake and destroy its foundations and infrastructures)."[49] In February 1998, bin Laden followed the Declaration of War by issuing a religious edict (fatwa) to all Muslims, declaring that "to kill the Americans and their allies – civilians and military – is an individual duty for every Muslim who can do it in any country in which it is possible to do it."[50] The fatwa further called on "every Muslim who believes in God and wishes to be rewarded to comply with God's order to kill the Americans and plunder their money wherever and whenever they find it."[51]

Subsequent events proved that bin Laden's al-Qaeda was not a mere group of "crackpots," making grandiose proclamations of war, but a well-funded, well-organized, and deadly new terrorist organization with franchise cells across the globe.[52] The targets of al-Qaeda attacks have included US forces in Yemen in 1992, the US embassies in Kenya and Tanzania in 1998, the USS *Cole* in Yemen in 2000, and the simultaneous attack on the World Trade Center and Pentagon on September 11, 2001.[53] The death toll from September 11 was over 3,000, which is higher than that of the American casualties in the war of 1812, the US–Mexican War, or the Japanese attack on Pearl Harbor in 1941.[54] In addition to the loss of life, the damage to the American economy has been appraised at over $650 billion.[55] Al-Qaeda attacks after 9/11 have included the November 2003 truck bombings in Istanbul which injured 700 and killed 74 people, the March 2004 train bombings in Madrid which injured 1,800 and killed 191 people, and the July 2005 train and bus bombings in London which injured 700 and killed 56 people.[56]

---

[49] Osama bin Laden, Ladenese Epistle: Declaration of War (Aug. 24, 1996), *quoted in* Davis Brown, *Use of Force against Terrorism After September 11th: State Responsibility, Self-Defense and Other Responses*, 11 CARDOZO J. INT'L & COMP. L. 1, 25 (2003).

[50] Osama bin Laden et al., Jihad against Jews and Crusaders: World Islamic Front Statement (February 23, 1998), *quoted id.*, at 26.

[51] *Id.*

[52] Joshua Bennett, *Exploring the Legal and Moral Bases for Conducting Targeted Strikes Outside of the Defined Combat Zone*, 26 NOTRE DAME J.L. ETHICS & PUB. POL'Y 549, 551 (2012).

[53] Brown, *supra* note 49, at 26–27.

[54] *Id.* at 27.

[55] Norman G. Printer, Jr., *The Use of Force against Non-State Actors under International Law: An Analysis of the U.S. Predator Strike in Yemen*, 8 UCLA J. INT'L L. & FOREIGN AFF. 331, 353 (2003).

[56] Paul Carlsten, *Al Qaeda Attacks in Europe Since September 11*, THE TELEGRAPH, Mar. 21, 2012.

The 9/11 attacks forced states to reevaluate the long-standing notion that only a state has the capacity to commit an armed attack against another state giving rise to the right to respond with force in self-defense. Post-9/11, terrorist threats come from stateless entities that possess many of the attributes of a state – wealth, willing forces, training, organization, and potential access to weapons of mass destruction. If such a non-state actor commits a series of attacks against a state, and the acts are of sufficient scale and effect to amount to an armed attack, then arguably force in self-defense should be permitted against the non-state actor which presents a continuing threat where the host state has manifested an inability or unwillingness to respond effectively to the threat.

2 The International Response to 9/11

The day after the 9/11 attack, the United States informed the UN Security Council that it had been the victim of an armed attack and declared its intent to respond under Article 51 of the UN Charter.[57] The North Atlantic Treaty Organization (NATO) for the first time in its history invoked Article 5 of the North Atlantic Treaty, which treats an armed attack on one member as an armed attack on all of them.[58] The Organization of American States (OAS) took a similar stance in OAS Resolution 797. Invoking the 1947 Inter-American Treaty of Reciprocal Assistance, which provides that in the event of an armed attack on an American state, the parties agree that "each one of [them] undertakes to assist in meeting the attack in the exercise of the inherent right of individual or collective self-defense,"[59] the OAS called upon "the government of the member States and all other governments to use all necessary means at their disposal to pursue, capture, and punish those responsible for the attacks, and to prevent additional attacks."[60] Meanwhile the United States and Australia jointly invoked the collective defense article of the ANZUS Treaty, which provides for the parties to collectively "resist armed attack" and "act to meet the common danger."[61] In addition, the Japanese government took the position that the September 11 attack was an attack on the

---

[57] Statement of Ambassador James B. Cunningham, US Deputy Representative to the United Nations, Transcript of the 4370th meeting of the Security Council, at 3, U.N. Doc. S/PV.4370 (Sept. 12, 2001).

[58] NATO Press Release 124, Sept. 12, 2001, *cited in* Brown, *supra* note 49, at 28.

[59] Inter-American Treaty for Reciprocal Assistance, Sept. 2, 1947, 21 U.N.T.S. 77.

[60] OEA/SER.G CP/RES. 797 (1293/01, Sept. 19, 2001).

[61] Security Treaty between Australia, New Zealand and the United States of America, Arts. II and IV, Sept. 1, 1951, 131 U.N.T.S. 83, 86.

United States, and soon thereafter enacted legislation to enable Japan to deploy its forces in support of US operations against al-Qaeda.[62]

Consistent with these developments, the Security Council adopted Resolution 1368, which condemned the 9/11 attacks and "recognized the inherent right of individual or collective self-defense in accordance with the Charter."[63] This action was not a Chapter VII authorization to use force, but rather a confirmation that the United States could invoke its right to respond with force under Article 51 of the UN Charter, despite the fact that al-Qaeda was a non-state actor. Consistent with that right, on October 7, 2001, the United States informed the Council that it had launched Operation Enduring Freedom.[64] Air strikes were directed at camps allegedly belonging to al-Qaeda and other Taliban military targets throughout Afghanistan. There was no international protest or condemnation of the operation;[65] rather, through word and actions, a long list of states expressed support for the operation.[66]

Had al-Qaeda been a state, its attacks (both in the aggregate but also some of the most spectacular individual attacks) would have passed the "scale and effect" test of the *Nicaragua* case. But as a non-state actor based in Afghanistan, under the *Nicaragua* precedent, use of force against al-Qaeda in Afghanistan would only be permissible if Afghanistan had "effective control" of the terrorist organization.

Some commentators argue that Afghanistan met the *Nicaragua* test of effective control because the Taliban and al-Qaeda were in effect partners. Yet, the facts do not establish that al-Qaeda acted as an agent or instrumentality of the Afghan State, but rather that al-Qaeda pursued an independent agenda and acted autonomously within Afghanistan.[67] Neither did the Taliban government of Afghanistan endorse the September 11 attack. Rather,

---

[62] Brown, *supra* note 49, at 29 (citing Government of Japan, Ministerial Meeting Concerning Measures against Terrorism and Press Conference of the Prime Minister, Wednesday, Sept. 19, 2001; Government of Japan, Basic Plan regarding Response Measures Based on the Anti-Terrorism Special Measures Law, Cabinet Decision of Nov. 16, 2001).

[63] S.C. Res. 1368 (2001), 3rd preambular paragraph.

[64] Letter dated Oct. 7, 2001, from the Permanent Representative of the United States of America, to the United Nations addressed to the President of the Security Council, UN SCOR, 56th session at 1, UN Doc. S/2001/946 (2001).

[65] Rebecca Kahan, *Building a Protective Wall Around Terrorists – How the International Court of Justice's Ruling in the Legal Consequences of the Construction of a Wall in the Occupied Palestinian Territory Made the World Safer for Terrorists and More Dangerous for Member States of the United Nations*, 28 FORDHAM INT'L L.J. 827, 842–843 (2005).

[66] Benjamin Langille, *It's Instant Custom: How the Bush Doctrine Became Law After the Terrorist Attacks of September 11, 2001*, 26 B.C. INT'L & COMP. L.R. 145, 146, 155 (2003).

[67] ALEX STRICK VAN LINSCHOTEN & FELIX KUEHN, AN ENEMY WE CREATED: THE MYTH OF THE TALIBAN-AL QAEDA MERGER IN AFGHANISTAN 1990–2010 (2012).

Taliban officials denied that bin Laden had anything to do with the attack, asserting that "bin Laden lacked the capability to pull off large-scale attacks," and proclaiming their confidence that a US investigation would find him innocent.[68]

On the other hand, the Taliban government knowingly harbored al-Qaeda, providing its members a place of refuge and allowing the organization to use Afghanistan as a base from which to plan, sponsor, and launch international terrorist operations. The Taliban government repeatedly ignored the Security Council's demands to close down the terrorist training facilities in Afghanistan and extradite bin Laden, thereby enabling al-Qaeda to represent a continuing threat to the United States.

3 The Bush Doctrine

A week after the terrorist attacks of 9/11, the United States announced the "Bush Doctrine" when President George Bush declared: "Our war on terror begins with al-Qaeda, but it does not end there. It will not end until every terrorist group of global reach has been found, stopped, and defeated. Either you are with us or you are with the terrorists."[69] The most important aspect of the doctrine was encapsulated in Bush's statement that "we will make no distinction between the terrorists who committed these acts and those who harbor them."[70] In a speech before a joint session of Congress on September 20, 2001, President Bush said, "[f]rom this day forward, any nation that continues to harbor or support terrorism will be regarded by the United States as a hostile regime."[71]

In the words of White House spokesman Ari Fleisher, the Bush Doctrine represented "a dramatic change in American policy."[72] Yet, in a five-day debate in the United Nations General Assembly, where state after state condemned the 9/11 attacks, not one objection was voiced to the newly announced US policy.[73]

---

[68] Facts on File World News Digest, Sept. 11, 2001, at 697A1, *quoted in* Brown, *supra* note 49, at 11.

[69] *See* President George Bush's Seminal Speech on Sept. 20, 2001 to the Joint Session of Congress, *quoted in* Obayemi, supra note 48, at 19.

[70] George W. Bush, Address to the Nation on the Terrorist Attacks, Sept. 11, 2001, *quoted in* Brown, *supra* note 49, at 17.

[71] Address to a Joint Session of Congress and the American People, Sept. 20, 2001, *quoted in* Greg Travalio & John Altenburg, *Terrorism, State Responsibility, and the Use of Military Force*, 4 Chi. J Int'l L. 98, 108 (2003).

[72] Statement of Ari Fleisher, Sept. 21, 2001, *quoted id.*

[73] Travalio & Altenburg, *supra* note 71, at 109.

Although it represented a clear departure from the *Nicaragua* case, the Bush Doctrine was rooted in historic provenance. The general affirmative obligation that every state not knowingly allow "its territory to be used for acts contrary to the rights of other States" was first articulated by the ICJ in the 1949 *Corfu Channel* case. There, the ICJ held Albania liable for damage to British warships that struck mines in Albanian territorial waters.[74] Although Great Britain could not prove that Albania had laid the mines or had engaged another state to do so, the ICJ found that Albania must have known of the existence of the mines because Albania was known to have jealously guarded its side of the Corfu Strait, and this was enough to establish Albania's liability.

This principle is analogous to the rules relating to neutrality adopted in the Hague Convention (v) some one hundred years ago.[75] According to the Hague Convention, "neutral powers" may not permit belligerents to move troops, munitions, or supplies across their territory, nor may they allow their territory to be used to form "corps of combatants" nor "recruiting agencies."[76] Should the neutral state prove unwilling or unable to uphold these proscriptions, the other belligerent state is justified in attacking the enemy forces in the territory of the neutral state.[77]

The application of this concept to terrorism was confirmed by Security Council Resolution 1373, adopted shortly after September 11, 2001.[78] In reaffirming the right of self-defense in the context of the September 11 attacks while at the same time stating that States are prohibited from allowing their territory from being used as a safe haven for terrorist groups, the resolution signifies that allowing known terrorists to operate freely in their territory triggers the right to self-defense against the non-state actors located within the host state's territory.

Summing up what he considers to be the current state of international law, UN Special Rapporteur Philip Alston has stated: "A targeted killing conducted by one State in the territory of a second State does not violate the second State's sovereignty [where] the first, targeting State has a right under international law to use force in self-defense under Article 51 of the UN Charter, [and] the second State is unwilling or unable to stop armed attacks against the

---

[74] The Corfu Channel (merits), 1949 I.C.J. 4 (Apr. 9).
[75] Hague Convention (v) Respecting the Rights and Duties of Neutral Powers and Persons in Case of War on Land, 36 Stat. 2310 (1907).
[76] *Id.* arts. 2, 4. 5.
[77] Deeks, *supra* note 7, at 497–501.
[78] S.C. Res. 1373, U.N. Doc. S/RES/1373 (Sept. 28, 2001).

first State launched from its territory."[79] The fact that the "unwilling or unable" test has its roots in the customary law of neutrality anchors the test's legitimacy as applied to use of force in self-defense against non-state actors present in a foreign country.[80]

The extent of permissible military action used to combat terrorists in a country unwilling or unable to control them depends on the level of support provided by the harboring state. Consistent with the Hague Convention (v) discussed above, with its precept of proportionality, "[i]f a State does nothing but allow terrorists to operate from its territory, providing no meaningful support, the extent of the permissible military force is only that which is necessary to deal with the terrorist threat itself. Neither the military of the harboring State nor its infrastructure is a permissible target."[81] In such case, there is a distinction between using force in a state but not against the state.[82] A swift, precision strike against terrorists or their training facilities in the territorial state (a so-called in-and-out operation) represents a reasonably limited interference with the territorial integrity or political independence of the territorial state under these circumstances.[83] The use of force against the non-state actor taken in self-defense is a lawful use of force, and the territorial state cannot therefore mount a forcible resistance in the name of its own self-defense.[84] If, on the other hand, the territorial state is implicated in the terrorist attack, than the victim state may have the right to use force against the territorial state and its agents, in addition to using it against the non-state actor.[85]

A more controversial aspect of the Bush Doctrine was its assertion of an expanded right of anticipatory self-defense against terrorist threats. In the National Security Strategy issued in the aftermath of 9/11, President Bush explained:

---

[79] Philip Alston, Special Rapporteur on Extrajudicial, Summary or Arbitrary Executions, *Study on Targeted Killings*, para. 29, Human Rights Council, U.N. Doc. a/HRC/14/24/Add.6 (May 28, 2010).

[80] Deeks, *supra* note 7, at 497.

[81] Travalio & Altenburg, *supra* note 71, at 112.

[82] Noam Lubell, Extraterritorial Use of Force against Non-State Actors 36 (2010).

[83] In 1976, Israel conducted a raid on the Ugandan airport in Entebbe to rescue Israeli hostages held by Palestinian hijackers. The hijackers were killed. At the UN Security Council meeting, the Israeli representative argued that the operation was not against the territorial integrity or political independence of Uganda. *See* Security Council Official Records, 31st Year, 1939th Meeting, July 9, 1976, U.N. Doc. S/PV.1939 (1976).

[84] Lubell, *supra* note 82, at 41.

[85] *Id.* at 40.

For centuries, international law recognized that nations need not suffer an attack before they can lawfully take action to defend themselves against forces that present an imminent danger of attack. Legal scholars and international jurists often conditioned the legitimacy of preemption on the existence of an imminent threat – most often a visible mobilization of armies, navies, and air forces preparing to attack. We must adapt the concept of imminent threat to the capabilities and objectives of today's adversaries. Rogue States and terrorists do not seek to attack us using conventional means ... Instead, they rely on acts of terror and, potentially, the use of weapons of mass destructions – weapons that can easily be concealed, delivered covertly and used without warning. The United States has long maintained the option of preemptive actions to counter a sufficient threat to our national security. The greater the threat, the greater is the risk of inaction – and the more compelling the case for taking anticipatory action to defend ourselves, even if the uncertainty remains as to the time and place of the enemy's attack. To forestall or prevent such hostile acts by our adversaries, the United States will, if necessary, act preemptively. The United States will not use force in all cases to preempt emerging threats, nor should nations use preemption as a pretext for aggression. Yet in an age where the enemies of civilization openly and actively seek the world's most destructive technologies, the United States cannot remain idle while dangers gather.[86]

As depicted in the National Security Strategy, the Bush Doctrine did not just advocate anticipatory self-defense – striking an enemy as it prepares an attack – but also "preventive self-defense" – striking an enemy even in the absence of specific evidence of an imminent attack. To that end, the Bush administration implemented a policy of targeted killing of key al-Qaeda figures in Afghanistan, Pakistan, Iraq, Yemen, Somalia, and elsewhere.

This expansion of the anticipatory self-defense concept was seen as warranted by the unique attributes of the continuing threat posed by the al-Qaeda terrorist organization.[87] Al-Qaeda and its affiliates are well funded with access to deadly means, potentially including chemical, biological, and nuclear weapons. They attack without warning, target civilians indiscriminately, and employ suicide missions on a regular basis. They had committed a series of prior attacks against the United States and publicly announced an intention to continue to attack in the future. Arguably, under these circumstances, it is

---

[86] National Security Council, the National Security Strategy of the United States of America 15 (2002), http://www.whitehouse.gov/nsc/nss.pdf

[87] National Defense Strategy of the United States of America, US Department of Defense, Mar. 2005, p. 9.

reasonable to deem an attack by such organizations as "continuing" or "always imminent" for purposes of the *Caroline* standard.[88]

In implementing the Bush Doctrine, the United States began to employ newly developed technology in the form of unmanned Predator drones equipped with laser-guided Hellfire missiles controlled by operators located thousands of miles away. Predator drones eliminate the risk to US pilots. They are capable of remaining in the air ten times longer and cost about one-twentieth as much as combat aircraft.[89] Because they are slow and vulnerable to signal jamming, the drones are not perceived to be a serious threat to an advanced military, but they are ideal for use against non-state actors in failed or struggling states.[90] The first drone strike outside Afghanistan occurred in 2002 in Yemen, killing alleged al-Qaeda leader Ali Aaed Senyan al-Harithi and four other men.[91]

When it came into office, the Obama administration embraced the Bush Doctrine's "unable and unwilling" principle, and relied on it in significantly expanding the drone targeted killing program. According to President Obama's CIA Director, Leon Panetta, due to their precision and effectiveness, drones have become "the only game in town in terms of confronting or trying to disrupt the al-Qaeda leadership."[92]

The Obama administration's State Department Legal Adviser, Harold Koh, delivered a major policy speech at the Annual Meeting of the American Society of International Law on March 25, 2010, in which he provided the legal justification for the administration's use of drones to fight terrorist groups around the world. Koh began by stressing that the attacks of 9/11 triggered the US right of self-defense against al-Qaeda and other terrorist organizations. Echoing the Bush administration's characterization of a "global war" against al-Qaeda,[93] Koh asserted "as a matter of international law, the United States is in an armed conflict with al-Qaeda, as well as the Taliban and associated

---

[88] Travalio & Altenburg, *supra* note 71, at 112. *Contra* Alston, *supra* note 79, at para. 45 (characterizing preventive self-defense as "deeply contested and lack[ing] support under international law").

[89] Michael W. Lewis, *Drones and Boundaries of the Battlefield*, 47 Tex. Int'l L.J. 293, 296 (2012).

[90] *Id.*

[91] Molly McNab & Megan Matthews, *Clarifying the Law Relating to Unmanned Drones and the Use of Force: The Relationships between Human Rights, Self-Defense, Armed Conflict, and International Humanitarian Law*, 39 Denv. J. Int'l L. & Pol. 661, 673 (2011).

[92] *See* Andrew C. Orr, *Unmanned, Unprecedented, and Unresolved: The Status of American Drone Strikes in Pakistan under International Law*, 44 Cornell Int'l L.J. 729, 735 (2011) (quoting LA Times story).

[93] Harold Hongju Koh, Remarks, Annual Meeting of the American Society of International Law, Mar. 25, 2010, http://www.state.gov/s/l/releases/remarks/139119.htm

forces, in response to the horrific 9/11 attacks, and may use force consistent with its inherent right to self-defense under international law."[94] Some commentators have argued that the armed conflict with al-Qaeda must be limited to territory on which the threshold of violence for an armed conflict is currently occurring, which at the time of this writing would include Afghanistan, parts of Pakistan, Yemen, Libya, Syria, and Iraq.[95] Koh's broader formulation recognizes that the limited approach would effectively create sanctuaries for terrorist organizations in failed and weak states such as Somalia and Sudan.

Next, Koh argued that the right to use force in self-defense against al-Qaeda was continuous in light of the continuous threat presented: "As recent events have shown, al-Qaeda has not abandoned its intent to attack the United States, and indeed continues to attack us. Thus, in this ongoing armed conflict, the United States has the authority under international law, and the responsibility to its citizens, to use force, including lethal force, to defend itself, including by targeting persons such as high-level al-Qaeda leaders who are planning attacks."[96] But then Koh walked back somewhat from the conception of preventive war enshrined in the Bush Doctrine, saying: "Of course, whether a particular individual will be targeted in a particular location will depend upon considerations specific to each case, including those related to the imminence of the threat, the sovereignty of the other States involved, and the willingness and ability of those States to suppress the threat the target poses."[97]

Two years later, US Attorney General Eric Holder provided further details about the Obama administration's criteria for authorizing a targeted killing. According to Holder, authorization would require three findings: "First, the U.S. government has determined, after a thorough and careful review, that the individual poses an imminent threat of violent attack against the United States; second, capture is not feasible; and third, the operation would be conducted in a manner consistent with applicable law of war principles."[98]

Until now, we've been examining principles related to *jus ad bellum* (the lawfulness of the resort to force). Attorney General Holder's statement reminds us that a forcible response to terrorists must also comply with the fundamental rules of *jus in bello* (the lawfulness of the means employed and target

---

[94] *Id.*

[95] Lewis, *supra* note 89, at 298.

[96] Harold Hongju Koh, Remarks, Annual Meeting of the American Society of International Law, Mar. 25, 2010, http://www.state.gov/s/l/releases/remarks/139119.htm

[97] Koh, *supra* note 93.

[98] *Contemporary Practice of the United States Relating to International Law, Attorney General Discusses Targeting of U.S. Persons*, 106 Am. J. Int'l L. 673, 675 (2012).

selected).In his speech before the American Society of International Law, Harold Koh described the applicable *jus in bello* principles as

> first, the principle of distinction, which requires that attacks be limited to military objectives and that civilians or civilian objects shall not be the object of the attack; and second, the principle of proportionality, which prohibits attacks that may be expected to cause incidental loss of civilian life, injury to civilians, damage to civilian objects, or a combination thereof, that would be excessive in relation to the concrete and direct military advantage anticipated.[99]

Koh's description assumes that the high-level members of al-Qaeda, themselves, are lawful targets. Since they are not part of a military, the laws of war would treat al-Qaeda members presumptively as civilians who are immune from targeting unless they either "directly participate in the hostilities" or take on a "continuous combat function" within the group.[100] In May 29, 2009, the International Committee of the Red Cross published a study titled "Interpretive Guidance on the Notion of Direct Participation in Hostilities under International Humanitarian Law," whose aim was in part to define when targeted killings of members of terrorist groups would be consistent with international humanitarian law.[101] The interpretive guidance states that "individuals whose continuous function involves the preparation, execution, or command of acts or operations amounting to direct participation in hostilities assume a continuous combat function."[102] The targeted killings to date appear to involve al-Qaeda figures that would meet this description.

Meanwhile, there has been little protest as other states have begun to cite the US response to al-Qaeda to justify their own acts against terrorist groups operating from neighboring states. Examples include:

- The April 2002 killing by Russian armed forces of "Chechen rebel warlord" Omar Ibn al Khattab.[103]
- The February 2008 offensive by Turkish forces against PKK bases in northern Iraq.[104]

---

[99] Koh, *supra* note 93.
[100] Lewis, *supra* note 89, at 298.
[101] Kenneth Watkin, *Opportunity Lost: Organized Armed Groups and the ICRC "Direct Participation in Hostilities" Interpretive Guidance*, 42 N.Y.U. J. INT'L L. & POL. 641 (2010).
[102] Nils Melzer, *Interpretive Guidance on the Notion of Direct Participation in Hostilities under International Humanitarian Law*, 90 INT'L REV. RED CROSS 991, 1007 (2009).
[103] Alston, *supra* note 79, at para. 7.
[104] Theresa Reinold, *State Weakness, Irregular Warfare, and the Right to Self-Defense Post-9/11*, 105 AJIL 244, 269 (2011).

- The March 2008, air strike by Colombia against a FARC terrorist camp just inside Ecuador's border, killing the FARC's second-in-command, Raul Reyes.[105]
- The December 2009 use of force by Ethiopian armed forces against the "Islamic Courts terrorist group" which had been conducting a series of cross-border attacks from Somalia.[106]
- The May 2011 mission by US Navy Seals to kill Osama bin Laden at his secret compound in northern Pakistan on a mission to kill bin Laden.[107]
- The September 2011 Predator drone attack by the United States that killed US national Anwar al-Awlaki in Yemen.[108]
- The October 2011 Kenyan incursion into Somalia in response to cross-border attacks by the Al-Shabaab terrorist group.[109]

C A Grotian Moment That Was Still One Case Away?

Several scholars have opined that "the attack of September 11th and the American response represent a new paradigm in the international law relating to the use of force."[110] This was manifested in the statements of the United States, NATO, the OAS, and other states that 9/11 constituted an armed attack by al-Qaeda which warranted force in self-defense; Security Council Resolutions 1368 and 1373 confirming the right to use self-defense in the context of the 9/11 attacks; the international community's positive reaction to the US invasion of Afghanistan to dismantle al-Qaeda and topple its Taliban supporters; and finally the UN Special Rapporteur's conclusion that force in self-defense could be used against terrorist groups operating in the territory of states unwilling or unable to control them. The reaction to 9/11 thus broke with the conception of Article 51 as a state-centered norm.

Moreover, in the aftermath of the 9/11 attack and response, the international community embraced the concept of anticipatory self-defense in the context

---

[105] Deeks, *supra* note 7, at 534. Unlike the other incidents listed above, in this case the OAS called the Colombian incursion "a violation of the sovereignty and territorial integrity of Ecuador," and declared that "the right of each State to protect itself ... does not authorize it to commit unjust acts against another State." Reinold, *supra* note 104, at 274.

[106] Awol K. Allo, *Ethiopia's Armed Intervention in Somalia: The Legality of Self-Defense in Response to the Threat of Terrorism*, 39 DENV. J. INT'L L. & POL. 139 (2010).

[107] Jordan J. Paust, *Permissible Self-Defense Targeting and the Death of bin Laden*, 39 DENV. J. INT'L L. & POL. 569, 579–580 (2011).

[108] Jordan J. Paust, *Propriety of Self-Defense Targeting of Members of Al Qaeda and Applicable Principles of Distinction and Proportionality*, 18 I.L.S.A. J. INT'L & COMP. L. 565, 574 (2012).

[109] International Crisis Group, *The Kenyan Military Intervention in Somalia*, Africa Report No. 184, Feb. 15, 2012.

[110] Brown, *supra* note 49, at 2.

of use of force against terrorists, confirming that the *Caroline* doctrine survived the UN Charter's limitations on resort to self-defense. Thus, the UN High-Level Panel concluded in its report that "a threatened State, according to long established international law, can take military action as long as the threatened attack is imminent, no other means would deflect it and the action is proportionate."[111]

What's more, the protracted quest of the international community to arrive at a consensus definition of terrorism got a substantial boost in 2011 when the Appeals Chamber of the Security Council-created Special Tribunal for Lebanon (STL)[112] concluded that "although it is held by many scholars and other legal experts that no widely accepted definition of terrorism has evolved in the world society because of the marked difference of views on some issues, closer scrutiny reveals that in fact such a definition has gradually emerged."[113] Based on its extensive review of state practice and indicators of *opinio juris*, the Appeals Chamber declared that the customary international law definition of terrorism consists of

> the following three key elements: (i) the perpetration of a criminal act (such as murder, kidnapping, hostage-taking, arson, and so on), or threatening such an act; (ii) the intent to spread fear among the population (which would generally entail the creation of public danger) or directly or indirectly coerce a national or international authority to take some action, or to refrain from taking it; (iii) when the act involves a transnational element.[114]

The STL's definition of terrorism, together with the listing of terrorist groups and individuals by the Security Council's sanctions committee,[115] removed

---

[111] The High-Level Panel, *Report of the High-Level Panel on Threats, Challenges and Change*, 188, U.N. Doc. a/59/565 (Dec. 2, 2004).

[112] The STL, established in 2007 by the United Nations Security Council to prosecute those responsible for the 2005 bombings that killed former Lebanese Prime Minister Rafiq Hariri and twenty-two others, is the world's first international court with jurisdiction over the crime of terrorism. *See* Statute of the Special Tribunal for Lebanon, *appended to* S.C. Res. 1757, U.N. Doc. S/RES/1757 (May 30, 2007).

[113] Interlocutory Decision on the Applicable Law: Terrorism, Conspiracy, Homicide, Perpetration, Cumulative Charging, Special Tribunal for Lebanon Appeals Chamber, Case No. STL-11–01/I (Feb. 16, 2011), paras. 83, 102, http://www.stl-tsl.org/x/file/TheRegistry/Library/CaseFiles/chambers/20110216_STL-11–01_R176bis_F0010_AC_Interlocutory_Decision_Filed_EN.pdf [Interlocutory Decision]

[114] *Id.* at para. 85.

[115] The UN Security Council adopted resolution 1267 on October 15, 1999 under Chapter VII of the UN Charter, authorizing the Security Council's Sanctions Committee to establish a list of sanctioned individuals, groups, and/or entities that were found to be associated with Al-Qaida and the Taliban. S.C. Res. 1267, U.N. Doc S/Res/1267 (Oct. 15, 1999).

one of the greatest obstacles to use of force against terrorists, namely the argument that "one person's terrorist was another's freedom fighter."

One commentator has asserted that "the Bush Doctrine, first proclaimed by the US in response to the terrorist attacks of September 11, 2011, became an instant custom during the days and weeks following the attacks."[116] Yet, 9/11 is better characterized as a Grotian moment that was until the crisis in Syria still one case away from coming to fruition. The problem is that the Bush administration's assertion that there is no difference between terrorists and states that harbor them, and its assertion of a right to preventive self-defense against such states, was unnecessarily broad and lacking nuance. A state may, for example, harbor a few terrorists or serve as the organization's headquarters. The terrorist may be poorly armed or possess weapons of mass destruction. The state may provide the terrorists funding, passports, training, and intelligence; or may simply be acquiescing to their presence. The Bush Doctrine provides no guidance on how these different scenarios should be treated. Concern that the imprecision of the Bush Doctrine would lead to assertions by other states to justify aggression in the name of self-defense prompted pushback which came in the form of two post-911 cases decided by the ICJ.

In its 2004 *Advisory Opinion on the Wall*, the ICJ rejected the Israeli claim to self-defense on the reasoning that self-defense under Article 51 is not available to Israel against non-state actors operating on territories under the control of Israel.[117] In its 2005 *Armed Activities in the Congo* case, the ICJ required the responsibility of the Congo for the attacks of Ugandan rebels operating from the Congolese territory in order to find Uganda's right to self-defense lawful.[118] These cases signaled the ICJ's "determination to counter a more permissive reading of Article 51" brought on by the international community's reaction to 9/11.[119]

Scholars and certain members of the ICJ have been highly critical of the ICJ's continued insistence after 9/11 that self-defense is only available in cases where the attack by non-state actors can be attributed to the territorial state.

---

[116] Langille, *supra* note 66, at 154.

[117] Legal Consequences of the Construction of a Wall in the Occupied Palestinian Territory, Advisory Opinion, 2004 I.C.J. 136, 194 (July 9).

[118] Dem. Rep. Congo v. Uganda (holding that Uganda could not rely on self-defense to justify its military operation in the Congo because (1) Uganda did not immediately report to the Security Council following its use of force as required by Article 51, (2) Uganda's actions were vastly disproportionate to the threat, and (3) there was no evidence from which to impute the attacks against Ugandan villages by rebel groups operating out of the Congo to the government of Congo).

[119] Theresa Reinold, *State Weakness, Irregular Warfare, and the Right to Self-Defense Post-9/11*, 105 AJIL 244, 261 (2011).

Scholars point out that the ICJ holdings are inconsistent with the wellspring of the customary law on self-defense, the *Caroline case*, which confirmed that anticipatory force in self-defense was lawful against non-state actors whose conduct was not attributable to a state.[120] Writing separately in the *Wall* case, Judge Higgins said, "There is, with respect, nothing in the text of Article 51 that thus stipulates that self-defense is available only when an armed attack is made by a State."[121] Similarly, writing separately in the *Congo* case, Judge Koojimans noted that in the era of al-Qaeda, it is "unreasonable to deny the attacked State the right to self-defense merely because there is no attacker State."[122] Judge Simma similarly concluded in his separate opinion in the *Congo* case that "Security Council resolutions 1368 (2001) and 1373 (2001) cannot but be read as affirmations of the view that large-scale attacks by non-State actors can qualify as 'armed attacks' within the meaning of Article 51."[123]

While the ICJ's *Wall* and *Congo* decisions may have put breaks on the rapidly crystallizing customary international law emerging from 9/11, their long-term impact on the development of the law of self-defense against terrorists will likely be negligible. This is because the situation in the *Wall* and *Congo* cases are quite distinguishable from that of a state using force against terrorists operating in a foreign state. In the *Wall* case, the ICJ stressed that the right to self-defense under Article 51 of the UN Charter only applied to attacks emanating from another state and did not apply to attacks coming from within the Occupied Territories, because the area was controlled by Israel.[124] In *Congo*, as in *Nicaragua*, the use of force was not limited to attacking the terrorist group itself, but involved widespread attacks throughout the territorial state.

The case study of use of force against non-state actors indicates how international courts are both capable of catalyzing and setting back the formation of customary international law during a potential Grotian moment. In light of these conflicting currents, the law could not be said to have been settled on the eve of the US military action against ISIS in Syria. Has the international response to the Syria situation provided the tipping point that has crystallized the new customary international law?

---

[120] *See* R.Y. Jennings, *The Caroline and McLeod Cases*, 32 AJIL 82, 82–89 (1938) (*quoting* 61 Parliamentary Papers (1843)).

[121] Legal Consequences of the Construction of a Wall in the Occupied Palestinian Territory, Advisory Opinion (separate opinion of Judge Higgins).

[122] Dem. Rep. Congo v. Uganda, para. 28.

[123] *Id.*, para. 11.

[124] Legal Consequences of the Construction of a Wall in the Occupied Palestinian Territory, Advisory Opinion, 139.

The US government has asserted that Syria is "unwilling or unable" to deal effectively with the ISIS threat emanating from within its borders to Iraq[125] and the United States.[126] This is the same argument that the United States has used elsewhere, most notably to justify its operation to kill Osama bin Laden without Pakistan's approval.

Experts believe that "the world reaction to the conflict against ISIS in Syria will help resolve the uncertain status of the unwilling or unable standard for force against non-state actors in third party territory."[127] There has been almost no protest of the use of force against ISIS in Syria. Even the Syrian government has been largely mute since ISIS is seen as a common enemy.[128] Since lack of protest is an important ingredient in the recognition of new rules of customary international law, this silence can be perceived as acquiescence. Yet, it is sometimes said that "good facts make bad law."[129] In the case of use of force against ISIS in Syria, ISIS is widely seen as "a rogue actor" that threatens all countries. This can cause governments to turn a "blind eye" to a troubling legal rationale.[130] In such a case, one must be careful about treating a lack of protest as acceptance of a new legal rule.

How a custom pioneer describes the new rule can greatly impact its international acceptance. Before settling on collective self-defense as its primary argument, the US officials tried out a variety of alternative legal arguments to justify using force in Syria. For example, US officials said that the strikes against ISIS "are in a part of Syria that is currently outside the authority of the Syrian government" and thus "in our eyes, a legal no-man's land."[131] The Chairman of the Joint Chiefs of Staff said ISIS has "to be addressed on both sides of what is essentially at this point a nonexistent border."[132] Perhaps the most remarkable of these arguments was put forth by Secretary of State John Kerry, who testified before the Senate that since ISIS attacks Iraq from and then retreats to Syria, a "right of hot pursuit" could provide a basis for

---

[125] Power, *supra* note 5.

[126] *Id.*

[127] Jens David Ohlin, *The Unwilling or Unable Doctrine Comes to Life*, http://opiniojuris.org/2014/09/23/unwilling-unable-doctrine-comes-life

[128] Reuters, *U.S. and Arab Allies Launch First Strikes on Militants in Syria*, N.Y. Times, Sept. 23, 2014, http://www.nytimes.com/reuters/2014/09/23/world/middleeast/23reuters-syria-crisis.html

[129] Mariana Bracic, *Good Facts Make Bad Law*, http://www.mbclegal.ca/assets/28_good-facts-make-bad-law.pdf

[130] Noah Feldman on NPR, *All Things Considered, Are US Airstrikes in Syria Legal?* Sept. 25, 2014, http://www.npr.org/2014/09/25/351529354/are-u-s-air-strikes-in-syria-legal

[131] Firman DeBrabander, *Drones and the Democracy Disconnect*, N.Y. Times, April 9, 2014.

[132] Associated Press, *Obama Again Faces Tug of Military Action in Syria*, N.Y. Times, Aug. 23, 2014, http://www.nytimes.com/aponline/2014/08/23/us/politics/ap-us-obama-syria.html

military force against ISIS in Syria.[133] While there is a recognized right of hot pursuit to pursue ships escaping in international waters, there is no authority for application of the doctrine to forces on land. Nevertheless, the United States has made the argument in the past, for example in relation to Maj. Gen. John Pershing's expeditionary force of 4,800 troops to pursue Mexican revolutionary Pancho Villa in 1916 into Mexican territory, in relation to the bombing of Cambodia and Laos in 1969 to pursue Vietcong who crossed into their territory from Vietnam, and in relation to pursuing Taliban forces from Afghanistan into Pakistan in 2007.[134] Notably, these incidents were met with widespread protest and condemnation. Moreover, if accepted, this land-based hot pursuit rationale could create a slippery slope, leading to border violations by many other states around the globe.

Yet, perhaps the most questionable aspect of the US self-defense argument is that Syria is not in fact unwilling to combat ISIS, which presents as much a threat to the government of Syria as to Iraq. The Syrian government has actively fought the group and has said that it is willing to cooperate in the effort to eradicate ISIS. At the same time, Syria has said, "Any strike which is not coordinated with the government will be considered as aggression."[135] But the United States does not want to provide what it considers to be a rogue regime the stature that would come with partnering with it against ISIS. Perhaps its best argument is that partnering with the Syrian military and intelligence would likely compromise the effectiveness of the operations against ISIS,[136] but to an objective observer, Syria does not fit neatly into the "unwilling and unable" formulation.

Finally, while the United States has made a credible collective self-defense argument to justify its attacks on ISIS, its argument for also attacking the Khorasan group has been less well received. Several of President Obama's aides told the media that air strikes against Khorasan were launched to foil an "imminent" terrorist attack.[137] But, later, US officials acknowledged that the Khorasan plot was only "aspirational" and that the group had not established a concrete plan, had not decided on a method of attack, and had not even selected a target.[138] As such, the attacks on

---

[133] Matthew Lee, Daily Mail, Sept. 23, 2014.

[134] *Id.*

[135] Ryan Goodman, *International Law on Airstrikes against ISIS in Syria*, Just Security (Aug. 28, 2014), at https://www.justsecurity.org/14414/international-law-airstrikes-isis-syria

[136] *Id.*

[137] White House Press Briefing, Airstrikes in Syria, Sept. 23, 2014, https://www.whitehouse.gov/the-press-office/2014/09/23/background-conference-call-airstrikes-syria

[138] Ivan Eland, *Legal Basis for U.S. War in Iraq and Syria Is Thin*, Independent Institute, Sept. 29, 2014.

Khorasan targets harken to President Bush's controversial preventive self-defense principle, and thus potentially undermined the crystallization of the Syrian crisis Grotian moment.

IV 2015: THE GROTIAN MOMENT COMES TO FRUITION

In the aftermath of the ISIS bombing of a Russian jetliner over the Sinai desert on October 31, 2015, and ISIS attacks on a Paris stadium and concert hall on November 13, 2015, the UN Security Council unanimously adopted Resolution 2249, which determined that ISIS is "a global and unprecedented threat to international peace and security," and called for "all necessary measures" to "eradicate the safe haven [ISIS] established" in Syria.[139]

The October 31 and November 13 ISIS attacks were a game changer, killing and injuring over 824 nationals of Russia, France, and twenty-two other countries. They showed that ISIS – the richest and most technologically advanced terrorist organization in the world – was no longer confining its objectives to territorial acquisition in Syria and Iraq, but had adopted the tactics of other terrorist groups, focusing on attacking vulnerable targets outside the Levant. Moreover, Russia was now just as much a target as the West.

Resolution 2249 did not provide a new stand-alone legal basis or authorization for use of force against ISIS in Syria.[140] Unlike past Security Council resolutions that have authorized force, Resolution 2249 does not mention Article 42, or even Chapter VII, of the UN Charter, which is the article and chapter under which the Security Council can permit states to use force as an exception to Article 2(4) of the UN Charter. Nor does the resolution use the word "authorizes" or even "decides" in relation to use of force. These textual differences led Mark Weller, Professor of International Law at the University of Cambridge, to conclude that "this language suggests that the resolution does not grant any fresh authority for states seeking to take action."[141]

But the resolution does stand as a confirmation by the Security Council that use of force against ISIS in Syria is permissible. Importantly, the French Security Council Representative, who had sponsored Resolution 2249, stated

---

[139] S.C. Res. 2249 (Nov. 20, 2015).

[140] Arabella Lang, Legal Basis for UK Military Action in Syria, House of Commons Library Briefing Paper No. 7404, Dec. 1, 2015, at 8, https://www.voltairenet.org/IMG/pdf/CBP-7404.pdf [https://perma.cc/FH4P-NPMH]

[141] Id.

in his explanation of vote on the resolution that "collective action could now be based on Article 51 [self-defense] of the United Nations Charter."[142] With a unanimous confirmation, Resolution 2249 will play an important role in crystallizing the new rule of customary international law regarding use of force in self-defense against non-state actors – a phenomenon colorfully described by Professor David Koplow of Georgetown as "helping to midwife the development of new norms of customary international law."[143]

Any doubt of the importance of the Security Council Resolution was dispelled when a few days after its adoption the UK parliament voted on December 2, 2015 to approve (397:223) air strikes against ISIS in Syria despite the earlier views of many MPs that such action could not be legally justified.[144] Immediately thereafter, the UK joined the United States in bombing ISIS targets throughout Syria.[145]

Perhaps the final chapter of the US war against ISIS was written on October 26, 2019, when the United States launched a Special Ops mission that resulted in the death of the leader of ISIS, Abu Bakr al-Baghdadi. The nighttime raid was conducted with eight US helicopters, accompanied by several fixed-wing aircraft, which flew over Turkish territory and Russian-controlled airspace in northwest Syria with Turkey's and Russia's permission. The raid involved seventy Delta Force troops. Al-Baghdadi had led ISIS since 2010.[146] There was no international protest of this military operation.

V CONCLUSION

This chapter has examined whether the use of force against ISIS during the Syrian conflict has given rise to a so-called Grotian moment: an instance of rapid formation of a new rule of customary international law, in this case

---

[142] Security Council "Unequivocally" Condemns ISIL Terrorist Attacks, Unanimously Adopting Text that Determines Extremist Group Poses "Unprecedented" Threat, U.N. Press Release (Nov. 20, 2015), http://www.un.org/press/en/2015/sc12132.doc.htm [https://perma.cc/2B2L-CJPF] (last visited Dec. 20, 2015).

[143] DAVID KAPLOW, *International Legal Standards and the Weaponization of Outer Space, in* SPACE: THE NEXT GENERATION – CONFERENCE REPORT, 31 MARCH–1 APRIL 2008, UNITED NATIONS INSTITUTE FOR DISARMAMENT RESEARCH 162 (2008).

[144] Steven Erlanger & Stephen Castle, *British Jets Hit ISIS in Syria after Parliament Authorizes Airstrikes*, N.Y. TIMES, Dec. 3, 2015, A16, http://www.nytimes.com/2015/12/03/world/europe/britainparliament-syria-airstrikes-vote.html?_r=0 [https://perma.cc/N4722RB6] (last visited Dec. 18, 2015).

[145] *Id.*

[146] Courtney Kube et al., *ISIS Leader Abu Bakr al-Baghdadi Killed in U.S. Raid in Syria, Trump Confirms*, NBC News, Oct. 27, 2019.

recognizing the right of states to attack non-state actors when the territorial state is unable or unwilling to suppress the threat they pose. Such a right would constitute a radical change from the prior-existing rule, which had required effective control of the non-state actors by the territorial state as a precondition to the use of force against them.

Ordinarily, customary international law takes many decades to crystallize. In this context, eighteen years would constitute almost instant custom. Historically, there has been a series of other instances of so-called Grotian moments, where a context of fundamental change served as an accelerating agent, enabling customary international law to form much more rapidly, and with less state practice, than is normally the case. Each represented a radical legal development. In each, the development was ushered in by the urgency of dealing with fundamental change. In some cases the change was the advent of new technology, as with offshore drilling and outer space flight. In others it was in the form of pervasive moral outrage regarding shocking revelations of crimes against humanity, as preceded the establishment of the Nuremberg Tribunal and the creation of the Yugoslavia Tribunal.

ISIS and al-Qaeda were widely viewed as representing a new kind of threat, in which a non-state actor possesses many of the attributes of a state: massive wealth, sophisticated training and organization, and access to destructive weaponry. To respond to the fundamental change presented by these uber-terrorist groups, the United States has argued that it is now lawful to attack such non-state actors when they are present in states that are unable or unwilling to curb them. In light of the Security Council approval of the 2001 invasion of Afghanistan to dislodge al-Qaeda and the absence of significant protest of the subsequent drone strikes against al-Qaeda leaders and operatives in Pakistan, Somalia, Iraq, and Yemen, international law seemed to be moving rapidly toward adoption of the "unable and unwilling" principle of self-defense. But in the 2004 *Wall* and 2005 *Congo* cases, the ICJ reaffirmed that international law permits extraterritorial attacks against non-state actors only when their actions are attributable to the territorial state, utilizing an effective control standard. Despite widespread criticism of these holdings, including from some of the ICJ's most respected members, these judicial decisions unquestionably set back the evolving customary international law of self-defense against non-state actors.

This chapter concludes that the international community's response to ISIS in Syria has provided the final push necessary to bring the Grotian moment to fruition. Despite its ambiguity, Resolution 2249 will likely be viewed as confirming that use of force in self-defense is now permissible against non-state actors where the territorial state is unable to suppress the threat that they pose. In the words of the Institute of International Law, "where a rule of customary law is (merely) emerging or there is still some doubt as to its status" a unanimous non-binding resolution of the General Assembly or Security Council "can consolidate the custom and remove doubts which might have existed."[147]

The implication of this newly accepted change in the international law of self-defense is that any state can now lawfully use force against non-state actors (terrorists, rebels, pirates, drug cartels, etc.) that are present in the territory of another state if the territorial state is unable or unwilling to suppress the threat posed by those non-state actors. The number of candidates for such action is quite large. The US Department of State maintains a list of terrorist organizations that pose a significant threat to the United States and its allies around the world, which includes fifty-eight terrorist groups headquartered in thirty-five different countries (in addition to ISIS in Syria/Iraq).[148]

The dangers inherent in this new doctrine of self-defense against non-state actors became apparent in October 2019 when Turkey launched a military offensive into northeast Syria, seeking to uproot the Kurdish-led militia and establish a 20-mile wide buffer zone.[149] Turkey submitted a letter to the UN Security Council, justifying its invasion as an effort to clear out terrorists in self-defense as permitted under Article 51 of the UN Charter.[150] Turkey considers the Kurdish militia in Syria an offshoot of the Kurdistan Workers' Party (PKK), which has waged a decades-long insurgency inside Turkey.[151] Citing Security Council Resolution 2249 confirming the right to use force against terrorists in Syria, Turkey said its operation would be "proportionate, measured and responsible."[152] "The operation will target only terrorists and their hideouts, shelters, emplacements, weapons, vehicles and equipment," the letter added.[153] But the UN Secretary General said that at least 160,000

---

[147] Committee on Formation of Customary (General) International Law, *Conference Report London*, ILA 25 (2000), http://www.ila-hq.org/en/committees/index.cfm/cid/30 [https://perma.cc/QG73-RLMH]

[148] Bureau of Counterterrorism, *Foreign Terrorist Organizations*, US Dep't of State, http://www.state.gov/j/ct/rls/other/des/123085.htm [https://perma.cc/U85H-7XRC] (last visited, Dec. 24, 2015).

[149] Ben Hubbard et al., *Abandoned by U.S. in Syria, Kurds Find New Ally in American Foe*, N.Y. Times, Oct. 13, 2019.

[150] Edith M. Lederer, *Turkey Says Ongoing Invasion into Syria Is Self-Defense*, Military Times, Oct. 14, 2019.

[151] Patrick Kingsley, *Who Are the Kurds, and Why Is Turkey Attacking Them in Syria?*, N.Y. Times, Oct. 14, 2019.

[152] *Id.*

[153] *Id.*

civilians had been displaced and that the military action had resulted in thousands of civilian casualties.[154]

Importantly, the right to use force against such non-state actors is subject to several limitations which may impede abuse of the doctrine. First, the individual or aggregate actions of the non-state actors must amount to the equivalent of an armed attack to trigger the right to use force in self-defense. Second, the use of force must be targeted against the non-state actors and not the state or its military unless the state is found to be in effective control of the non-state actors. Third, military action must still meet the principles of necessity, proportionality, and discrimination. It is not at all clear that the October 2019 Turkish offensive would meet those requirements. Further limitations are likely to develop in relation to international reaction to state invocation and application of the new rule.

[154] *Id.*

5

Humanitarian Intervention in Response to Use
of Chemical Weapons

I INTRODUCTION

This chapter[1] examines whether the allied air strikes against Syria on April 14, 2018 may have crystalized an emerging customary norm of humanitarian intervention, thereby representing a historic development in international law.[2]

The United States, France, and United Kingdom have said that they launched the April 2018 air strikes to prevent the Assad regime from continuing to use chemical weapons against the Syrian population. Before the Syrian air strikes, most countries and experts had taken the position that there was no international law right of humanitarian intervention under customary international law or the UN Charter except when authorized by the UN Security Council. As detailed in this chapter, however, the international response to the Syrian air strikes has been overwhelmingly supportive. Is this a Grotian moment?

The chapter begins by setting forth the background of the April 6, 2017 and April 14, 2018 air strikes against Syria. This is followed by an examination of the evolving view of humanitarian intervention, starting with the 1999 NATO air strikes against Serbia to save the Kosovo Albanians from ethnic cleansing. Finally, it explores the articulated justification for the Syrian air strikes and the response of the international community to determine whether or how the air strikes and the international response have altered international law.

---

[1] Parts of this chapter previously appeared as Michael P. Scharf, *Striking a Grotian Moment: How the 2018 Airstrikes on Syria Have Changed International Law Related to Humanitarian Intervention*, 19.2 CHI. J. INT'L L. 586–614 (2019).

[2] Customary international law means those rules of international law that derive from and reflect a general practice accepted as law. International Law Commission, Second Report on the Identification of Customary International Law, 22 May 2014, U.N. Doc. A/CN.4/672 (Draft Conclusion 2).

II BACKGROUND ON THE SYRIAN AIR STRIKES

A *President Obama Draws a Red Line*

Since the civil war in Syria began in 2011, Syria has presented the international community with its greatest challenges to international peace and security.[3] Responding to the crisis has been complicated by the unique geopolitical situation. Dating back to the 1970s, Russia has been a close ally of the Assad regime, which allows Russia to keep its only naval base outside the former Soviet Union at the Syrian Mediterranean port of Tartus.[4] As such, Russia has vetoed Security Council resolutions condemning Assad's harsh actions against the civilian population, blocked the Security Council from authorizing investigations into Syria's use of chemical weapons, and prevented the Council from referring the situation to the International Criminal Court.[5]

In reaction to reports that the Assad regime had amassed chemical weapons, on October 20, 2012, US President Barack Obama declared that Syria's use of chemical weapons would be a "red line."[6] If the Assad regime deployed the internationally banned weapons, it would trigger an immediate American military response. He reiterated this threat on several occasions in the following months. Then on August 21, 2013, the Assad regime used chemical weapons on a large scale in the opposition-held Ghouta area of Damascus, causing 1,400 civilian casualties.[7]

In response, President Obama tried and ultimately failed to gain support from Congress and international allies to launch a narrowly tailored attack on Syria.[8] At the time, polls revealed that only 36 percent of Americans favored

---

[3] Provisional Verbatim Record of the Security Council, Threats to International Peace and Security: The Situation in the Middle East, U.N. Doc. S/PV.8233, Apr. 14, 2018.

[4] Sam LaGrone, *Russia, Syria, Agree on Mediterranean Naval Base Expansion, Refit of Syrian Ships*, USNI NEWS, Jan. 20, 2017, https://news.usni.org/2017/01/20/russia-syria-agree-tartus-naval-base-expansion-refit-syrian-ships

[5] Provisional Verbatim Record of the Security Council, *supra* note 3.

[6] Glen Kessler, *President Obama and the "Red Line" on Syria's Chemical Weapons*, WASHINGTON POST, Sept. 6, 2013, https://www.washingtonpost.com/news/fact-checker/wp/2013/09/06/president-obama-and-the-red-line-on-syrias-chemical-weapons/?utm_term=.5d70c53d0668

[7] Secretary-General's remarks to the Security Council on the report of the United Nations Missions to Investigate Allegations of the Use of Chemical Weapons on the incident that occurred on Aug. 21, 2013 in the Ghouta area of Damascus, Sept. 16, 2013, https://www.un.org/sg/en/content/sg/statement/2013-09-16/secretary-generals-remarks-security-council-report-united-nations

[8] Pater Baker & Jonathan Weisman, *Obama Seeks Approval by Congress for Strike in Syria*, N.Y. TIMES, Aug. 31, 2013, http//www.nytimes.com/2013/09/01/world/middleeast/syria.html

the United States taking military action to prevent Syria's chemical weapons use, while 51 percent of those surveyed opposed such military action.[9] Lacking congressional and popular support, the Obama administration never took military action. Rather, it accepted a Russian-brokered deal under which the Assad regime agreed to give up its chemical weapons and submit to international inspections.[10]

B *The April 6, 2017 Unilateral Air Strikes*

It soon became clear that the Russian-brokered deal had failed to prevent Syrian possession and use of chemical weapons. On April 7, 2017, four months after President Donald Trump came into office, the United States fired fifty-nine Tomahawk missiles at the Shayrat Airfield in Syria. President Trump said the air strike was conducted in response to the Assad regime's chemical weapons attack on the town of Khan Sheikhoun using deadly sarin gas, which killed seventy-two people including a number of children on April 4.[11] Shayrat Airfield was selected because it had been used to store chemical weapons and aircraft employed in the April 4 attack.[12]

The United States acted alone, and President Trump did not articulate a legal rationale but said the air strikes were necessary "to secure the national security interests of the U.S."[13] US ambassador to the UN, Nikki R. Haley, said that the United States was "justified" in striking the airbase as "a very measured step" and warned that the United States is "prepared to do more."[14]

Despite the lack of a stated legal justification, many of America's allies defended the missile strikes. British Secretary of State for Defense, Michael Fallon announced that Britain "fully supported" the strike in its limited scope and appropriate proportional response."[15] The European Union was similarly

[9] Clare Malona, *America's Fickle Relationship with Humanitarian Intervention*, FIVETHIRTYEIGHT, Apr. 10, 2017, https://fivethirtyeight.com/features/americas-fickle-relationship-with-humanitarian-intervention

[10] Michael R. Gordon, *U.S. and Russia Reach Deal to Destroy Syria's Chemical Arms*, N.Y. TIMES, Sept. 14, 2013, https://www.nytimes.com/2013/09/15/world/middleeast/syria-talks.html

[11] Statement by President Trump on Syria, White House Press Secretary, Apr. 6, 2017, https://www.whitehouse.gov/the-press-office/2017/04/06/statement-president-trump-syria

[12] Id.

[13] *Id.*

[14] Somini Sengupta, Neil MacFarquhar, and Jennifer Steinhauer, *US Airstrikes in Syria: Fallout Around the World*, N.Y. TIMES, Apr. 7, 2017, https://www.nytimes.com/2017/04/07/us/politics/trump-syria-airstrikes.html

[15] Anushka Asthana, *Syria Airstrikes: UK Offers Verbal But Not Military Support to US*, THE GUARDIAN, Apr. 7, 2017, 2017, https://www.theguardian.com/world/2017/apr/07/syria-airstrikes-uk-offers-verbal-but-not-military-support-to-us

supportive, saying that Syria's use of chemical weapons cannot go unanswered.[16] In the Middle East, Saudi Arabia, Jordan, and Turkey said they supported the missile strikes as a "necessary and appropriate response."[17]

Only Russia, Iran, Bolivia, and Syria opposed the air strikes. Russian Foreign Minister Sergei Lavrov called the strikes "an act of aggression under a completely invented pretext."[18]

C *The April 14, 2018 Multilateral Air Strikes*

With Russia's assistance, in 2018 the Assad regime began the end game in its civil war, using overwhelming force to punish local populations where insurgents remained active.[19] On April 7, 2018, there was an attack using chlorine gas in the eastern Damascus suburb of Douma that killed more than eighty civilians. In response, on April 14, 2018, the United States, France, and Britain together launched another round of missile strikes against Syria.

"The nations of Britain, France and the United States of America have marshalled their righteous power against barbarism and brutality," President Trump said in an address from the White House announcing the military action. "The purpose of our actions tonight is to establish a strong deterrent against the production, spread, and use of chemical weapons," he said. He added, "[w]e are prepared to sustain this response until the Syrian regime stops its use of prohibited chemical agents."[20]

A variety of naval vessels and jets fired 103 missiles – about double what was launched in April 2017. The Chairman of the US Joint Chiefs of Staff, Joseph Dunford, said the targets were "specifically associated" with Syria's chemical weapons program. They included a scientific research facility in Damascus, a chemical weapons storage facility west of Homs, and a chemical weapons equipment storage site and command post, near Homs.[21,22]

---

[16] Syria War: World Reaction to US Missile Attack, BBC, Apr. 7, 2017, http://www.bbc.com/news/world-us-canada-39526089

[17] Madison Park, Who's with the US on Syria Strike and Who Isn't, CNN, Apr. 8 2017, http://www.cnn.com/2017/04/07/world/syria-us-strike-world-reaction/index.html

[18] *Id.*

[19] Daniel Brown, *A Compelling Theory Explains the Latest Chemical Attack in Syria – And It Looks Like Assad Got What He Wanted*, Business Insider, Apr. 9, 2018, https://www.businessinsider.com/why-assad-probably-used-chemical-weapons-syria-2018-4

[20] BBC, Syria Air Strikes: US and Allies Attack "Chemical Weapons Sites," Apr. 14, 2018, https//www.bbc.com/news/world-middle-east-43762251

[21] *Id.*

[22] *Id.*

"This is going to set the Syrian chemical weapons program back for years," Lt. General Kenneth McKenzie, a director of the US Joint Chiefs of Staff, told reporters.[23]

Decrying that the international investigators had just arrived in Douma to begin their examination of the suspected use of chemical weapons there, Russia called the air strikes "an act of aggression" and "a violation of the UN Charter and the norms and principles of international law."[24] But a Russian-sponsored Security Council resolution that would have condemned the attack was soundly defeated by a vote of three in favor, eight against, and four abstentions.[25] Both inside and outside the Council, the international reaction to the air strikes reflected broad support.[26]

III THE CHANGING LAW OF HUMANITARIAN INTERVENTION

This section describes how the NATO air strikes against Serbia in an effort to prevent ethnic cleansing of Kosovar Albanians in 1999 laid the groundwork for an eventual paradigm shift concerning the international community's view of the legality of humanitarian intervention in the absence of Security Council authorization.

A *Historic Status of Humanitarian Intervention*

Since the 1648 Peace of Westphalia, state sovereignty has been regarded as the fundamental paradigm of international law. Leading scholars have described the prohibition of the threat or use of force in Article 2(4) of the UN Charter as "the cornerstone of the Charter system."[27] This prohibition goes hand in hand with the nonintervention principle enshrined in Article 2(7) of the UN

---

[23] Laris Karklis et al., *Airstrikes in Syria Hit 3 Chemical Weapons Facilities, Including One in Damascus,* Washington Post, Apr. 14, 2018 (page unavailable, online version).

[24] Alonso Gurmendi Dunkelberg et al., *Mapping States Reactions to the Syria Strikes of April 2018,* Just Security, Apr. 22, 2018, https://www.justsecurity.org/55157/mapping-states-reactions-syria-strikes-april-2018

[25] Provisional Verbatim Record of the Security Council, *supra* note 3. Russia told the Security Council, "Just as it did a year ago, when it attacked Syria's Al-Shayrat airbase in Syria, the United States took a staged use of toxic substances against civilians as a pretext, this time in Douma, outside Damascus. Having visited the site of the alleged incident, Russian military experts found no traces of chlorine or any other toxic agent." *Id.*

[26] Gurmendi Dunkelberg et al., *supra* note 24.

[27] James L. Brierly, The Law of Nations: An Introduction to the International Law of Peace 414 (6th ed. 1963); Ian Brownlie, Principles of Public International Law 732 (7th ed. 2008).

Charter, which prohibits coercive intervention into the exclusively domestic affairs of a state.[28]

As discussed in Chapter 3, there are only three exceptions to the nonuse of force rule enumerated in the UN Charter. The first covers situations that qualify as self-defense in the face of an armed attack under Article 51 of the Charter. The second covers situations where the use of force has been authorized by the Security Council under Article 42 of the Charter in response to a threat to the peace, a breach of the peace, or an act of aggression. And the third involves situations where the territorial state has consented to the use of force within its borders.

In the last fifty years, the Security Council has significantly broadened what it considers as qualifying as a threat to the peace. Thus, the Council found threats to the peace in situations involving widespread human rights violations and humanitarian atrocities in Southern Rhodesia (1969), South Africa (1977), Somalia (1992), Rwanda (1994), East Timor (1999), Kosovo (1999), and Libya (2011). In 1992, the president of the Security Council acknowledged this conceptual shift, stating "the mere absence of war and military conflict among States does not itself ensure international peace and security – rather, intrastate humanitarian situations can also become threats peace and security."[29] Yet, Security Council action is often thwarted by the threat or use of the veto by its Permanent Members, and consequently, the Council has failed to authorize humanitarian intervention in situations such as Rwanda in 1994, where 800,000 deaths would likely have been prevented had the Council acted.

While the Security Council was increasing its ability to respond to atrocities within a state, the United Nations General Assembly adopted a number of instruments designed to limit resort to humanitarian intervention outside the framework of the United Nations. These include the 1965 Declaration on the Inadmissibility of Intervention that denied legal recognition to intervention "for any reason whatsoever"; the 1970 Declaration on Principles of International Law concerning Friendly Relations and Cooperation that confirmed that "[n]o State or group of States has the right to intervene ... in the internal or external affairs of any other State"; and the 1987 Declaration on the Enhancement of the Effectiveness of the Principle of Refraining from the

---

[28] Military and Paramilitary Activities (Nicaragua v. United States), 1986 I.C.J. 14, 107–108 (June 27).

[29] Mehrdad Payandeh, *With Great Power Comes Great Responsibility? The Concept of the Responsibility to Protect within the Process of International Lawmaking*, 35 Yale J. Int'l L. 470, 495 (2010) (quoting Note by the President of the Security Council, U.N. Doc. S/23500 (Jan. 31, 1992)).

Threat or Use of Force in International Relations, which stated that "no consideration of whatever nature may be invoked to warrant resorting to the threat or use of force in violation of the Charter."[30]

Prior to the 1999 NATO bombing campaign, there had been several cases where foreign intervention was employed to halt widespread atrocities without Security Council approval. Hence, India stopped the slaughter in East Pakistan in 1971, Tanzania ended Idi Amin's mass killing in Uganda in 1978, Vietnam's intervention brought an end to Pol Pot's killing fields in Cambodia in 1979, and the US and UK unilaterally imposed a no-fly zone over the northern and southern thirds of Iraq following the 1991 conflict in order to protect the Kurds and Marsh Arabs from Saddam Hussein's retaliation.[31] In the first three cases, self-defense, rather than humanitarian concern, was the primary justification asserted, and in the case of Iraq, the U.S. claimed residual authority from Security Council Resolution 688 which ended the 1991 war.[32] In none of these cases did the international community endorse a right of unilateral humanitarian intervention. And in the case of the Iraq no-fly zone, three Permanent Members of the Security Council – Russia, China, and France – repeatedly protested the legality of the U.K. and U.S. action.[33]

B *The 1999 NATO Intervention*

The Kosovo crisis in 1998–1999 emerged out of the same historic backdrop of ethnic tensions that had engulfed the former Yugoslavia in a brutal ethnic conflict in 1991–1995. Kosovo was a Serbian province where the population was 90 percent ethnic Albanian Muslims and 10 percent Serbian Eastern Orthodox.[34] In 1998, purportedly in response to the threat posed by Kosovar insurgents, Serb military and security forces launched a series of attacks that appeared intended to ethnically cleanse the region.

---

[30] NICHOLAS J. WHEELER, *Reflections on the Legality and Legitimacy of NATO's Intervention in Kosovo*, in THE KOSOVO TRAGEDY: THE HUMAN RIGHTS DIMENSIONS 149 (Ken Booth, ed., 2001).

[31] *Id.* 150.

[32] SIMON CHESTERMAN, *No More Rwandas No More Kosovos: Intervention and Prevention*, in Velaso & Daniel Ortega Nieto (eds.), THE PROTECTION OF HUMAN RIGHTS: A CHALLENGE IN THE 21ST CENTURY 175–200 (2007).

[33] Christine Grey, *From Unity to Polarization: International Law and the Use of Force against Iraq*, 13 EJIL 1, 10 (2002).

[34] Noel Cox, *Developments in the Laws of War: NATO Attacks on Yugoslavia and the Use of Force to Achieve Humanitarian Objectives*, in NEW ZEALAND ARMED FORCES LAW REVIEW 13–24 (2002).

In Resolution 1199 of March 31, 1998, the UN Security Council determined that the situation in Kosovo constituted a threat to the peace and, acting under Chapter VII of the UN Charter, called upon the parties to comply with certain provisional measures for quelling the conflict.[35] The preamble of the resolution referred to the "recent intense fighting in Kosovo" and "in particular the excessive and indiscriminate use of force by Serbian security forces and the Yugoslav Army which had resulted in numerous civilian casualties and, according to the Secretary-General, the displacement of over 230,000 persons from their homes."

Resolution 1203 of October 24, 1998, repeated that the Kosovo situation constituted a threat to the peace; insisted upon the cessation of hostilities, withdrawal of certain forces and the commitment of the parties to seek a political resolution; and authorized an OSCE Kosovo Verification Mission and a NATO Air Verification Mission to monitor compliance with the provisional measures required under Resolution 1199.[36] But the Security Council resolutions did not authorize the use of force, and Russia made it clear that it would veto any attempt to do so.

Nevertheless, after peace negotiations broke down in March 1999, NATO decided to launch a series of aerial attacks against military and strategic targets in Serbia with the intent to persuade the Serbian government, headed by Slobodan Milošević, to comply with United Nations Security Council Resolutions 1199 and 1203. Following the massacres of Kosovars in Drenica, Gornje Obrinje, and Racak, the NATO States had come to the conclusion that unless action was taken a humanitarian catastrophe would unfold, potentially eclipsing that of Bosnia.[37] The bombing campaign, called "Operation Allied Force," involved 912 aircraft, which flew a total of 37,225 bombing missions.[38] A significant feature of the Kosovo incident is the purity of the actors' motives – "there were no strategic or material interests of NATO nations in Kosovo."[39]

In explaining its decision to issue an activation order to use NATO force in the Kosovo crisis, the North Atlantic Council stated, "[T]he unrestrained assault by Yugoslav military, police and paramilitary forces, under the direction of President Milošević, on Kosovar civilians has created a massive

---

[35] S.C. Res. 1160, para. 8 (Mar. 31, 1998).

[36] S.C. Res. 1203, paras. 1–3 (Oct. 24, 1998).

[37] Steven Haines, *The Influence of Operation Allied Force on the Development of the Jus Ad Bellum*, 85 INT'L AFF. 477, 480 (2009).

[38] Patrick T. Egan, *The Kosovo Intervention and Collective Self-Defense*, 8 INT'L PEACEKEEPING 39, 40 (2001).

[39] Fernando R. Teson, *Kosovo: A Powerful Precedent for the Doctrine of Humanitarian Intervention*, 2 AMSTERDAM L.F. 119 (2009).

humanitarian catastrophe, which also threatens to destabilize the surrounding region ... These extreme and criminally irresponsible policies, which cannot be defended on any grounds, have made necessary and justify the military action by NATO."[40]

In the early days of the bombing campaign, British Prime Minister Tony Blair explained the humanitarian justification for the action. "This is not a battle for NATO; this is not a battle for territory; this is a battle for humanity. This is a just case, it is a rightful cause."[41] When pressed in parliament for the legal rationale for the NATO bombing campaign, Blair's Secretary for Defense, George Robertson, provided the following elucidation:

> Our legal justification rests upon the accepted principle that force may be used in extreme circumstances to avert a humanitarian catastrophe. Those circumstances clearly existed in Kosovo. The use of force in such circumstances can be justified as an exceptional measure in support of purposes laid down by the Security Council, but without the Council's express authorisation, when that is the only means to avert an immediate and overwhelming humanitarian catastrophe.[42]

Similar statements were issued by the Canadian and Dutch ambassadors. Thus, the Canadian ambassador claimed that "[h]umanitarian considerations underpin our action. We cannot simply stand by while innocents are murdered, an entire population is displaced, and villages are burned."[43] The Dutch ambassador acknowledged that his government would always prefer to base action on a specific Security Council resolution when taking up arms to defend human rights, but if "due to one or two permanent members' rigid interpretation of the concept of domestic jurisdiction such a resolution is not attainable, we cannot sit back and simply let the humanitarian catastrophe occur." Rather, he concluded, "we will act on the legal basis we have available, and what we have available in this case is more than adequate."[44]

Later, when Serbia attempted to bring a case against the NATO States before the International Court of Justice,[45] the United States listed the following factors in defense of Operation Allied Force:

---

[40] NATO, The Situation in and around Kosovo: Statement Issued at the Extraordinary Ministerial Meeting of the North Atlantic Council held at NATO Headquarters, Brussels, on Apr. 12, 1999, Press Release M-NAC-1(99)51, Brussels, Apr. 12, 1999.

[41] Dino Kritsiotis, *The Kosovo Crisis and NATO's Application of Armed Force against the Federal Republic of Yugoslavia* 49 INT'L & COMP. L.Q. 330, 341 (2000).

[42] *Id.* 342 (quoting UK Parliamentary Debate, Mar. 25, 1999).

[43] WHEELER, *supra* note 30, at 153.

[44] *Id.*

[45] The Court later concluded that it lacked jurisdiction over the case brought by Serbia.

– the humanitarian catastrophe that has engulfed the people of Kosovo as a brutal and unlawful campaign of ethnic cleansing has forced many hundreds of thousands to flee their homes and has severely endangered their lives and well-being;

– the acute threat of the actions of the Federal Republic of Yugoslavia [Serbia] to the security of neighboring States, including the threat posed by extremely heavy flows of refugees and armed incursions into their territories;

– the serious violation of international humanitarian law and human rights obligations by forces under the control of the Federal Republic of Yugoslavia [Serbia], including widespread murder, disappearances, rape, theft and destruction of property; and finally

– the resolutions of the Security Council, which have determined that the actions of the Federal Republic of Yugoslavia [Serbia] constitute a threat to peace and security in the region and, pursuant to Chapter VII of the Charter, demanded a halt to such actions.[46]

Belgium was even more explicit in its defense before the International Court of Justice, claiming that the NATO action was necessary "to rescue a people in peril, in deep distress." Belgium then went on to characterize the application of force as "an armed humanitarian intervention, compatible with Article 2(4) of the Charter, which covers only intervention against the territorial integrity or political independence of a State."[47] Similarly, Germany told the Court that the NATO action had been undertaken "as a last resort in order to put a stop to the massive human rights violations perpetrated by the Federal Republic of Yugoslavia [Serbia] in Kosovo and to protect the population of Kosovo from the unfolding humanitarian catastrophe."[48] Professor Bruno Simma, who was soon thereafter elected to be a judge of the International Court of Justice, commented that the German government "called a spade a spade and spoke of the NATO threat as an instance of 'humanitarian intervention.'"[49]

On March 25, 1999, Russia sponsored a draft resolution in the Security Council which sought to condemn the NATO action as an unlawful act in violation of the UN Charter.[50] According to the Russian delegation, the vote

---

[46] CR 99/24, Verbatim Record of May 11, 1999, http://www.icj-cij.org/icjwww/idocket/iybe/iybeframe.htm

[47] CR 99/15, Verbatim Record of May 10, 1999, http://www.icj-cij.org/icjwww/idocket/iybe/iybeframe.htm

[48] CR 99/18, Verbatim Record of May 10, 1999, http://www.icj-cij.org/icjwww/idocket/iybe/iybeframe.htm

[49] Bruno Simma, NATO, *the UN and the Use of Force: Legal Aspects*, 10 EJIL 1, 12–13 (1999).

[50] U.N. Doc. S/1999/328 (Mar. 25, 1999).

was to be a choice between law and lawlessness.[51] The Independent International Commission on Kosovo, chaired by the former Chief Prosecutor of the International Criminal Tribunal for the Former Yugoslavia, Richard Goldstone, would later conclude that the 1999 NATO intervention was "illegal but legitimate."[52] But during the Security Council debate the NATO states did not take the position that the air strikes were illegal but morally justified. Rather, they argued that their action had the backing of international law.[53] In the end, the proposed resolution was defeated 12:3, with only China and Namibia joining Russia in support of the measure.[54] Voting in opposition were the five NATO members on the Security Council (the United Kingdom, Canada, France, the Netherlands, and the United States), joined by Argentina, Bahrain, Gabon, the Gambia, Malaysia, and Slovenia.[55] The sizable rejection of the draft resolution indicated that there was a broad base of support for the NATO action. Outside of the Council, NATO's intervention was endorsed by the European Union, the Organisation of Islamic States, and by the Organization of American States.[56] Moreover, key states in the area, including Romania, Slovenia, and Bulgaria, granted NATO access to their air space for Operation Allied Force, transforming their support into action.[57] Other than Russia, China, India, and Iraq, there was virtually no public protest of the NATO action across the globe.[58]

After seventy-eight days, the NATO bombing campaign ultimately succeeded in driving Milošević back to the negotiating table, where he signed an agreement providing autonomy for Kosovo under the temporary administration of the United Nations and protection of NATO forces. Subsequently, the Security Council adopted Resolution 1244 of June 10, 1999, which some have interpreted as providing a sort of after-the-fact ratification of Operation Allied Force. The resolution put in place the foundations for the international civil and security presence in Kosovo that accompanied the end of hostilities.[59]

---

[51] Kritsiotis, *supra* note 41, at 347.
[52] INDEPENDENT INTERNATIONAL COMMISSION ON KOSOVO, THE KOSOVO REPORT: CONFLICT, INTERNATIONAL RESPONSE, LESSONS LEARNED (2000).
[53] WHEELER, *supra* note 30, at 154.
[54] Kritsiotis, *supra* note 41, at 342.
[55] *Id.*
[56] WHEELER, *supra* note 30, at 158.
[57] Kritsiotis, *supra* note 41, at 346.
[58] Antonio Cassese, *Ex Injuriaius Oritur: Are We Moving towards Legitimatization of Forcible Humanitarian Countermeasures in the World Community?*, 10 EJIL 23, 28 (1999).
[59] Kritsiotis, *supra* note 41, at 348.

C *Development of the Responsibility to Protect Doctrine*

In the aftermath of the 1999 NATO bombing campaign, the issue of humanitarian intervention emerged as an important aspect of Secretary-General Kofi Annan's reform agenda at the United Nations. When Annan delivered his annual report to the UN General Assembly later that year, he presented in stark terms the dilemma facing the international community with respect to the idea of unauthorized humanitarian intervention:

> To those for whom the greatest threat to the future of international order is the use of force in the absence of a Security Council mandate, one might ask – not in the context of Kosovo – but in the context of Rwanda: If, in those dark days and hours leading up to the genocide, a coalition of States had been prepared to act in defense of the Tutsi population, but did not receive prompt Council authorization, should such a coalition have stood aside and allowed the horror to unfold?[60]

In his *Millennium Report* to the General Assembly in 2000, Annan posed a similar question: "If humanitarian intervention is, indeed, an unacceptable assault on sovereignty, how should we respond to a Rwanda, to a Srebrenica – to gross and systematic violations of human rights that offend every precept of our common humanity?"[61]

Rising to the challenge posed by the Secretary-General's appeal, the government of Canada established the International Commission on Intervention and State Sovereignty (ICISS), which in December 2001 submitted its report to Secretary-General Annan. The ICISS report, titled *The Responsibility to Protect*,[62] contained two important innovations. The first was its suggestion that the debate be shifted from focusing on the right to intervene to the responsibility to protect (R2P) victims of serious human rights violations, a concept that comprises prevention, reaction, and post-conflict support.[63] The second was its assertion that sovereignty implies a responsibility of the state to protect its citizens from human rights violations, and when the state is unable or unwilling to fulfill its sovereign responsibility, "it becomes the responsibility of the international community to act in its place."[64]

---

[60] U.N. Doc. SG/SM/7136-GA/9596, Sept. 20, 1999.

[61] The Secretary-General, *Report of the Secretary-General, We the Peoples: The Role of the United Nations in the Twenty-First Century*, paras. 215–219, U.N. Doc. A/54/2000 (Mar. 27, 2000).

[62] INTERNATIONAL COMMISSION ON INTERVENTION AND STATE SOVEREIGNTY [ICISS], THE RESPONSIBILITY TO PROTECT (2001).

[63] *Id.*, paras. 2.28–2.29.

[64] *Id.*, para. 2.29.

Drawing from principles of "just war theory,"[65] the ICISS report sets forth criteria for deciding when military humanitarian intervention is warranted. According to the ICISS, such action should only be employed in extreme cases of large-scale loss of life or ethnic cleansing and where (1) the action is motivated by the "right intention"; (2) the action is a "last resort"; (3) the action is proportional to the threat; and (4) the action carries with it a reasonable chance of ending the suffering.[66]

On the most important question of who can authorize humanitarian intervention, the ICISS report emphasizes the primary role of the Security Council. However, should the Security Council fail to react (as when it is paralyzed by a Permanent Member's veto), the report states that action by the General Assembly under the Uniting for Peace Resolution[67] is a possible alternative that would "provide a high degree of legitimacy for an intervention."[68]

The report also mentions the possibility of action by regional organizations, while pointing out that the UN Charter requires that they act with authorization of the Security Council.[69] Following the reference to the Security Council, however, the ICISS report refers to cases in which regional organizations have carried out an intervention and only subsequently sought the approval of the Security Council, concluding that "there may be certain leeway for future action in this regard."[70]

As to whether individual states or regional organizations can ever legally act without Security Council authorization, the report is intentionally ambiguous. While observing the lack of a global consensus on the issue, the report avoids deeming such interventions illegal.[71] Further, the report points out that there will be damage to the international order if the Security Council is

---

[65] Luke Glanville, *The Responsibility to Protect beyond Borders*, HUM. RTS. L. REV. 1, 197 (2012).

[66] ICISS, *supra* note 62, at paras. 4.19, 4.32, 4.43.

[67] Uniting for Peace, G.A. Res. 377 (v), U.N. Doc. A/1775 (Nov. 3, 1950).

[68] ICISS, *supra* note 62, at paras. 6.29–6.30. Adopted in 1950, the Uniting for Peace Resolution provides:

> That if the Security Council, because of lack of unanimity of the permanent members, fails to exercise its primary responsibility for the maintenance of international peace and security in any case where there appears to be a threat to the peace, breach of the peace or act of aggression, the General Assembly shall consider the matter immediately with a view to making appropriate recommendations to Members for collective measures, including in the case of a breach of the peace or act of aggression the use of armed force when necessary, to maintain or restore international peace and security.
>
> *See* Uniting for Peace, G.A. Res. 377(v), U.N. Doc. A/1775 (Nov. 3, 1950)

[69] ICISS, *supra* note 62, at paras. 6.31–6.35.

[70] *Id.* paras. 6.35, 6.5.

[71] *Id.* paras. 6.36–6.37.

bypassed, but also emphasizes that there will be "damage to that order if human beings are slaughtered while the Security Council stands by."[72] The ICISS finds it intolerable that "one veto can override the rest of humanity on matters of grave humanitarian concern."[73] Thus, the ICISS urges the Permanent Members of the Security Council to refrain from using the veto in cases of genocide and large-scale human rights abuses, and cautions that coalitions might take action if the Council fails to live up to its responsibility.[74]

D Was the International Reaction to the NATO Intervention a Grotian Moment?

In the 1986 *Nicaragua* case, the International Court of Justice observed that "[r]eliance by a State on a novel right or an unprecedented exception to the principle [of nonintervention] might, if shared in principle by other States, tend toward a modification of customary international law."[75] In contrast to the past instances of humanitarian intervention described above, in the case of the 1999 NATO intervention in Serbia, a major application of armed force had taken place for humanitarian purposes without Security Council authorization but with widespread support by the international community. According to one scholar, the NATO intervention was "a case that expanded, rather than breached, the law, similar to the Truman proclamation about the Continental Shelf."[76] Others have described the NATO intervention as "a watershed event" and "an important transition point in the shift from one international order to the next."[77]

Moreover, the NATO intervention led to the ICISS's articulation of the R2P doctrine, a concept that has been described as the "most dramatic normative development of our time"[78] and a "revolution in consciousness in international affairs."[79] The 2001 ICISS report characterized the R2P as

---

[72] *Id.* para. 6.37.

[73] *Id.* paras. 6.13, 6.20.

[74] *Id.* paras. 6.39, 256.

[75] Case Concerning Military and Paramilitary Activities in and against Nicaragua (1986) I.C.J. Reports 14, 109 (para. 207).

[76] Fernando R. Teson, *Kosovo: A Powerful Precedent for the Doctrine of Humanitarian Intervention*, 2 AMSTERDAM L. F. 119 (2009).

[77] Heiko Borchert & Mary N. Hampton, *The Lessons of Kosovo: Boon or Bust for Transatlantic Security?*, ORBIS 369 (2002).

[78] Ramesh Thakur & Thomas G. Weis, *R2P: From Idea to Norm – And Action?*, 1 GLOBAL RESPONSIBILITY TO PROTECT 22 (2009).

[79] Jeremy Sarkin, *Is the Responsibility to Protect an Accepted Norm of International Law in the Post-Libya Era?*, 1 CRONINGEN J. INT'L L. 11, 16 (2012).

"an emerging principle of customary international law,"[80] and the 2005 High-level Panel report described it as an "emerging norm,"[81] an assessment shared by the Secretary-General.[82] The R2P doctrine was then unanimously endorsed at the 2005 World Summit by the Heads of State and Government of every UN member state, and later by the United Nations Security Council. Based on these developments, Professor Ved Nanda of Denver University School of Law argues that a government can no longer "hide behind the shield of sovereignty, claiming non-intervention by other States in its internal affairs, if it fails to protect the people under its jurisdiction from massive violations of human rights."[83] And Antonio Cassese, who served as President of the International Criminal Tribunal for the former Yugoslavia and later as President of the Special Tribunal for Lebanon, argued that NATO's action may support an emerging custom allowing the use of forcible countermeasures to impede a State from committing large-scale atrocities within its own territory, in circumstances where the Security Council is incapable of responding to the crisis.[84]

Yet, two roadblocks prevented humanitarian intervention without Security Council authorization from actually ripening into a norm of customary international Law following the 1999 intervention and the promulgation of the R2P doctrine. The first impediment was the ambiguity of the initial manifestation of *opinio juris* that accompanied the acts of the NATO States. The participating NATO States were not comfortable with the idea that the bombing campaign would create a new rule of customary international law justifying a broad notion of unilateral humanitarian intervention. Thus, in July 1999, US Secretary of State Madeleine Albright stressed that the air strikes were a "unique situation *sui generis* in the region of the Balkans," concluding that it was important "not to overdraw the various lessons that come out of it."[85] UN Prime Minister Tony Blair, who had earlier suggested that humanitarian interventions might become

---

[80] ICISS, *supra* note 62, at paras. 2.24, 6.17.

[81] Report of the High-Level Panel on Threats, Challenges and Change: A More Secure World: Our Shared Responsibility, U.N. Doc. A/59/565 (Dec. 2, 2004), para. 203.

[82] United Nations Secretary-General, *In Larger Freedom: Towards Development, Security and Human Rights for All – Report of the Secretary-General*, U.N. GAOR, 59th Sess., U.N. Doc. a/59/2005 (2005), at para. 135.

[83] Ved Nanda, *The Protection of Human Rights under International Law: Will the U.N. Human Rights Council and the Emerging New Norm "Responsibility to Protect" Make a Difference?*, 35 DENV. J. INT'L L. & POL. 353, 373 (2007).

[84] Cassese, *supra* note 58, at 23.

[85] US Secretary of State Madeleine Albright, Press Conference with Russian Foreign Minister Igor Ivanov, Singapore, July 26, 1999, http://secretary.state.gov./www/statements/1999/990726b .html

more common,[86] subsequently retreated from that position, emphasizing the exceptional nature of the Kosovo operation.[87]

The reason for the reluctance of the United States and United Kingdom to acknowledge a precedent that could ripen into customary international law was explained by Michael Matheson, the Acting Legal Adviser of the US Department of State at the time of the intervention, in the following terms:

> About six months before the actual conflict, at the time when NATO was considering giving an order to threaten the use of force, the political community of NATO got together and had a discussion about what the basis of such threat of force would be. At the end of the discussion, it was clear that there was no common agreement on what might be the justification. There were some NATO members who were prepared to base it on a new doctrine of humanitarian intervention; but most members of the NATO Council were reluctant to adopt a relatively open-ended new doctrine. So at the end of that week, the NATO political community said, here is a list of all of the important reasons why it is necessary for us to threaten the use of force. And at the bottom, it said that under these unique circumstances, we think such actions would be legitimate. There was deliberate evasion of making a "legal" assertion.
>
> And this same process occurred in the U.S. Government. There were some who wanted to articulate that humanitarian intervention in now the basis for U.S. action. There was another theory from the Department of Defense, which wanted to adopt sort of an expanded idea of self-defense based on the general interest of the United States in the region; but on reflection, nobody was really prepared to throw all the eggs into either of those baskets. So we ended up with a formulation similar to that of NATO, where we listed all of the reasons why we were taking action and, in the end, mumbled something about its being justifiable and legitimate but not a precedent. So in a sense, it was something less than a definitive legal rationale – although it probably was taken by large parts of the public community as something like that.[88]

When the principal state actors assert that their actions are *sui generis* and not intended to constitute precedent, this does not create a favorable climate for the cultivation of a new rule of customary international law.[89]

---

[86] Colin Brown, *Blair's Vision of Global Police*, INDEPENDENT, Apr. 23, 1999.

[87] UK Parliamentary Debates, Commons, Apr. 26, 1999, col. 30 (Prime Minister Blair).

[88] MICHAEL P. SCHARF & PAUL R. WILLIAMS, SHAPING FOREIGN POLICY IN TIMES OF CRISIS, THE ROLE OF INTERNATIONAL LAW AND THE STATE DEPARTMENT LEGAL ADVISER 124–125 (2010) (quoting remarks by Michael Matheson).

[89] Bruno Simma, *NATO, the UN and the Use of Force: Legal Aspects*, 10 EJIL1 (1999).

The formation of a new customary rule of humanitarian intervention hit a second obstruction when the 2004 High-Level Panel report, which was endorsed by the UN Secretary-General, and the 2005 *World Summit Outcome Document*, which was endorsed by the General Assembly and Security Council, were written to reflect a much narrower conception in which humanitarian intervention is only lawful when authorized by the Security Council.

The ICISS report was the subject of unfortunate timing. Shortly after the report was issued, in March 2003, the United States and a "coalition of the willing" invaded Iraq without Security Council authorization in part to prevent Iraq from deploying weapons of mass destruction and in part in response to Saddam Hussein's historic record of atrocities against Iraq's Kurdish and Shi'ite populations.[90] The action was controversial and widely unpopular across the globe. By November 2003, the worry over the "lack of agreement amongst Member States on the proper role of the United Nations in providing collective security" prompted the UN Secretary-General to create the High-Level Panel on Threats, Challenges and Change.[91]

The High-Level Panel's report, published in December 2004, specifically endorsed "the emerging norm that there is a collective international responsibility to protect, exercisable by the Security Council authorizing military intervention as a last resort," and urged the Permanent Members to refrain from using the veto in cases of genocide and large-scale human rights abuses.[92] But, while the High-Level Panel supported the conceptual change in the understanding of sovereignty as responsibility and that the responsibility is shared between the state and the international community, the panel's characterization of the R2P doctrine was much more restrictive than that of the ICISS. Influenced by the widespread criticism of the March 2003 invasion of Iraq, the High-Level Panel, departing from the approach of the ICISS report, focused exclusively on action taken by the Security Council and did not mention the possibility of authorization by the General Assembly or actions by states or regional organizations outside the UN framework.

The Secretary-General returned to the R2P concept in his 2005 report, *In Larger Freedom*. Like the High-level Panel, the Secretary-General's 2005 report focused only on the Security Council and did not discuss the possibility of humanitarian interventions without authorization of the Council. In the

---

[90] Nanda, *supra* note 83, at 371–372.
[91] Report of the High-Level Panel on Threats, Challenges and Change, *supra* note 81.
[92] *Id.* paras. 203, 256.

Secretary-General's words, "The task is not to find alternatives to the Security Council as a source of authority but to make it work better."[93]

Up through 2005, the R2P had only been considered by the Secretary-General and specialized commissions. The R2P doctrine received its first endorsement by states at the September 2005 World Summit, attended by the world's heads of state and government at the United Nations. While unanimously endorsing the general concept, the *World Summit Outcome Document* reflected an even more restrictive approach than then the High-level Panel report. The heads of state and government vaguely affirmed that they are prepared to act in a timely manner and on the bases of a case-by-case evaluation. Yet, "they neither recognize specific responsibilities of the Security Council, nor mention the possibility of unilateral or collective action with the authorization of the General Assembly or outside the U.N. framework."[94]

A year later, the R2P made its first appearance in a Security Council Resolution when the Council referred to the relevant paragraphs of the *World Summit Outcome Document* and explicitly reaffirmed the R2P with regard to the protection of civilians in armed conflict.[95] Later that year, the Security Council acknowledged the concept with regard to the situation in Darfur.[96] In 2011, the Council again referenced R2P in the context of Security Council authorization for force in Libya.[97]

In 2009, ten years after the NATO intervention, the Secretary-General issued a report titled *Implementing the Responsibility to Protect*.[98] The report suggests a three-pillar approach: first, is the state's responsibility to protect its population from serious crimes; second, is the international community's commitment to support the state in complying with its obligations under the first pillar; and third is the timely and decisive response by the international community should a state not live up to its R2P.[99] The General Assembly scheduled a formal debate on the Secretary-General's 2009 report.

In anticipation of the General Assembly's debate, the president of the General Assembly circulated a concept note, in which he emphasized that the 2005 Summit Document does not entail any "legally binding commitment" but that it is for the General Assembly to develop and elaborate a legal

---

[93] United Nations Secretary-General, Report of the Secretary-General, *supra* note 82, at para. 126.

[94] Payandeh, *supra* note 29, at 476.

[95] S.C. Res. 1674, para. 4, U.N. Doc. S/RES/1674 (Apr. 28, 2006).

[96] S.C. Res. 1706, preamble, U.N. Doc. S/RES/1706 (Aug. 31, 2006).

[97] S.C. Res. 1973, preamble, U.N. Doc. S/RES/1973 (Mar. 17, 2011).

[98] The Secretary-General, *Report of the Secretary-General, Implementing the Responsibility to Protect*, U.N. Doc. A/63/677 (Jan. 12, 2009).

[99] *Id.* paras. 13–27, 28–48, 49–66.

basis for the R2P concept.[100] In the ensuing General Assembly debate, ninety-four speakers representing 180 states submitted statements (some speakers spoke on behalf of regional groups). Unfortunately, nothing close to a consensus on the content of the R2P doctrine emerged. Significantly, a number of states voiced serious concerns about "the concept's potential for abuse as a pretext for unilateral intervention and equated the responsibility to protect with humanitarian intervention."[101] Ultimately, the General Assembly adopted a resolution which reaffirmed the principles and purposes of the UN Charter as well as the commitment to the R2P in the *World Summit Outcome Document* in its preamble. In its operative paragraphs, the resolution merely "takes note" of the Secretary General's report and decided to continue its consideration of the topic in the future.[102]

These developments signify that the R2P doctrine had been morphed into a conceptual framework for discourse, which may be quite politically useful but is without legal force. The prohibition of the use of force in the absence of Security Council authorization had been left intact, leading the Rapporteur of the UN Working Group on Enforced or Involuntary Disappearances to comment that "the last few years has shown that the political context within which the doctrine has to operate has severely limited its operation."[103] These developments prompted former US Secretary of State Madeleine Albright to decry in 2008 that "[t]he notion of national sovereignty as sacred is [once again] gaining ground."[104]

The issue of whether R2P doctrine was inextricably coupled to Security Council authorization was tested in 2008, when Russia cited the R2P doctrine to justify its use of force to protect threatened Russian populations in the neighboring country of Georgia that year.[105] Perceiving the military action as a land grab, the United States, European Union, and many other countries protested the Russian invasion of the South Ossetia and Abkhazia provinces of Georgia.[106] As Nancy Soderberg, former US ambassador to the United

---

[100] Letter and Concept Note from Office of the President, U.N. General Assembly, to Permanent Missions and Permanent Observer Missions to the United Nations (July 17, 2009), http://www.un.org/ga/president/63/letters/ResponsibilitytoProtect170709.pdf

[101] Payandeh, *supra* note 29, at 479.

[102] G.A. Res. 63/308, U.N. Doc. A/RES/63/308 (Oct. 7, 2009).

[103] Jeremy Sarkin, *Is the Responsibility to Protect an Accepted Norm of International Law in the Post-Libya Era?*, 1 CRONINGEN J. INT'L L. 11, 13 (2012).

[104] Madeleine Albright, *The End of Intervention*, N.Y. TIMES, June 11, 2008.

[105] Brian Barbour & Brian Gorlick, *"Embracing the Responsibility to Protect": A Repertoire of Measures Including Asylum for Potential Victims*, 20 INT'L J. REFUGEE L. 533, 559 (2008).

[106] RONALD D. ASMUS, A LITTLE WAR THAT SHOOK THE WORLD: GEORGIA, RUSSIA, AND THE FUTURE OF THE WEST (2010).

Nations has explained, "The Georgia case was really an abuse of power by Russia under an abuse of the Responsibility to Protect Doctrine, and it was not authorized by the UN and was resoundingly condemned by the international community."[107] In a *Los Angeles Times* op ed, Gareth Evans, one of the principal authors of the ICISS report, argued that the Russian action was clearly invalid because Russia failed to obtain authorization from the Security Council.[108] As Evans explained:

> The 2005 General Assembly position was very clear that, when any country seeks to apply forceful means to address an R2P situation, it must do so through the Security Council. The Russia–Georgia case highlights the risks of states, whether individually or in a coalition, interpreting global norms unilaterally. The sense of moral outrage at reports of civilians being killed and ethnically cleansed can have the unintended effect of clouding judgment as to the best response, which is another reason to channel action collectively through the United Nations. That other major countries may have been indifferent to this constraint in the past doesn't justify Russian actions in Georgia.[109]

While the US invasion of Iraq in 2003 and the Russian pretextual invocation of the R2P doctrine for its invasion of Georgia in 2008 constituted a setback for the idea that humanitarian intervention can be lawful outside the UN framework, developments in Iraq and Syria in 2014–2018 may have supplied the tipping point to bring aspects of the law of humanitarian intervention to fruition.

E Use of Force against ISIS on Mount Sinjar

As described in Chapter 3, in 2014, the ISIS terrorist group took over two-thirds of the territory of Syria and Iraq. The UN Security Council adopted Resolution 2170, condemning the "continued gross, systematic and widespread abuses of human rights" that ISIS was committing against populations that fell under its control.[110] Then, in August 2014, ISIS captured the town of Sinjar in northern Iraq and targeted the majority ethnic group who lived in the town

---

[107] National Public Radio, Talk of the Nation, Feb. 6, 2012, transcript available at www.npr.org/2012/02/06/146474734/the-worlds-responsibility-to-protect

[108] Gareth Evans, *Russia and the Responsibility to Protect*, LOS ANGELES TIMES, Aug. 31, 2008, http://www.gevans.org/opeds/oped93.html

[109] *Id.*

[110] S.C. Res. 2170, Aug. 15, 2014, http://www.un.org/press/en/2014/sc11520.doc.htm

known as the Yazidis for extermination.[111] Forty thousand Yazidis fled to nearby 4,800-foot Mount Sinjar, where they were trapped by ISIS forces that had cut off their egress.[112]

Without authorization by the Iraqi government or UN Security Council, President Obama ordered US aircraft to conduct air strikes on the ISIS forces at the base of the mountain to save the starving Yazidis. Explaining his decision to authorize limited force under the circumstances, President Obama said: "The Yazidis faced a terrible choice: starve on the mountain or be slaughtered on the ground. That's when America came to help."[113]

President Obama had signaled his advocacy for recognition of a right of humanitarian intervention a year earlier in a September 2013 speech to the United Nations General Assembly:

> Different nations will not agree on the need for action in every instance, and the principle of sovereignty is at the center of our international order. But sovereignty cannot be a shield for tyrants to commit wanton murder, or an excuse for the international community to turn a blind eye. While we need to be modest in our belief that we can remedy every evil, while we need to be mindful that the world is full of unintended consequences, should be really accept the notion that the world is powerless in the face of a Rwanda or Srebrenica? If that's the world that people want to live in, they should say so and reckon with the cold logic of mass graves . . . I believe we can embrace a different future.[114]

While the United States would later justify its attacks on ISIS in Syria using a novel theory of self-defense against non-state actors,[115] consistent with President Obama's remarks to the UN, its initial justification was purely humanitarian.[116] Under these dire circumstances, there was no international protest by

---

[111] Helene Cooper & Michael D. Schear, *Militants Seize of Mountain in Iraq Is Over, Pentagon Says*, N.Y. Times, Aug. 14, 2014, http://www.nytimes.com/2014/08/14/world/middleeast/iraq-yazidi-refugees.html?_r=0; Helene Cooper et al., *Obama Allows Limited Airstrikes on ISIS*, N.Y. Times, Aug. 7, 2014, http://www.nytimes.com/2014.08/08/world/middleeast/obama-weighs-military-strikes-to-aid-trapped-iraqis-officials-say.html

[112] Cooper & Schear, *supra* note 111; Cooper et al., *supra* note 111.

[113] Erin Dooley, *Obama: We Broke the ISIL Siege of Mt. Sinjar*, ABC News, Aug. 14, 2014, https://abcnews.go.com/Politics/obama-broke-isil-siege-mt-sinjar/story?id=24978440

[114] *Text of President Obama's Remarks to the United Nations General Assembly*, N.Y. Times, Sept. 24, 2013, https://www.nytimes.com/2013/09/25/us/politics/text-of-obamas-speech-at-the-un.html

[115] *See* Michael P. Scharf, *How the War on ISIS Changed International Law*, 48 Case W. Res. J. Int'l L. 15–68 (2016).

[116] Cooper et al., *supra* note 111.

any state against this limited military action. The stage was set for the 2017 and 2018 Syrian air strikes.

IV DID THE 2018 SYRIAN AIR STRIKES CONSTITUTE A GROTIAN MOMENT?

A *Articulation of a Clear Legal Rationale*

States broadly condoned the April 6, 2017 US air strikes against Syria, but in the absence of a clear legal rationale, the case was viewed as *sui generis*, lacking in clear precedential value. In contrast, there were three particularly noteworthy aspects of the April 14, 2018 air strikes that may have rendered the air strikes a Grotian moment.

First, unlike the April 6, 2017, on April 14, 2018 the United States did not act alone. It is harder for critics to argue pretext when a country acts in concert with others for a humanitarian goal. The case would be stronger, however, if the United States had acted under the auspices of NATO as it did in 1999 and not just its two close allies.

Second, whereas the United States avoided conveying a legal case for the April 2017 air strikes, this time the three countries unequivocally stated that they believed they had a right under international law in these circumstances to undertake the air strikes. Importantly, they did not suggest that the action was unlawful but legitimate, as some have characterized the 1999 NATO action discussed above.[117]

In its statement to the Security Council, France asserted that the air strikes were in compliance with "principles and values of the United Nations Charter," adding that "they serve the law and our political strategy to put an end to the Syrian tragedy."[118]

The United States told the Security Council, "[w]e acted to deter the future use of chemical weapons by holding the Syrian regime responsible for its atrocities against humanity ... The responses were justified, legitimate, and proportionate."[119] And, in a press briefing, the US Secretary of Defense added, "We did what we believe was right under international law, under our nation's laws."[120] Notably, the Department of Justice Office of Legal Counsel issued an official opinion on the legality of the air strikes on May 31, 2018, which

---

[117] INDEPENDENT INTERNATIONAL COMMISSION ON KOSOVO, *supra* note 52.
[118] Gurmendi Dunkelberg et al., *supra* note 24.
[119] Provisional Verbatim Record of the Security Council, *supra* note 3.
[120] Gurmendi Dunkelberg et al., *supra* note 24.

observed a convergence in the domestic and international law justifications focusing on "the U.S. interest in mitigating humanitarian disasters" and in "the deterrence of the use and proliferation of chemical weapons."[121]

In contrast to its statements following the April 2017 air strikes, it is significant that the United States did not employ the language of armed reprisal, as such is considered unlawful under international law.[122] Thus, at the United Nations, the US ambassador stated, "[t]he United Kingdom, France and the United States acted not in revenge, not in punishment and not in a symbolic show of force. We acted to deter the future use of chemical weapons by holding the Syrian regime responsible for its crimes against humanity."[123]

It is also significant that the United States recognized that chemical weapons presented a special case. As President Trump explained after the Syrian air strikes, "[c]hemical weapons are uniquely dangerous not only because they inflict gruesome suffering, but because even small amounts can unleash widespread devastation."[124] The use of chemical weapons have been outlawed for over a century,[125] and the UN Security Council has specifically condemned the use of chemical weapons in Syria in a series of resolutions.[126] The United States has concluded that Syria's continued use of chemical weapons would "desensitize the world to their use and proliferation, weaken prohibitions against their use, and increase the likelihood that additional states will acquire and use these weapons."[127] The US argument, then,

---

[121] Opinions of the Office of Legal Counsel, *April 2018 Airstrikes against Syrian Chemical-Weapons Facilities*, May 31, 2018, at 11, https://www.justice.gov/olc/opinion/file/1067551/download

[122] Marry Ellen O'Connell, *The Popular but Unlawful Armed Reprisal*, 44 OHIO N.U.L. REV. 325, 338–345 (2018), https://papers.ssrn.com/sol3/papers.cfm?abstract_id=3159510

[123] Provisional Verbatim Record of the Security Council, *supra* note 3.

[124] Opinions of the Office of Legal Counsel, *April 2018 Airstrikes*, at 16.

[125] *Id.* at 17.

[126] *See* S.C. Res. 2319 (Nov. 17, 2016) ("Condemning again in the strongest terms any use of any toxic chemicals as a weapon in the Syrian Arab Republic and expressing alarm that civilians continue to be killed and injured by toxic chemicals as weapons in the Syrian Arab Republic"); S.C. Res. 2235 (Aug. 7, 2015) ("Condemning in the strongest terms any use of any toxic chemical as a weapon in the Syrian Arab Republic and noting with outrage that civilians continue to be killed and injured by toxic chemicals as a weapons in the Syrian Arab Republic, Reaffirming that the use of chemical weapons constitutes a serious violation of international law, and stressing again that those individuals responsible for any use of chemical weapons must be held accountable"); S.C. Res. 2209 (Mar. 6, 2015) ("Reaffirming that the use of chemical weapons constitutes a serious violation of international law and reiterating that those individuals responsible for any use of chemical weapons must be held accountable"); S.C. Res. 2118 (Sept. 17, 2013) ("Determining that the use of chemical weapons in the Syrian Arab Republic constitutes a threat to international peace and security").

[127] Opinions of the Office of Legal Counsel, *April 2018 Airstrikes*, at 17.

is that "the prohibition of chemical weapons is nearly sacrosanct and can, in certain circumstances, justify a forcible response"[128]

Third, the United Kingdom specifically relied on the theory of "humanitarian intervention" in the context of preventing use of chemical weapons to justify the April 2018 air strikes.[129] The UK representative told the Security Council that "[a]ny State is permitted under international law, on an exceptional basis, to take measures in order to alleviate overwhelming humanitarian suffering."[130] Echoing the main elements of the R2P doctrine, the UK explained that such humanitarian intervention is lawful when three conditions are met:

(1) There is convincing evidence, generally accepted by the international community as a whole, of extreme humanitarian distress on a large scale, requiring immediate and urgent relief.
(2) It must be objectively clear that there is no practicable alternative to the use of force if lives are to be saved; and
(3) The proposed use of force must be necessary and proportionate to the aim of relief of humanitarian suffering and must be strictly limited in time and in scope to this aim (i.e., the minimum necessary to achieve that end and for no other purpose).[131]

The United Kingdom then detailed why it reasonably considers that the air strikes met these requirements, concluding "there was no practicable alternative to the truly exceptional use of force to degrade the Syrian regime's chemical weapons capability and deter their further use by the Syrian regime in order to alleviate humanitarian suffering."[132]

This clearly articulated legal rationale distinguishes the 2018 air strikes from the vague and equivocal justifications for the NATO action in 1999. While the UK had first made public its views on humanitarian intervention in 2014,[133]

---

[128] Monica Hakimi, *The Attack on Syria and the Contemporary Jus ad Bellum*, EJIL TALK!, Apr. 15, 2018, https://www.ejiltalk.org/the-attack-on-syria-and-the-contemporary-jus-ad-bellum

[129] A policy paper issued by the UK Prime Minister's Office stated: "The UK is permitted under international law, on an exceptional basis, to take measures in order to alleviate overwhelming humanitarian suffering. The legal basis for the use of force is humanitarian intervention" (Gurmendi Dunkelberg et al., *supra* note 24).

[130] Provisional Verbatim Record of the Security Council, *supra* note 3.

[131] UK Policy Paper, Syria Action – UK Government Legal Position, Apr. 14, 2018, https://www.gov .uk/government/publications/syria-action-uk-government-legal-position/syria-action-uk-government-legal-position

[132] *Id.*

[133] *Written Evidence from the Rt Hon Hugh Robertson, MP, Minister of State, Foreign and Commonwealth Office to the Foreign Affairs Committee on Humanitarian Intervention and the Responsibility to Protect*, Jan. 14, 2014, www.publications.parliament.uk/pa/cm201415/cmselect/ cmdfence/582/58205.htm

this was the first time the rationale was tied to concrete action taken by armed UK forces. Further, although the United States did not similarly formulate a detailed justification, it did tell the Security Council that "[t]he United States is deeply grateful to the United Kingdom and France for their part in the coalition to defend the prohibition of chemical weapons. We worked in lock step: we were in complete agreement."[134] As such, the United States can be held to have implicitly adopted the rationale of the United Kingdom.[135] This is particularly significant because the United States has never before recognized a right of humanitarian intervention under international law.

B The Response of the International Community

The UK's clear legal rationale may have laid the groundwork for a Grotian moment, but it takes widespread state action in support to crystalize an emerging rule of customary international law.[136]

Fifty-six separate states and NATO (consisting of twenty-eight member states) – for a total of over seventy countries – publicly expressed opinions about the April 14, 2018 air strikes.[137] Of those, only a handful, including Russia and Syria, explicitly stated that the air strikes violated international law. For a case in which there was not a debate in a large international forum such as the UN General Assembly, seventy states from every region of the world is actually a fairly large sample from which to discern widespread state practice. In fact, scholars who have carefully dissected the judgments of the International Court of Justice have concluded that "most customs are found to exist on the basis of practice by fewer than a dozen States."[138] This is because international law considers states that elect not to weigh in on an issue of general concern as providing silent support or acquiescence.[139] In the case of

---

[134] Provisional Verbatim Record of the Security Council, *supra* note 3.

[135] International Law Commission, Draft Articles on State Responsibility, art. 11 (2008), http://legal
.un.org/ilc/texts/instruments/english/commentaries/9_6_2001.pdf (citing international cases where a state's unequivocal acknowledgment and adoption of another's position will render the State retroactively responsible for it).

[136] International Law Commission, Second Report on the Identification of Customary International Law, May 22, 2014, U.N. Doc. A/CN.4/672, at paras. 53, 63, 69.

[137] Gurmendi Dunkelberg et al., *supra* note 24.

[138] Anthea E. Roberts, *Traditional and Modern Approaches to Customary International Law: A Reconciliation*, 95 AJIL 757, 767 (2001) (citing the works of Charney, Chodosh, Schacter, and Weisburd).

[139] David Kaplow, *International Legal Standards and the Weaponization of Outer Space*, in SPACE: THE NEXT GENERATION – CONFERENCE REPORT, 31 MARCH–1 APRIL 2008, UNITED NATIONS INSTITUTE FOR DISARMAMENT RESEARCH (2008), at 160; ILC, Second Report on the Identification of Customary International Law, *supra* note 136, at para. 42 ("Inaction by States

the *S.S. Lotus*, for example, the Permanent Court of International Justice (the forerunner of the ICJ) relied on the absence of protest against legislation based on the "objective territoriality" doctrine of jurisdiction in finding that such an exercise of jurisdiction was permissible under customary international law.[140]

The state reactions to the April 2018 air strikes can be characterized as falling into four categories. First, there were those states that expressed recognition of the lawful nature of the military action. This was typified by the statements of the United States, United Kingdom and France, as described above, which each affirmatively asserted that the air strikes complied with international law.[141]

Second, nineteen states and NATO (thirty-eight states in all) expressed approval of the air strikes without an explicit statement concerning legality. These states represented Latin America, Africa, the Middle East, Europe, Asia, and the Pacific.[142] Typical of the language used was the statement of Germany, which stated, "[t]he military strike was *necessary and appropriate* in order to preserve the effectiveness of the international ban on the use of chemical weapons and to warn the Syrian regime against further violations" (emphasis added).[143] Similarly, Italy said "[t]he U.S. France and the UK action against this use of chemical weapons was justified."[144] And Spain said "[t]he strikes are a legitimate and proportionate response to the brutal attacks committed by the Syrian regime against the civilian population."[145] While terms such as "necessary and appropriate," "justified," and "legitimate" are somewhat ambiguous, they can be read as a statement regarding legality under the circumstances.

Third, there were a couple of states that expressed disapproval of the air strikes without a statement concerning illegality. The Brazilian Ministry of Foreign Affairs, for example, said "Brazil reiterates its understanding that the

---

may be central to the development and ascertainment of rules of customary international law, in particular when it qualifies (or is perceived) as acquiescence").

[140] S.S. Lotus (1927), P.C.I.J., Ser. A, No. 10, p. 23.

[141] Gurmendi Dunkelberg et al., *supra* note 24.

[142] The states of this type included Columbia, Saint Lucia, Australia, Belgium, Canada, Germany, Israel, Italy, Spain, the Netherlands, Turkey, Georgia, Poland, Ukraine, Oman, Qatar, UAE, Japan, South Korea. *Id.* NATO is made up of twenty-eight states: Albania, Belgium, Bulgaria, Canada, Croatia, the Czech Republic, Denmark, Estonia, France, Germany, Greece, Hungary, Iceland, Italy, Latvia, Lithuania, Luxemburg, Montenegro, the Netherlands, Norway, Poland, Portugal, Romania, Slovakia, Slovenia, Spain, Turkey, United Kingdom, and the United States. *See* https://www.nato.int/cps/en/natolive/nato_countries.htm

[143] Gurmendi Dunkelberg et al., *supra* note 24.

[144] *Id.*

[145] *Id.*

end of the conflict can only be reached through political means, through negotiations undertaken in the framework of the United Nations and based on Security Council resolutions."[146] Other states in this category indicated their concern that the Organization of the Prohibition of Chemical Weapons (OPCW) had not yet completed an investigation of whether Syria was behind the use of chemical weapons at the time of the air strikes. Thus, the Prime Minister of Algeria said "Algeria can only regret the strikes ... It would have been necessary to wait for the findings of an investigation into the alleged chemical attack before taking any steps."[147] Equatorial Guinea likewise said, "[u]ntil we have reliable proof of the alleged chemical attack which took place last weekend in Douma, the Republic of Equatorial Guinea believes that no aggression is justified."[148] These statements suggest that had the US, France, and UK waited until the OPCW completed its investigation and concluded that Syria was responsible for the use of the chemical weapons, Algeria and Guinea would have accepted the legality of the air strikes.

And, finally, there were eleven states that expressed disapproval while including an explicit statement that humanitarian intervention without Security Council authorization is contrary to international law.[149] The clearest statement of this type was by South Africa, which said "[t]he alleged use of chemical weapons in Syria cannot be a justification for military airstrikes in a territory of a sovereign state without the authorization of the UN Security Council."[150] Bolivia was likewise clear, saying "Bolivia condemns the illegal use of force and calls for compliance with international norms that prevent violations of peace and security and keep the most powerful states from attacking the weakest states with impunity."[151] Eleven states are a small number out of the nearly 200 that make up the modern community of nations.

Arguably more significant as evidence of state practice than public statements are a country's votes in the UN Security Council. In this case, only Bolivia, China, and Russia voted in favor of the Russian draft resolution to condemn the April 14, 2018 air strikes.[152] Russia's position was undercut by its

---

[146] *Id.*

[147] *Id.*

[148] *Id.*

[149] States in this category included South Africa, Bolivia, Costa Rica, Cuba, Venezuala, China, Iran, and Kazakhstan. *Id.*

[150] *Id.*

[151] *Id.*

[152] The text of the Russian draft resolution is available at: https://www.securitycouncilreport.org/atf/cf/%7B65BFCF9B-6D27-4E9C-8CD3-CF6E4FF96FF9%7D/s_2018_355.pdf. It stated:

focus in its explanation of vote on the lack of proof that Syria was behind the chemical weapons attack rather than an unequivocal statement that unauthorized humanitarian intervention is always unlawful,[153] probably because such a statement would have been contrary to the legal argument Russia had invoked as justification for its invasion of South Ossetia Georgia in 2008.[154] China's vote may be discounted because it had declined to condemn the April 6, 2017 air strikes a year earlier, and its 2018 vote came in the context of strained relations brought on by a US-initiated trade war commenced a few months earlier.[155] Cote d'Ivoire, France, Kuwait, the Netherlands, Poland, Sweden, United Kingdom, and the United States voted against condemnation; Equatorial Guinea, Ethiopia, Kazakhstan, and Peru abstained.[156]

V CONCLUSION

In the years since the 1999 NATO air strikes on Serbia to prevent the slaughter of the Kosovar Albanians, international law has been moving in fits and starts toward recognition of a limited right of humanitarian intervention. But all the ingredients necessary for a so-called Grotian moment to come to fruition were not present until the April 2018 air strikes on Syria.

As discussed in this chapter, there were several circumstances that made the 2018 air strikes distinctive. First, for the past nine years, Syria has represented the greatest humanitarian crisis on the planet. As with the changes to

> The Security Council,
>
> Appalled by the aggression against the Syrian Arab Republic by the US and its allies in violation of international law and the UN Charter,
>
> Expressing grave concern that the aggression against the sovereign territory of the Syrian Arab Republic took place at the moment when the Organization for the Prohibition of Chemical Weapons Fact-Finding Mission team has just begun its work to collect evidence of the alleged use of chemical weapons in Douma and urging to provide all necessary conditions for the completion of this investigation,
>
> 1. Condemns the aggression against the Syrian Arab Republic by the US and its allies in violation of international law and the UN Charter,
> 2. Demands that the US and its allies immediately and without delay cease the aggression against the Syrian Arab Republic and demands also to refrain from any further use of force in violation of international law and the UN Charter,
> 3. Decides to remain further seized on this matter.

[153] Provisional Verbatim Record of the Security Council, *supra* note 3. See text quoted *supra* note 26.

[154] ASMUS, *supra* note 106.

[155] Lauren Kyger & Andrea Durkin, *U.S.–China Tradewar Timeline*, Hinrich Foundation, https://tradevistas.org/u-s-china-trade-war-timeline

[156] Provisional Verbatim Record of the Security Council, *supra* note 3. See text quoted *supra* note 26.

international law ushered in by World War II and the conflicts in the former Yugoslavia of the 1990s, the urgency created by the Syrian crisis set the stage for rapid development of customary international law. As with the other Grotian moments discussed in Chapter 3, this context serves as a kind of accelerating agent, enabling customary international law to form much more rapidly and with less state practice than is normally the case.

Second, the 2018 air strikes were undertaken collectively, rather than by a single state. Unlike the 2008 Russian invasion of South Ossetia Georgia,[157] the 2014 US air strikes against ISIS at Mount Sinjar, or the 2017 US air strikes against the Syrian airbase, collective action like that undertaken in April 2018 helps ensure that the military force will not be perceived as a pretext for a land grab or regime change.

Third, the participating countries asserted the legality of the April 2018 air strikes and embraced a common justification – humanitarian intervention – rather than cite only factual considerations that render use of force morally defensible. For customary international law to rapidly crystallize, norm pioneers must be consistent in their articulation of the new rule, its contours, and application. Two former state department legal advisers, Harold Koh and John Bellinger, have criticized the US failure to articulate a legal argument for its past humanitarian interventions.[158] That approach not only makes it harder for customary international law to form, but at the same time it makes it easier for the precedent to be abused by other countries since its contours are left purposely ambiguous. This time, by telling the Security Council that it was acting "lock step" and "in complete agreement" with the UK, the United States associated itself with a clearly annunciated legal principle.

Fourth, the underlying humanitarian need in the case of the April 2018 air strikes was to stop the use of chemical weapons against a civilian

---

[157] *See* Peter Roudik, *Library of Congress Report, Russian Federation: Legal Aspects of War in Georgia*, Aug. 2008, https://www.loc.gov/law/help/russian-georgia-war.php

[158] John Bellinger, *The Trump Administration Should Do More to Explain the Legal Basis for the Syrian Airstrikes*, Lawfare Blog, Apr. 14, 2018, https://www.lawfareblog.com/trump-administration-should-do-more-explain-legal-basis-syrian-airstrikes (as former state department legal adviser John Bellinger has said, "When the United States uses military force, especially under controversial circumstances, it should explain the legal basis for its actions. When the United States does not do so, it appears to act lawlessly and invites other countries to act without a legal basis or justification"); Harold Hongju Koh, *The Legal Adviser's Duty to Explain*, 41 Yale J. Int'l L. 189 (2016); Harold Hongju Koh, *The War Powers and Humanitarian Intervention*, 53 Houston L. Rev. 972, 977 (2016) ("I thought it is outrageous that the U.S. government would fail to state a legal rationale to justify its use of force").

population – a *jus cogens* norm.[159] Rather than target infrastructure, airfields, or government buildings, as had been the case of past humanitarian interventions, the targets of the April 2018 strikes were chemical weapons production and storage facilities.[160] While a wider principle of humanitarian intervention might be too much for the international community to buy into at this time, the large majority of states were more concerned about the Assad regime's attempt to normalize the use of chemical weapons and Russia's willingness to prevent the Security Council from taking action against Syria than they were about the potential for abuse of a precedent that would condone future humanitarian interventions without Security Council authorization.[161]

Finally, many countries from all parts of the globe expressed support and only a handful opposed the air strikes. China had not criticized the 2017 air strikes and its criticism in 2018 came in the context of strained US–China relations at the height of their trade war. Russia's opposition was weakened by its argument that Syria's responsibility for the chemical attack had not been sufficiently proved, and its draft resolution condemning the April 2018 air strikes was soundly defeated by the Security Council.

Some commentators have argued that even if there were a newly emergent customary international law right to humanitarian intervention, customary international law simply cannot prevail over the UN Charter.[162] But as former State Department legal adviser Harold Koh points out, "it is not nearly so black and white as the absolutists claim, because textual ambiguity in Article 2 (4), the broader structural purposes of the UN Charter, and some recent significant state practice give far more legal play in the joints than textual absolutists would concede."[163] In this case, the UN Charter is being

---

[159] Charlie Dunlap, Do the Syria Strikes Herald a New Norm of International Law? LAWFARE BLOG, Apr. 14, 2018, https://sites.duke.edu/lawfire/2018/04/14/do-the-syria-strikes-herald-a-new-norm-of-international-law. The term "jus cogens" designates a peremptory principle or norm from which no derogation is permitted. *Jus cogens* norms are recognized as being fundamental to the maintenance of the international legal order.

[160] The 1999 NATO air strikes comprised a seventy-eight-day bombing campaign of Serbia's infrastructure, military targets, and government buildings. The April 2017 air strikes targeted an airbase in general use.

[161] Youssef Badawi, *Syria Strikes Violated International Law – Are the Rules of Foreign Intervention Changing?*, The Conversation, Apr. 18, 2018, http://theconversation.com/syria-strikes-violated-international-law-are-the-rules-of-foreign-intervention-changing-95184

[162] *See, e.g.,* Dapo Akande, *The Legality of the UK's Air Strikes on the Assad Government in Syria,* Apr. 6, 2018, https://www.scribd.com/document/376483861/Akande-Opinion-UK-Government-s-Legal-Position-on-Syria-Strike-April-2018 (memo prepared by Oxford professor for MP Tom Watson, then Deputy Leader of the UK Labour Party).

[163] Harold Hongju Koh, *The War Powers and Humanitarian Intervention*, 53 HOUSTON L. REV. 972, 1017 (2016).

interpreted to allow for a customary international law right of humanitarian intervention in the narrow circumstances of preventing the use of chemical weapons. This is consistent with the Charter's Purposes and Principles, which include "maintaining international peace and security," "promoting and encouraging respect for human rights," and "sav[ing] succeeding generations from the scourge of war."

Since the Security Council declined to condemn the air strikes, the question that this chapter addresses – whether a limited customary international law right of humanitarian intervention has crystalized from the 2018 Syrian air strikes – may not require a definitive answer at this time, as there is no pending International Court of Justice or International Criminal Court case arguing that the strikes were an unlawful act of aggression. But the precedent may render it easier for the United States and its allies to marshal support for follow-up air strikes against Syria or any other state that uses chemical weapons in the future. Canada and Germany, for example, have indicated their readiness to join air strikes if the Syrian government uses chemical weapons in the last rebel stronghold of Idlib.[164] Advocates of a right of humanitarian intervention should be careful, however, in reading this development too broadly, for there is unlikely to be broad international approval at this time for its application outside the context of responding to repeated use of chemical weapons against civilians.

---

[164] Michael P. Scharf, The Conversation, Dec. 6, 2018, https://theconversation.com/syria-may-be-using-chemical-weapons-against-its-citizens-again-heres-how-international-law-has-changed-to-help-countries-intervene-108162

6

Transformation of Accountability Paradigms

I INTRODUCTION

As the Syrian civil war presses on, the need for accountability for atrocities committed by Syrian officials, rebel commanders, and terrorist leaders grows. As documented by the UN Human Rights Council's Independent and International Commission of Inquiry, the atrocities in Syria are among the worst in history. They include mass executions, widespread rapes, systematic torture, intentionally targeting hospitals, and repeated use of chemical weapons against civilians.[1] The vast majority of international crimes have been committed in a methodical fashion by the Syrian government, encouraged by the long-standing culture of impunity. These crimes require prosecution to bring justice for the victims, deter vigilantism, and prevent recurrence.[2]

Eventually, there will be a regime change (if nothing else, President Assad will eventually die of natural causes), and the road to peace in Syria may include a period of transitional justice.[3] But in the near term, Syrian domestic courts are unable and unwilling to prosecute the culpable officials.[4] And

The authors thank PILPG Fellow Taylor Frank, J.D., Case Western Reserve University School of Law 2019, and the following Cox Center Fellows for research assistance for this Chapter: Philip Albers, Christopher Glass, and Amanda Makhoul.

[1] Wolfgang Kaleck & Patrick Kroker, *Syrian Torture Investigations in Germany and Beyond: Breathing New Life into Universal Jurisdiction in Europe?* 16 J. INT'L CRIM. L. 165, 166 (2018).

[2] GARY JONATHAN BASS, STAY THE HAND OF VENGEANCE: THE POLITICS OF WAR CRIMES TRIBUNALS 284 (2000).

[3] As described in the Prologue, the authors have worked with Syrian jurists to create a blueprint for an eventual regional or hybrid court to prosecute war crimes and crimes against humanity committed during the conflict. The blueprint is reproduced in the Appendix to this book.

[4] The rights of prisoners are not strictly respected, military courts are employed to suppress dissent, and the judiciary is commonly used as a tool of the ruling regime. *See* Hilly Moodrick-Even Khen, *Revisiting Universal Jurisdiction: The Application of the Complementarity Principle by National Courts and Implications for Ex-Post Justice in the Syrian Civil War*, 30 EMORY INT'L L. REV. 261, 308 (2015).

Russia and China have used their veto to block attempts to refer the prosecution of Syrian atrocities to the International Criminal Court (ICC).[5]

As a result, after falling out of favor during the past twenty years, countries around the world are expanding the use of the global enforcer approach to universal jurisdiction to prosecute Syrian officials and rebels for war crimes and crimes against humanity. Perhaps most prominently, Germany which has Europe's greatest number of Syrian refugees, issued an international arrest warrant in June 2018 for alleged Syrian war criminal General Jamil Hassan.[6] Significantly, the United States threw its support behind this exercise of universal jurisdiction, even though Germany itself has no tie to the alleged crimes and the perpetrator is not present in Germany.[7]

Meanwhile, the UN General Assembly has circumvented the paralysis of the Security Council by creating its own International Investigative Mechanism for Syria over the objections of Russia. This chapter examines how the Syrian conflict is transforming international criminal law to fill an accountability gap in regard to the Syrian conflict. We begin with the story of the International Impartial and Independent Mechanism for Syria (the IIIM).

II A POWER SHIFT WITHIN THE UN: THE STORY OF THE IIIM

Despite significant evidence of atrocity crimes being committed by all sides to the conflict – particularly by government forces – the UN Security Council has been paralyzed by the Russian veto, unable to take any steps toward accountability in Syria. In May 2014, Russia vetoed a Security Council resolution that would have referred the situation in Syria to the ICC.[8] Later,

---

[5] *See* UN Security Council, *Referral of Syria to International Criminal Court Fails as Negative Votes Prevent Security Council from Adopting Draft Resolution*, UNGAOR, 7180th mtg., UN Doc SC/11407 (May 22, 2014). Since Syria has not ratified the ICC Statute, the ICC can prosecute crimes in Syria only if committed by nationals of states parties or if the UN Security Council refers the situation to the ICC as it did with Libya and Sudan. The Security Council cannot, however, make such a referral or take other action if any of the five Permanent Members of the Security Council (China, France, Russia, the United Kingdom, and the United States) vote against the resolution.

[6] *See German Authorities Issue Arrest Warrant against Jamil Hassan, Head of the Syrian Air Force Intelligence*, EUROPEAN CENTER FOR CONSTITUTIONAL AND HUMAN RIGHTS, https://www.ecchr.eu/en/case/german-authorities-issue-arrest-warrant-against-jamil-hassan-head-of-the-syrian-air-force-intellige [hereinafter *Hassan Arrest Warrant*].

[7] *See* Ryan Goodman, *Breaking: United States Support's Germany's International Arrest Warrant for Accused Syrian War Criminal*, JUST SECURITY (Mar. 6, 2019), https://www.justsecurity.org/63079/breaking-united-states-supports-germanys-international-arrest-warrant-accused-syrian-war-criminal-a-rare-exercise-universal-jurisdiction-general-jamil-hassan

[8] I. Black, *Russia and China Veto UN Move to Refer Syria to International Criminal Court*, THE GUARDIAN, May 22, 2014.

Russia vetoed a Security Council resolution that would have established an investigative mechanism to document Syrian use of chemical weapons and other atrocities. In all, Russia has vetoed twelve resolutions to prevent accountability of the Syrian government since the outbreak of the Syrian civil war.[9]

The situation is to be contrasted with the former Yugoslavia and Rwanda, in which the Security Council first condemned atrocities, then established an investigative commission to document them, and finally created ad hoc tribunals to prosecute the perpetrators.[10] It is to be contrasted with the Sudan and Libya, in which the Security Council referred the situations to the ICC for prosecution.[11] Here, the Security Council could do nothing.

Enter Liechtenstein's UN Ambassador Christian Wenaweser, who had formerly served as President of the ICC Assembly of State Parties. In the fall of 2016, Ambassador Wenaweser hatched a bold plan for an end run around the Security Council. If the Council won't act, why shouldn't the General Assembly? For months, Wenaweser canvassed UN delegates, arguing: "We have postponed any meaningful action on accountability too often and for too long."[12] Commenting on the outsized role Wenaweser played, Harvard law professor Alex Whiting writes, "the short history of international criminal justice, from Nuremberg to the present, is full of heroic individuals and their improbable and creative ideas that have pushed the project forward."[13] This is the very essence of a custom pioneer.

Galvanized by Ambassador Wenaweser's efforts, on December 21, 2016, the United Nations General Assembly took a historic step in establishing a mechanism to investigate and preserve evidence of international crimes in Syria, the first time the Assembly has established such a body.[14] Despite objection by Russia, the General Assembly adopted Resolution 71/248 by a vote of 105:15 with 52 abstentions, creating the International, Impartial and Independent Mechanism to Assist in the Investigation and Prosecution of

---

[9]   *Russia's 12 Vetoes on Syria*, RTE, Apr. 11, 2018, https://www.rte.ie/news/world/2018/0411/953637-russia-syria-un-veto

[10] *See generally*, Milena Sterio & Michael Scharf, The Legacy of Ad Hoc International Tribunals in international Criminal Law (2019).

[11] Security Council Press Release, Security Council Refers Situation in Darfur, Sudan, to Prosecutor of ICC, Mar. 31, 2005, https://www.un.org/press/en/2005/sc8351.doc.htm; Situation in Libya, ICC-01/11, https://www.icc-cpi.int/libya.

[12] Michelle Nichols, *UN Creates Team to Prepare Cases on Syria War Crimes*, Reuters, Dec. 21, 2016, https://www.reuters.com/article/us-mideast-crisis-syria-warcrimes-idUSKBN14A2H7?il=0

[13] Alex Whiting, *An Investigation Mechanism for Syria: The General Assembly Steps Into the Breach*, 15 J. Int'l Crim. Just. 231, (2017).

[14] *Id.*

Those Responsible for the Most Serious Crimes under International Law Committed in the Syrian Arab Republic since March 2011, known in short-hand as the IIIM.[15]

The IIIM is empowered to collect evidence from other bodies including the Independent International Commission of Inquiry established by the Human Rights Council, and to conduct its own investigations "including interviews, witness testimony, documentation and forensic material."[16] The General Assembly Resolution further envisages that the IIIM will analyze the collected evidence and prepare files of evidence that could be provided to "national, regional or international courts or tribunals that have or may in the future have jurisdiction over these crimes, in accordance with international law."[17]

This was the first time in history that the General Assembly had established an investigative body to assemble and analyze evidence of international crimes for the purpose of preserving evidence for future international or domestic trials. Was it consistent with international law? During the debate on the resolution and subsequently in a *note verbale* dated February 8, 2017, the Russian government complained that "the General Assembly acted *ultra vires* – going beyond its powers as specified" in the UN Charter.[18] Specifically, Russia argued that "[a] number of powers vested in the mechanism under resolution 71/248, including those of 'analys[ing] evidence' and 'prepa[ring] files,' are prosecutorial in nature. However, prosecutions, criminal investigations, and support of criminal investigations are not among the functions of the General Assembly. It cannot create an organ that has more powers than the General Assembly itself."[19]

There was a time when it was not settled whether the Security Council, itself, had the power to establish a prosecutorial institution, let alone whether the General Assembly could do so. But that question was answered in the affirmative by the Appeals Chamber of the Yugoslavia Tribunal in 1995 based on the extraordinary powers vested in the Security Council under Chapter VII of the

---

[15] UN Doc. A/71/L.48, Dec. 21, 2016.

[16] Secretary-General, *Report of the Secretary-General on the Implementation of the resolution establishing the International, Impartial and Independent Mechanism to Assist in the Investigation and Prosecution of Persons Responsible for the Most Serious Crimes under International Law Committed in the Syrian Arab Republic since March 2011*, UN Doc. A/71/ 755, Jan. 19, 2017, at §12.

[17] UN Doc. A/71/L.48, 21 Dec. 2016, at § 4.

[18] Secretary-General, *Note verbale dated 8 February 2017 from the Permanent Mission of the Russian Federation to the United Nations addressed to the Secretary-General*, UN Doc. A/71/ 793, Feb. 14, 2017.

[19] *Id.*

UN Charter to maintain international peace and security.[20] The General Assembly has no such powers. Yet, it is not clear that the powers of the IIIM are "prosecutorial in nature" in the sense that they entail the prosecution of individuals, a power that could only be conferred by the Security Council. Rather, the resolution and Secretary-General's report describe a "prosecutorial" body only in respect to the *standards* that will be adopted by the IIIM when collecting and analyzing evidence. If one views the IIIM not as a sort of investigative judge or prosecutor but simply as a fact-finding body that will adhere to a criminal law standard in performing its functions, its creation would seem to be within the powers of the General Assembly.

Article 10 of the UN Charter gives the General Assembly the power to "discuss" and make "recommendations" concerning "any questions or matters within the scope of the present Charter or relating to the powers and functions of any organs provided for in the present Charter."[21] A limitation on this power is set forth in Article 12 of the Charter, which stipulates that the General Assembly cannot make recommendations when the Security Council is exercising its functions with respect to a particular dispute or situation, unless the Council requests the General Assembly to do so.[22] But this limitation has been honored increasingly in the breach[23] and was not seen as limiting the General Assembly's involvement in major crises including the former Yugoslavia, Rwanda, Libya, and Syria over the past thirty years. As such, it is within the mandate of the General Assembly to consider questions of threats to peace and security in Syria and whether a referral to the ICC or the establishment of an ad hoc tribunal is warranted. Further, Article 22 of the Charter empowers the General Assembly to "establish such subsidiary organs as it deems necessary for the performance of its functions."[24] Therefore, the General Assembly has the authority to establish a "subsidiary organ" to collect and assess the available evidence of international crimes in Syria in order to inform the General Assembly's discussion and recommendations on these matters. Now, the evidence collected by the IIIM would undeniably not be used solely (or even primarily) for the purpose of the General Assembly's discussion and recommendations, but it is not clear that

---

[20] Prosecutor v. Tadić, Case No. IT-94-1-T (Trial Chamber, Decision on the Defense Motion: Jurisdiction of the Tribunal, Aug. 10, 1995), affirmed, Prosecutor v. Tadić, Case No. IT-94-1-AR72 (Appeals Chamber, Decision on the Defense Motion for Interlocutory Appeal on Jurisdiction, Oct. 2, 1995); VIRGINIA MORRIS & MICHAEL P. SCHARF, THE INTERNATIONAL CRIMINAL TRIBUNAL FOR RWANDA, Vol. 1 at 95–97 (1998).

[21] UN Charter, art. 10.

[22] *Id.*, art. 12.

[23] MORRIS & SCHARF, *supra* note 20, at 81.

[24] UN Charter, art. 22.

additional uses of the information would render the creation of the IIIM beyond the power of the General Assembly.

Whatever the merits of Russia's legal argument, the establishment of this novel institution by the General Assembly clearly evinces a fundamental power shift away from the Security Council and to the General Assembly caused by the international community's frustration with the abuse of the veto to prevent action to deal with international atrocities. Professor Jennifer Trahan of New York University argues

> that the veto power is being abused in a way never anticipated when the Charter was drafted, and in a way that is at odds with other bodies of international law (such as the highest level *jus cogens* norms) and the "purposes and principles" of the UN Charter, with which the Security Council (including its permanent members), are bound, under article 24.2 of the Charter, to act in accordance.[25]

The *Guardian* newspaper reported in 2015 that "[t]he United States has warned that Russia's continued blanket use of its UN veto will jeopardize the security council's long-term legitimacy and could lead the US and like-minded countries to bypass it as a decision-making body."[26] As the US

---

[25] Jennifer Trahan, *Russia's Illegitimate Veto*, Opinio Juris, Apr. 23, 2018, https://opiniojuris.org/2018/04/23/the-narrow-case-for-the-legality-of-strikes-in-syria-and-russias-illegitimate-veto.
Trahan argues that there are three ways in which the Russian veto of the proposal to refer the matter of Syria to the ICC, or to at least establish an international investigative mechanism for Syria was incompatible with the UN Charter. First, the veto power derives from the UN Charter, which is subsidiary to *jus cogens* norms. Thus, a veto that violates *jus cogens* norms, or permits the continued violation of *jus cogens* norms, would be illegal. The Charter (and veto power) must be read in a way that is consistent with *jus cogens*. Second, the veto power derives from the UN Charter, which states in Article 24(2) that the Security Council "[in] discharging [its] duties . . . shall act in accordance with the Purposes and Principles of the United Nations." A veto in the face of a credible draft resolution aimed at curtailing or alleviating the commission of genocide, crimes against humanity, or war crimes does not accord with the Charter's purposes and principles. And, finally, a Permanent Member of the Security Council that utilizes the veto power also has other treaty obligations, such as those under the Genocide Convention, which contains an obligation to "prevent" genocide. A Permanent Member's use of the veto that would enable genocide, or allow its continued commission, would violate that state's legal obligation to "prevent" genocide. A similar argument can be made as to allowing the perpetration of at least certain war crimes, such as "grave breaches" and violations of Common Article 3 of the 1949 Geneva Conventions.
For a contrary view, *see* Mohamed Helal, *On the Legality of the Russian Vetoes and the Harsh Realities of International Law: A Rejoinder to Professor Jennifer Trahan*, Opinio Juris, May 4, 2018, http://opiniojuris.org/2018/05/04/on-the-legality-of-the-russian-vetoes-in-the-un-security-council-and-the-harsh-reality-of-international-law-a-rejoinder-to-professor-jennifer-trahan

[26] Julian Borger & Bastien Inzaurralde, *Russian Vetoes Are Putting UN Security Council Legitimacy at Risk, US Says*, THE GUARDIAN, Sept. 23, 2015.

Permanent Representative to the UN told the *Guardian*: "It's a Darwinian universe here. If a particular body reveals itself to be dysfunctional, then people are going to go elsewhere."[27]

A year later, the General Assembly took the first step in implementing those prophetic words by establishing the IIIM. On July 3, 2017, the Secretary-General appointed as the head of the IIIM Catherine Marchi-Uhel, a former French judge with broad international experience trying and adjudicating war crimes. During her twenty-seven-year career, Marchi-Uhel has provided legal support to the International Criminal Tribunal for the Former Yugoslavia, the UN Mission in Liberia, and the UN Interim Administration Mission in Kosovo. She has also adjudicated for the Extraordinary Chambers in the Courts of Cambodia and served as ombudsperson to the UN Security Council's Sanctions Committee. Before, that, she has served as Head of Chambers at the International Criminal Tribunal for the Former Yugoslavia, and as an international judge at the Pre-Trial Chamber of the Extraordinary Chambers in the Courts of Cambodia.

At a lecture at Case Western Reserve University School of Law soon after her appointment, Marchi-Uhel said: "I believe that the creation of the Mechanism is an important demonstration of the international community's will to ensure that crimes committed in Syria do not go unpunished."[28] She notes that an international, regional, or hybrid tribunal for Syria may not be on the horizon, but "several criminal proceedings relating to Syria have been initiated in various countries. In relation to these cases, the Mechanism can play an immediate, significant role in supporting ongoing and future investigation of crimes committed in Syria by national prosecutors."[29] And that brings us to how the Syrian situation is changing the international approach to universal jurisdiction.

III CHANGES TO THE PARADIGM OF UNIVERSAL JURISDICTION

A *What Is Universal Jurisdiction?*

Universal jurisdiction provides every state with the authority to prosecute a limited category of offenses generally recognized as of universal concern, regardless of where the offense occurred, the nationality of the perpetrator,

---

[27] *Id.*

[28] Catherine Marchi-Uhel, Klatsky *Endowed Lecture in Human Rights*, 51 CASE W. RES. J. INT'L L. 223–235 (2019).

[29] *Id.*

or the nationality of the victim.[30] While other bases of jurisdiction require connections between the prosecuting state and the offense, the perpetrator, or the victim, universal jurisdiction assumes that every state has a sufficient interest in exercising jurisdiction to combat egregious offenses that states universally have condemned.[31]

There are two premises underlying universal jurisdiction.[32] The first involves the gravity of the crime. Crimes subject to universal jurisdiction are so threatening to the international community or so heinous in scope and degree that they offend the interest of all humanity, and any state may, as humanity's agent, punish the offender. The second involves the *locus delicti* (place of the act). Crimes subject to universal jurisdiction occur in territory over which no country has jurisdiction or in situations in which the territorial state and state of the accused's nationality are unlikely to exercise jurisdiction, because, for example, the perpetrators are state authorities or agents of the state.[33]

There are two approaches to universal jurisdiction. The first is the "no safe haven" approach, pursuant to which states may exercise universal jurisdiction over perpetrators found in their territory to avoid becoming a refuge for perpetrators of grave international crimes.[34] The second is the "global enforcer" approach, under which domestic courts conduct prosecutions on behalf of humanity. Under this second approach, investigations, indictments, and requests for extradition may be initiated even where the perpetrator is not located within the state's territory.[35]

The first widely accepted crime of universal jurisdiction was piracy. For 500 years, states have exercised jurisdiction over piratical acts on the high seas, even when neither the pirates nor their victims were nationals of the prosecuting state.[36] Piracy's fundamental nature and consequences explained why it was subject to universal jurisdiction. Piracy often consists of heinous acts of violence or depredation, which are committed indiscriminately against the vessels

---

[30] *See* Kenneth C. Randall, *Universal Jurisdiction under International Law*, 66 Tex. L. Rev. 785, 786 (1988).

[31] *See id.* at 787.

[32] *See* Lee A. Steven, *Genocide and the Duty to Extradite or Prosecute: Why the United States Is in Breach of Its International Obligations*, 39 Va. J. Int'l L. 425, 435 (1999).

[33] *See generally* Leila Sadat Wexler & S. Richard Carden, *The New International Criminal Court: An Uneasy Revolution*, 88 Geo. L.J. 381 (2000).

[34] Devika Hovell, *The Authority of Universal Jurisdiction*, 29 EJIL 427, 439 (2018).

[35] *Id.* at 448.

[36] Like other international criminals, pirates can retain their nationality and still be subject to universal jurisdiction. *See* Kenneth C. Randall, *Universal Jurisdiction under International Law*, 66 Tex. L. Rev. 785, 793 (1988).

and nationals of numerous states.[37] Moreover, pirates can quickly flee across the seas, making pursuit by the authorities of particular victim states difficult.[38]

There are a handful of academics that have taken the position that piracy is a unique crime and does not provide a valid basis for expansion of universal jurisdiction by analogy to war crimes, crimes against humanity, and torture. Their argument is based on the view that historical pirates were not prone to atrocities of the level of the war criminal or torturer, but rather were simply maritime plunderers and thieves.[39] Thus, Professor Kontorovich asserts, "[t]he rationale for piracy's unique jurisdictional status had nothing to do with the heinousness or severity of the offense. Indeed, piracy was not regarded in earlier centuries as being an egregiously heinous crime, at least not in the way that most human rights offenses are heinous."[40] Contrary to this benign view of piracy, the Archeological Institute of America has documented a catalogue of pirate cruelties.[41] The Institute's report begins with this warning: "The accounts that follow, taken from contemporary reports, are not for the faint of heart. As these shocking examples of cruelty show, pirates of the Golden Age were not the same lovable or admirable rogues portrayed in popular literature and film today."[42] The report goes on to describe widely practiced sadistic acts of barbarism toward captured crew and passengers such as gang rape, mutilation, disembowelment, burning prisoners alive, using captured friars and nuns as human shields, and pouring salt water into open wounds of victims in what was called "pickling."[43]

In 1820, the US Supreme Court upheld the exercise of universal jurisdiction by US courts over piracy in *United States v. Smith*.[44] The Court reasoned that "pirates being *hostis humani generis* [enemies of all humankind], are

---

[37] *See* Hari M. Osofsky, *Domesticating International Criminal Law: Bringing Human Rights Violators to Justice*, 107 YALE L.J. 191 (1997); Randall, *supra* note 36, at 793; Daniel Bodansky, *Human Rights and Universal Jurisdiction*, in WORLD JUSTICE? U.S. COURTS AND INTERNATIONAL HUMAN RIGHTS 9 (Mark Gibney ed., 1991).

[38] *See* Osofsky, *supra* note 37, at 191; Randall, *supra* note 36, at 793; Bodansky, *supra* note 37, at 9.

[39] Anthony R. Reeves, *Liability to International Prosecution: The Nature of Universal Jurisdiction* 28 EJIL 1047, 1052 (2018), citing Eugene Kontorovic, *The Piracy Analogy: Modern Universal Jurisdiction's Hollow Foundation*, 45 HARV. INT'L L.J. 183, 186 (2004).

[40] Kontorovich, *supra* note 39, at 186.

[41] Archeology, A publication of the Archeological Institute of America, Archeology's Top Ten Vicious Pirate Acts, https://archive.archaeology.org/online/reviews/pirates/poll.html

[42] *Id.*

[43] *Id.*

[44] 18 U.S. (5 Wheat.) 153 (1820). The piracy Statute of 1819 provided "if any person or persons whatsoever, shall, on the high seas, commit the crime of piracy, as defined by the law of nations, and ... shall afterwards be brought into or found in the United States, every such offender ... shall, upon conviction ... be punished with death." The Supreme Court upheld this statute over the objection that it failed to define the crime with sufficient particularity. *Id.* at 162.

punishable in the tribunals of all nations. All nations are engaged in a league against them for the mutual defence and safety of all."[45]

In the aftermath of the atrocities of World War II, the international community extended universal jurisdiction to war crimes and crimes against humanity. Trials exercising this jurisdiction took place in international tribunals at Nuremberg,[46] as well as domestic courts across the globe.[47] Some individuals faced trial in the states in which they had committed their crimes, but others were tried by other states in which they were later captured, surrendered, or found – including such far off countries as Canada and Australia.[48] Thus, on the basis of universal jurisdiction, Israel tried Adolph Eichmann in 1961[49] and John Demjanjuk

---

[45] *Id.* at 156. *Accord*, U.S. v. Klintock, in which the Supreme Court stated:

> A pirate, being hostis humani generis, is of no nation or State ... All the States of the world are engaged in a tacit alliance against them. An offense committed by them against any individual nation, is an offense against all. It is punishable in the Courts of all ... So, in the present case, the offense committed on board a piratical vessel, by a pirate, against a subject of Denmark, is an offense against the United States, which the Courts of this country are authorized and bound to punish.
>
> Klintock, 18 U.S. (5 Wheat.) at 147–148

[46] *See* Michael P. Scharf, *Universal Jurisdiction and the Crime of Aggression*, 53 HARV. INT'L L.J. 357, 390 (2012) (providing a detailed response to the argument that Nuremberg was not based on universal jurisdiction).

[47] Between 1945 and 2010, there were prosecutions for crimes under international law based on universal jurisdiction in seventeen states (Argentina, Australia, Austria, Belgium, Canada, Denmark, Finland, France, Germany, Israel, the Netherlands, Norway, Spain, Sweden, Switzerland, United Kingdom, and the United States). Amnesty Int'l, UN Should Support this Essential International Justice Tool (2010), https://www.amnesty.org/download/Documents/40000/ior530152010en.pdf

[48] R. v. Imre Finta [1994] 28 C.R. (4th) 265 (S.C.) (Canada) (reaffirming universal jurisdiction over crimes against humanity committed against Jews in Hungary during World War II, but finding that the available evidence did not meet the requisite standard for such crimes); Polyukhovich v. Commonwealth, (Austl. 1991) 172 C.L.R. 501 (reaffirming universal jurisdiction over crimes against humanity and war crimes committed against Jews in the Ukraine during World War II).

[49] Israel kidnapped Adolph Eichmann in Argentina and prosecuted him in Jerusalem in 1961 for crimes against humanity and war crimes. As chief of the Gestapo's Jewish Section, Eichmann had primary responsibility over the persecution, deportation, and extermination of hundreds of thousands of Jews. Although the Security Council condemned Israel for violating Argentina's territorial sovereignty in apprehending Eichmann, there was no averment that Israel lacked jurisdiction to try him. In upholding the District Court's conviction and death sentence, the Supreme Court of Israel stated:

> There is full justification for applying here the principle of universal jurisdiction since the international character of crimes against humanity ... dealt with in this case is no longer in doubt ... The basic reason for which international law recognizes the right of each State to exercise such jurisdiction in piracy offenses ... applies with even greater

in 1988[50] for crimes committed before Israel even existed as a state. In extending universal jurisdiction to war crimes and crimes against humanity, an analogy was made between those offenses and piracy. Like piracy, the Nazi offenses during the war involved violent and predatory action and were typically committed in locations where they would not be prevented or punished through other bases of jurisdiction.[51]

On December 11, 1946, the United Nations General Assembly unanimously affirmed the "principles of international law recognized by the Charter of the Nuremberg Tribunal and the Judgment of the Tribunal,"[52] thereby "codifying the jurisdictional right of all States to prosecute perpetrators of the offenses

> force to the above-mentioned crimes. Not only do all the crimes attributed to the appellant bear an international character, but their harmful and murderous effects were so embracing and widespread as to shake the international community to its very foundations. The State of Israel therefore was entitled, pursuant to the principle of universal jurisdiction and in the capacity of a guardian of international law and an agent for its enforcement, to try the appellant. That being the case, no importance attaches to the fact that the State of Israel did not exist when the offenses were committed.
>
> Attorney General of Israel v. Eichmann, 36 I.L.R. 277, 299, 304 (Isr. S. Ct. 1962)

[50] The United States granted Israel's request for the extradition of John Demjanjuk, a retired auto worker accused of being the infamous Treblinka Nazi death camp guard, "Ivan the Terrible." *See* Demjanjuk v. Petrovsky, 776 F.2d 571 (6th Cir. 1985). The Court held that Israel had the right to try Demjanjuk under universal jurisdiction for crimes committed in Poland during 1942 or 1943, prior to the establishment of the Israeli State. *See id.* at 582–583. Demjanjuk was found guilty and sentenced to death for crimes against humanity by the Israeli court, but his conviction was subsequently overturned when new evidence discovered after the collapse of the Soviet Union was considered by the Israeli Supreme Court. *See* Cr. A. 347/88, Demjanjuk v. State of Israel (Special Issue), 395–396; Mordechai Kremnitzer, *The Demjanjuk Case*, in War Crimes in International Law 321, 323 (Yoram Dinstein & Mala Tabory eds., 1996). Ultimately, Demjanjuk was tried, convicted, and sentenced to five years' imprisonment by Germany in 2011 on charges stemming from his participation in crimes at a different concentration camp (Sobibor). Janet Stobart, *Nazi Camp Guard Gets 5-Year Sentence in Germany*, L.A. Times, May 13, 2011, at A3.

[51] *See* Randall, *supra* note 36, at 793. As Col. Willard Cowles wrote on the eve of the establishment of the Nuremberg Tribunal:

> Basically, war crimes are very similar to piratical acts, except that they take place usually on land rather than at sea. In both situations there is, broadly speaking, a lack of any adequate judicial system operating on the spot where the crime takes place – in the case of piracy it is because the acts are on the high seas and in the case of war crimes because of a chaotic condition or irresponsible leadership in time of war. As regards both piratical acts and war crimes there is often no well-organized police or judicial system at the place where the acts are committed, and both the pirate and the war criminal take advantage of this fact, hoping thereby to commit their crimes with impunity.
>
> Willard B. Cowles, Universality of Jurisdiction Over War Crimes,
> 33 Cal. L. Rev. 177, 194 (1945)

[52] G.A. Res. 95, U.N. Doc. A/64/Add.1, at 188 (1946).

addressed by the IMT [Nuremberg Tribunal], namely war crimes, crimes against humanity, and the crime of aggression."[53] The General Assembly has subsequently confirmed that no statute of limitations or amnesty may be applied to bar prosecution of such crimes and that all states have a duty to cooperate in their prosecution.[54] International courts have repeatedly cited the Nuremberg precedent as crystallizing universal jurisdiction for the core international crimes under customary international law.[55]

In the 1990s, domestic courts of Denmark, Austria, and Germany relied on universal jurisdiction in trying Croatian and Bosnian Serb nationals for war

---

[53] *See* Randall, *supra* note 36, at 834.

[54] *See, e.g.,* Declaration on Territorial Asylum, G.A. Res. 2312, 22 U.N. GAOR, 22d Sess., Supp. No. 16, at 81, U.N. Doc. A/6716 (1967) *reprinted in* BLAINE SLOAN, UNITED NATIONS GENERAL ASSEMBLY RESOLUTIONS IN OUR CHANGING WORLD 351–352 (1991) (stating that states shall not grant asylum "to any person with respect to whom there are serious reasons for considering that he has committed … a war crime or crime against humanity"); United Nations Resolution on War Criminals, G.A. Res. 2712, U.N. GAOR, 25th Sess., Supp. No. 28, at 78–79, U.N. Doc. A/8028 (1970), *reprinted in* M. CHERIF BASSIOUNI, CRIMES AGAINST HUMANITY IN INTERNATIONAL CRIMINAL LAW 698–700 (1992) (adopted by a vote of 55:4 with 33 abstentions) (condemning war crimes and crimes against humanity and "calls upon the States concerned to bring to trial persons guilty of such crimes"); Questions of the Punishment of War Criminals and of Persons Who Have Committed Crimes against Humanity, G.A. Res. 2840, U.N. GAOR, 26th Sess., Supp. No. 29, at 88, U.N. Doc. A/8429 (1971), *reprinted in* UN–GENERAL ASSEMBLY RESOLUTIONS, 311–312 (Ausgewahlt & Zusammengestelit eds., 1975) (adopted by a vote of 71 in favor to none against with 42 abstentions) (affirming that a State's refusal "to cooperate in the arrest, extradition, trial and punishment" of persons [accused or convicted] of war crimes or crimes against humanity is "contrary to the purposes and principles of the United Nations Charter and to generally recognized norms of international law"); United Nations Resolution on Principles of International Cooperation in the Detection, Arrest, Extradition, and Punishment of Persons Guilty of War Crimes and Crimes against Humanity, G.A. Res. 3074, U.N. GAOR, 28th Sess., Supp. No. 30 at 79, U.N. Doc. A/9030 (1973), *reprinted in* M. CHERIF BASSIOUNI, CRIMES AGAINST HUMANITY IN INTERNATIONAL CRIMINAL LAW 701–703 (1992) (adopted by a vote of 94 in favor to none against with 29 abstentions) (stating "war crimes and crimes against humanity … shall be subject to investigation and the persons against whom there is evidence that they have committed such crimes shall be subject to tracing, arrest, trials and, if found guilty, to punishment").

[55] Prosecutor v. Tadić, Case No. IT-94-1-1, Decision on Defence Motion for Interlocutory Appeal on Jurisdiction 62 (Int'l Crim. Trib. for the Former Yugoslavia Oct. 2, 1995); Prosecutor v. Ntuyuhaga, Case No. ICTR-96-40-T, Decision on the Prosecutor's Motion to Withdraw the Indictment (Int'l Crim. Trib. for Rwanda Mar. 18, 1999); Prosecutor v. Kallon and Kamara, Case Nos. SCSL-2004-15 AR72(E), SCSL-2004-16-AR72(E), Decision on Challenge to Jurisdiction: Lome Accord Amnesty 67–71 (Special Ct. for Sierra Leone, Mar. 13, 2004); Case No. STL-11-01/1 Interlocutory Decision on the Applicable Law: Terrorism, Conspiracy, Homicide, Perpetration, Cumulative Charging 103 (Special Trib. for Leb. Feb. 16, 2011) (citing *Tadić* for test for establishing a crime under customary international law).

crimes and crimes against humanity committed in Bosnia in 1992,[56] and courts in Belgium cited universal jurisdiction as a basis for issuing arrest warrants and prosecuting persons involved in the atrocities in Rwanda in 1994, including cases that did not involve Belgian victims.[57]

In 2001, a group of academics from around the world drafted the Princeton Principles on Universal Jurisdiction in an effort to codify universal jurisdiction in international law.[58] The Princeton Principles define universal jurisdiction as "criminal jurisdiction based solely on the nature of the crime, without regard to where the crime was committed, the nationality of the alleged or convicted perpetrator, the nationality of the victim, or any other connection to the state exercising such jurisdiction,"[59] and apply to seven crimes[60]: (1) piracy,[61] (2) slavery,[62] (3) war crimes,[63] (4) crimes against peace,[64]

---

[56] In the 1994 case of Director of Public Prosecutions v. T, the defendant was tried by a Denmark court for war crimes committed against Bosnians in the territory of the former Yugoslavia. *See* Mary Ellen O'Connell, *New International Legal Process*, 83 Am. J. Int'l L. 334, 341 (1999). On April 30, 1999, the German Federal Supreme Court upheld the conviction of a Bosnian Serb convicted for committing acts of genocide in Bosnia. *See* 5 International Law Update 52 (May 1999) (a press release on this case – No. 39/1999 – is available on the German Federal Supreme Court's website). In 1993, an Austrian domestic court prosecuted a Bosnian Serb for atrocities committed in Bosnia despite the fact that the defendant was not an Austrian citizen and he was not alleged to have committed any crimes against Austrian citizens. *See* Eve La Haye, War Crimes in Internal Armed Conflict 244 (2008). The US Second Circuit Court of Appeals similarly relied on universal jurisdiction in a tort case arising under the Alien Tort Claims Act and the Torture Victim Protection Act against Radovan Karadžić, the Bosnian Serb leader accused of crimes against humanity and war crimes in Bosnia. *See* Kadić v. Karadžić, 70 F.3d 232, 240 (2d Cir. 1995).

[57] *See* Theodor Meron, *International Criminalization of Internal Atrocities*, 89 Am. J. Int'l L. 554, 577 (1995) (stating while several of the warrants involved the killing of Belgian peacekeepers, one of the warrants was issued against a Rwandan responsible for massacres of other Rwandans in Rwanda).

[58] Jeff Milgram, *University-Led Panel Eyes World Crime*, Princeton Packet (July 24, 2001) (Richard Falk, a drafter of the Princeton Principles, describes them as "the most serious attempt ever made to guide national courts in meeting the challenge of crimes of state").

[59] The Princeton Principles on Universal Jurisdiction 28 (Stephen Macedo ed., 2001) (Principle 1.1) [hereinafter Princeton Principles].

[60] *Id.* at 29 (Principle 2.1).

[61] Included because piracy is "crucial to the origins of universal jurisdiction." *Id.* at 45.

[62] Included because of "its historical ties to piracy." *Id.*

[63] Supposedly encompassing all breaches of the 1949 Geneva Conventions and Additional Protocol I, though the drafters noted that "it would be inappropriate to invoke universal jurisdiction for the prosecution of minor transgressions of the 1949 Geneva Conventions and Protocol I." *Id.* at 46–47.

[64] *Id.* at 47; *see* Charter of the International Military Tribunal, Aug. 8, 1945, art. 6(a), 82 U.N.T.S. 284, *annexed to* Agreement for the Prosecution and Punishment of the Major War Criminals of the European Axis, Aug. 8, 1945, 82 U.N.T.S. 279 ("planning, preparation, initiation or waging of a war of aggression, or a war in violation of international treaties,

(5) crimes against humanity,[65] (6) genocide,[66] and (7) torture.[67] Universal jurisdiction has been extended by treaty to other crimes, including several terrorist offenses.[68]

B *The Rise and Fall of the Global Enforcer Approach to Universal Jurisdiction*

In the 1990s, Belgium and Spain became the most aggressive countries in asserting universal jurisdiction under the global enforcer approach. The gutting of Belgium's and Spain's universal jurisdiction law a decade later was seen at the time as the death knell of this type of universal jurisdiction. But that was before Syria.

The saga of Belgium's universal jurisdiction law began in 1993, when the government amended its penal code to authorize prosecution of violations of the 1949 Geneva Conventions and 1977 Additional Protocols, regardless of the nationality of the perpetrator and victim and where such crimes were committed.[69] In 1999, the law was amended to add universal jurisdiction over genocide, as defined in the 1948 Genocide Convention, and over Crimes against Humanity, as defined in the Statute of the ICC.[70] The 1999 amendment also clarified that official immunity would not be a bar to prosecutions under the law.[71]

---

agreements or assurance, or participation in a common plan or conspiracy for the accomplishment of any of the foregoing").

[65] PRINCETON PRINCIPLES, *supra*, at 47; *see* Rome Statute for the International Criminal Court, July 17, 1998, U.N. Doc. A/Conf.183/9, art. 7.1 [hereinafter Rome Statute]; *see also*, Leila Sadat, ASIL Insight, *the UN International Law Commission Progresses toward a Global Treaty on Crimes against Humanity*, Jan. 25, 2017, https://www.asil.org/insights/volume/21/issue/2/un-international-law-commission-progresses-towards-new-global-treaty

[66] PRINCETON PRINCIPLES, *supra*, at 47 (noting that Article 6 of the Genocide Convention – which provides that a person accused of genocide shall be tried in a court of "the State in the territory of which the act was committed" – does not specifically preclude the exercise of universal jurisdiction); *see* Convention on the Prevention and Punishment of Genocide, Dec. 9, 1948, 78 U.N.T.S. 277, art. 6.

[67] "[I]ntended to include the 'other cruel, inhuman, or degrading treatment or punishment' as defined in the Convention Against Torture and Other Cruel, Inhuman or Degrading Treatment or Punishment." PRINCETON PRINCIPLES, at 47–48; *see* Convention Against Torture and Other Cruel, Inhuman or Degrading Treatment or Punishment, Dec. 10, 1984, 1465 U.N.T.S. 85, art. 1.1 [hereinafter Convention Against Torture].

[68] As of December 2019, there were 185 states party to the Hijacking Convention; 188 states are party to the Aircraft Sabotage Convention; 170 states are party to the Airport Security Protocol; 176 are party to the Hostage Taking Convention; 166 are party to the Maritime Terrorism Convention; and 180 states are party to the Internationally Protected Persons Convention.

[69] Steven R. Ratner, *Belgium's War Crimes Statute: A Postmortem*, 97 AJIL 888, 889 (2003).

[70] *Id.*

[71] *Id.*

Things started off well enough in 2001 when the Belgian government tried two Rwandan nuns and two Rwandan men who had relocated to Belgium for participating in the Rwandan genocide of 1994. There was no international outcry when all four were convicted and sentenced to prison terms ranging from twelve to twenty years.[72]

But soon thereafter, twenty-three survivors of the 1982 massacre of Palestinian refugees by Lebanese militiamen at the Sabra and Shatila camps in an area under the control of Israel filled a criminal complaint against Amos Yaron, who had been the Israeli general in charge of the sector and Ariel Sharon, who had been Israeli Defense Minister at the time of the massacre and was now Prime Minister of Israel. Like many civil law countries, Belgium's criminal system permitted victims to initiate cases.

Within months, the Belgium Court received victim-initiated complaints against Cuban President Fidel Castro, Iraqi President Saddam Hussein, former Democratic Republic of the Congo Foreign Minister Abuldaye Yeridia,[73] and former Iranian President Hashemi Rafsanjani. These cases were all controversial, engendering protests from the various states involved. Then, in March 2003, Iraqi families filed a complaint against US President George H. W. Bush, Vice President (and former Secretary of Defense) Dick Cheney, Secretary of State (and former chairman of the Joint Chiefs of Staff) Colin Powell, and retired general Norman Schwarzkopf for alleged war crimes committed during the 1991 Gulf War.[74] This was a bridge too far.

In response, the United States warned Belgium that unless it amended its universal jurisdiction law, Belgium risked losing its status as the host state of NATO. To bolster its position, the Universal Jurisdiction Rejection Act was introduced in the US House of Representatives, declaring in its preamble that universal jurisdiction "is an assault on the internationally accepted concept of state sovereignty."[75] The bill was not ultimately passed, but it had its desired effect. The Belgium parliament immediately amended the law in April 2003 such that only the federal prosecutor could initiate cases brought under

---

[72] *Id.*

[73] The Yuridia case went to the International Court of Justice, which held that head-of-state immunity applied to the former foreign minister of the Congo and prevented Belgium from lawfully requesting his extradition. The Court did not opine on whether Belgium had a legitimate basis under universal jurisdiction for issuing the extradition request. *See* Case Concerning the Arrest Warrant of Apr. 11, 2000 (Democratic Republic of the Congo v. Belgium), ICJ 14/II/2002, opinion of President Guillaume and opinion of JJ. Higgins, Kooigmans, and Buergenthal.

[74] Ratner, *supra* note 69, at 890.

[75] Hovell, *supra* note 34, at 441.

universal jurisdiction. The amendment further stipulated that the federal prosecutor could refuse to proceed in the interest of the administration of justice, a vague term providing broad discretion.[76] But these amendments were not sufficient for the United States, which announced that it would refuse to fund a new headquarters building for NATO in Belgium and bar its officials from traveling to meetings there unless Belgium rescinded the universal jurisdiction statute altogether. The Belgium parliament responded with another set of amendments in August 2003 stipulating that Belgian courts can hear cases regarding war crimes, genocide, and crimes against humanity committed outside Belgium only if the defendant or victim is a citizen or resident of Belgium.[77]

At about the same time, Spain was experiencing a similar repudiation of its universal jurisdiction law. Spain catapulted itself into the center of the human rights movement when it invoked universal jurisdiction to request the extradition from the UK of former Chilean President, Augusto Pinochet, in 1998 for crimes against humanity committed during his reign. The UK House of Lords found Pinochet extraditable for acts of torture under the Torture Convention,[78] but the UK ended up returning him to Chile for health reasons.[79]

In 2009, a Spanish judge had invoked universal jurisdiction to investigate six former Bush administration officials alleged to have violated the Torture Convention by giving legal cover to torture of detainees at Guantanamo Bay. In another case, a Spanish judge launched an investigation of former Israeli officials over an air attack in Gaza that killed fourteen civilians including nine children.[80] Under pressure from the United States, and concerned that Spain's judicial system was being hijacked by activist judges pursuing a political agenda, Spanish lawmakers in the Congress of Deputies (lower house) voted in June 2009 to restrict the scope of universal jurisdiction to cases in which: (1) the victims are Spanish; (2) the alleged perpetrators are in Spain; or (3) there exists some other clear link to Spanish interests. That bill was approved by the Spanish Senate in October 2009 and became law in November 2009, thereby transforming Spain's universal jurisdiction from the

---

[76] Ratner, *supra* note 69, at 891.

[77] "Belgium: Universal Jurisdiction Law Repealed," HUMAN RIGHTS WATCH (Aug. 1, 2003), https://www.hrw.org/news/2003/08/01/belgium-universal-jurisdiction-law-repealed

[78] In Re Pinochet, House of Lords, Mar. 24, 1999, http://www.iilj.org/wp-content/uploads/2016/08/Regina-v.-Bartle-ex.-p.-Pinochet.pdf

[79] Kevin G. Hall, *Pinochet Released to Return to Chile*, MIAMI HEROLD, Mar. 3, 2000, http://www.latinamericanstudies.org/chile/released.htm

[80] Victoria Burnett & Marlise Simons, *Push in Spain to Limit Reach of the Courts*, N.Y. TIMES, May 20, 2009.

"global enforcer" approach to the "no safe haven" approach.[81] Then, when a Spanish court issued arrest warrants for five high-ranking Chinese officials over alleged human rights abuses in Tibet, the Congress of Deputies voted to further restrict the reach of Spain's law on universal jurisdiction only to those cases directly involving Spanish citizens or foreign nationals habitually resident in Spain.[82]

Following Belgium's and Spain's amendments to their universal jurisdiction statutes, observers opined that the global enforcer approach to universal jurisdiction was "on its last legs, if not already in its death throes."[83] Reflecting the rising international ambivalence toward this practice, in 2009 the African Group requested that the UN General Assembly include an item on its agenda entitled "the abuse of universal jurisdiction."[84] During the General Assembly discussion, several delegations opined that to avoid abuse, universal jurisdiction should be used only where the crimes are exceptionally serious, the territorial state and state of nationality of the accused refrain from prosecuting, the accused is present in the prosecuting state's territory, and an appropriate government authority (such as the Attorney General) consents to the prosecution.[85]

C The Revival of the Global Enforcer Approach

With the advent of the Syrian crisis, the global enforcer approach to universal jurisdiction is making a comeback. Soon after the outbreak of the Syrian civil war, the German Federal Prosecutor's War Crimes Unit opened several "structural investigations" into more than 2,800 crimes committed in Syria.[86] This involves investigating specific structures within which international crimes have been allegedly committed rather than investigating specific persons.

---

[81] Soeren Kern, *Spain Re-thinks Universal Jurisdiction*, Jan. 31, 2014, Gatestene Institute, https://www.gatestoneinstitute.org/4149/spain-universal-jurisdiction

[82] *Id.*

[83] Antonio Cassese, *Is the Bell Tolling for Universality? A Plea for a Sensible Notion of Universal Jurisdiction*, 1 J. INT'L CRIM. J. 589 (2003).

[84] Amnesty Int'l, Universal Jurisdiction: UN General Assembly Should Support this Essential International Justice Tool, at 5, IOR 53/015/2010 (Oct. 5, 2010). Since 2009, the scope and application of the principle of universal jurisdiction has been an agenda item for the United Nations General Assembly. Country Reports, UN Secretary-General Summaries, and record of debates are available at: http://lawguides.scu.edu/c.php?g=5750&p=25270

[85] UN General Assembly, The Scope and Application of Universal Jurisdiction, Summary of Work (2011), https://www.un.org/en/ga/sixth/66/ScopeAppUniJuri.shtml

[86] Hovell, *supra* note 34, at 448.

This technique serves several purposes.[87] First, it can enable the prosecutor to react swiftly when a suspect enters Germany in the future. Second, it can facilitate future proceedings in a third state or before an international court. Third, it can lead to the opening of an investigation against a specific individual and can serve as the basis for an international arrest warrant or extradition request.[88]

Established in 2010, in its first years of existence the German War Crimes Unit declined to open investigations in cases against US officials regarding the torture in Abu Ghraib, Guantanamo Bay, and other sites where alleged terrorists were being held. But taking advantage of the thousands of Syrian refugees pouring into Germany starting in 2011, the staff of the German War Crimes Unit interviewed 200 witnesses in two structural investigations. One, based on the "Caesar photos," is focused on crimes committed by the Syrian regime as captured in thousands of photos smuggled out by a former Syrian official. The other, based on interviews of Yazidi refugees in Germany, is focused on crimes committed by the ISIS terrorist organization against that ethnic group in Syria.[89] So far, the structural investigations have led to twenty-two person-specific investigations against twenty-eight suspects.[90] While most of the alleged perpetrators are outside of the country, Germany has gained custody over and tried four Syrian defendants to date.[91]

In June 2018, Germany issued an international arrest warrant for Syrian General Jamil Hassan, a member of Assad's inner circle, charging him with war crimes and crimes against humanity.[92] In February 2019, after the general traveled to Lebanon seeking medical treatment, Germany made a formal extradition request of Lebanon for Hassan's surrender. A few days later, the US government issued a statement supporting Germany's extradition request for the high-ranking Syrian official. By taking this step, the United States placed itself on the record in support of Germany's exercise of universal jurisdiction, a move that marks a major reversal in US legal practice.[93] Commenting on this development, Beth Van Schaack, former Deputy US Ambassador at Large for War Crimes Issues, said "[t]he exercise of universal jurisdiction is making a comeback, and so far the German model represents one of the most responsibly managed, highly professional exercises of this form

---

[87] Kaleck & Kroker, *supra* note 1, at 179–180.
[88] *Id.*
[89] *Id.*
[90] *Id.* at 181.
[91] Hovell, *supra* note 34, at 448.
[92] *See Hassan Arrest Warrant.*
[93] *See* Goodman, *supra* note 7.

of criminal justice especially when used in directed manner to address the world's most heinous crimes."[94]

Germany was the first country to have launched these structural investigations related to Syria, "but it established a model for other states wishing to serve the interests of a broader international fight against impunity."[95] France has also embraced the strategy of structural investigations, with the limitation that French law requires that one or more of the victims of each case be a French national or that the suspect is located in French territory.[96] Using this authority, in 2018, a French court issued international arrest warrants for three high-level Assad regime officials (Ali Mamluk, director of the National Security Bureau; Jamil Hassan, head of Syrian Air Force Intelligence, and Abdel Salam Mahmoud, director of an Air Force Intelligence investigative branch), charging them with complicity in the disappearance of dual French-Syrian nationals.[97]

Meanwhile, a number of other European states have begun prosecuting Syrian perpetrators found in their territory under the "no safe haven approach." Most of these have ended with convictions, such as the Austrian case against a 27-year-old Syrian asylum seeker and former member of the opposition Farouq Brigade, who was sentenced to life in May 2017 for the multiple murders of government soldiers near Homs between 2013 and 2014.[98] In Sweden, a 28-year-old Syrian Asylum seeker and former member of the Free Syrian Army was sentenced to eight years in 2013 for war crimes and torture.[99] And, in September 2017, a collective of Swiss lawyers disclosed the existence of a criminal investigation into Rifaat Al-Assad–Syrian President Bashar Al-Assad's uncle, often referred to as the "Butcher of Hama"– for war crimes allegedly committed in 1982.[100]

IV CONCLUSION

The massive number of Syrians that have fled the violence in Syria has had an undeniable impact on the international community's approach to

---

[94] *Id.*

[95] Hovell, *supra* note 34, at 448.

[96] Kaleck & Kroker, *supra* note 1, at 173.

[97] Trial International, Universal Jurisdiction Annual Review 2019, https://trialinternational.org/wp-content/uploads/2019/03/Universal_Jurisdiction_Annual_Review2019.pdf

[98] Kaleck & Kroker, *supra* note 1, at 173.

[99] *Id.*

[100] *Switzerland Judicial Development, in* TRIAL International Make Way for Justice #4: Momentum towards accountability 78, 79 (2018).

international criminal justice. Over one million Syrian refugees have migrated to Europe, with 530,000 settling in Germany, 110,000 in Sweden, 50,000 in Austria, and smaller numbers in other countries.[101] Many of the refugees are victims of international crimes. Others are perpetrators. The issue of accountability was quite literally delivered to the doorsteps of the European states by the refugees arriving from Syria and there is reason to believe that the stream of universal jurisdiction cases will continue to increase in the coming years.

As this chapter has documented, the need to establish accountability for atrocities committed during the Syrian conflict has provided the catalyst for altering the power relationship in the United Nations between the Security Council and General Assembly. But the novel approach to creating the IIIM would never have been pursued if not for the pioneering efforts of Lichtenstein. The widespread view that Russia had abused its use of the veto set the stage for the General Assembly's bold power grab, which is likely to reverberate beyond just the creation of the IIIM. Conflict, intrepid leadership, and Security Council paralysis were the ingredients for profound change.

At the same time, Germany's adoption of the global enforcer approach to universal jurisdiction to prosecute Syrian perpetrators after that approach was abandoned earlier by Belgium and Spain, and the assistance of the IIIM, may presage a resurgence in this far-reaching type of universal jurisdiction. If other states begin to follow Germany's structural investigation model, as seems likely, this will constitute yet another way the Syrian conflict has fundamentally transformed customary international law.

---

[101] Phillip Connor, The PEW Research Center, Fact Sheet, Jan. 29, 2018, https://www.ethicsandinternationalaffairs.org/2017/rebirth-universal-jurisdiction

7

The Syrian Migration Crisis

I INTRODUCTION

As the above chapters have described, the UN High Commissioner for Refugees has recognized the Syrian refugee crisis as the world's single largest refugee crisis since World War II.[1] This chapter will analyze how the international community has attempted to deal with more than six million Syrians who have sought refuge around the globe while still protecting against the infiltration of terrorists. The global approach to the Syrian migration crisis, described in this chapter, includes novel legislation, executive and judicial actions, as well as new policy approaches related to the rights of Syrian refugees. This chapter will also examine how the Syrian refugee crisis affected the negotiation of the Global Compact on Refugees and the Global Compact on Safe, Orderly and Regular Migration, which were adopted in 2018. Finally, this chapter will assess whether the Syrian migration crisis has contributed to the development of new Grotian moments.

II DISPLACED SYRIANS: REFUGEES OR MIGRANTS?

This chapter examines the Syrian migration crisis by discussing both refugees and migrants. Because it is difficult to distinguish between refugee and migrant legal status in many cases of displaced Syrians, this chapter will refer to the Syrian migration crisis on the whole, and the impact that it has had throughout the world, without separating the cases of refugees from those of migrants. The section below will briefly discuss the legal difference between refugees and migrants; moreover, this section will demonstrate why it has

---

[1] *See* Chapters 2 and 6.

become increasingly difficult to attach these labels to individual cases of displaced Syrians.

A refugee is defined in the 1951 Refugee Convention as someone who has fled his or her country because of a "well-founded fear of being persecuted for reasons of race, religion, nationality, membership of a particular social group or political opinion."[2] This refugee definition, which is widely accepted and has reached the status of customary law, deliberately excludes individuals who have been forced from their homes by economic disaster or climate change. In addition, the Refugee Convention does not oblige its member states to grant anybody asylum; instead, member states are obligated to hear asylum cases and not to send asylum seekers to countries where they may face danger. In most countries, only individuals who satisfy the legal definition of a refugee qualify for asylum protection. Others fall in the "migrant" category. Migrants are not defined in any legal instruments, but most migration experts argue that migrants are individuals who move from their home country for other reasons, including in search of economic prosperity. In reality, however, the line between refugees and migrants is often blurred, and people do not fall neatly within one or the other category. "The system tries to place them into categories – refugee or economic migrant, legal or illegal, deserving or under-serving – that do not always fit the reality of their lives. And if the system breaks down, people are cast into a legal and moral grey zone that lasts for many months or even years."[3]

In addition, all individuals, including Syrians, who flee their country of origin have two main ways of obtaining protected status in third countries. First, they can travel to a third state and claim asylum there, and, second, they can seek to be recognized as a refugee for resettlement selection from a country in which they choose to seek asylum.[4] The main difference between these two procedures, which are complementary, is where the person seeking to migrate is located at the time of his or her application. Refugee designations and resettlement decisions are made while the person is outside of their destination country (the person can be in his or her country of origin, or in another state). A person seeking asylum, however, typically submits an

---

[2] UN General Assembly, Convention Relating to the Status of Refugees, July 28, 1951, United Nations, Treaty Series, vol. 189, p. 137, https://www.refworld.org/docid/3be01b964 .html (hereinafter "Refugee Convention").

[3] Daniel Trilling, *Five Myths about the Refugee Crisis*, THE GUARDIAN, June 5, 2018, https://www.theguardian.com/news/2018/jun/05/five-myths-about-the-refugee-crisis

[4] Nicole Ostrand, *The Syrian Refugee Crisis: A Comparison of Responses by Germany, Sweden, the United Kingdom, and the United States*, 3 J MIGRATION & HUM. SEC. 255, 257 (2015), https://journals.sagepub.com/doi/pdf/10.1177/233150241500300301

application while he or she is physically present or at a port of entry in the territory where they are seeking refuge.[5]

In the cases of many displaced Syrians, it is impossible to legally label someone as a refugee or as a migrant – many Syrians have fled their country because of war and in search of economic prosperity, but it is increasingly difficult to recognize which Syrians have faced a well-founded fear of persecution in a way which would satisfy the legal criteria of the 1951 Refugee Convention. Many fleeing Syrians do not carry supporting documentation, and may not understand the distinction between refugee versus migrant status. And government officials from host countries processing large numbers of Syrian arrivals may be ill-equipped to make such distinctions. This chapter will address the Syrian migration crisis globally, by discussing cases of Syrians who seek refugee status and resettlement outside of their destination country, as well as cases where Syrians enter their destination country and apply for asylum. In fact, as this chapter will discuss, some host countries, such as Germany and Turkey, have focused on resettlement and protected status policies, and have turned away from traditional asylum-focused routes toward legalizing a newly arrived person's status. This chapter will thus focus on the Syrian migration crisis, by including all Syrians, refugees and migrants, in its discussion, and by analyzing different countries' responses to the crisis, whether they entail refugee or non-refugee protections.

III SYRIAN MIGRATION: BACKGROUND

As Chapters 2 and 6 have described, the Syrian conflict has, since its beginning in 2011, escalated into a global migration crisis, causing massive regional and international refugee and migrant movements. According to most recent data, there are over six million internally displaced Syrians and nearly five million seeking refuge abroad.[6] According to the Syria Center for Policy Research, the Syrian conflict has been marked by widespread and brutal atrocities, including a death toll exceeding 470,000.[7] In addition, there have been over 14,000 documented cases of death by torture, and there has been widespread Syrian government use of internationally prohibited chemical weapons, inherently indiscriminate barrel bombs, cluster munitions, and the indiscriminate use of incendiary weapons in civilian-populated areas.

---

[5] *Id.*

[6] World Vision, *Syrian Refugee Crisis: Facts, FAQs, and How to Help*, https://www.worldvision .org/refugees-news-stories/syrian-refugee-crisis-facts

[7] Simon Lewis, *The Death Toll from Syria's War Is Actually 470,000, New Research Claims*, Time, Feb. 11, 2016, https://time.com/4216896/death-toll-syria-war-470000

Syria's war has had a ripple effect throughout both the Middle East as well as Europe and other parts of the world. The war has caused the largest humanitarian crisis since the end of World War II. Millions of refugees and migrants have poured into Turkey, Jordan, Lebanon, Iraq, and Egypt as well as European countries.[8] As this chapter will discuss, the Syrian refugee crisis has had a significant political impact in Europe in particular, and it may be argued that this crisis has been one of the main causes of Brexit. The Syrian refugee crisis has wreaked havoc domestically as well: more than half of Syria's population has been displaced and dependent on humanitarian aid for daily subsistence.[9] Numerous homes, schools, businesses, hospitals, roads, and infrastructure have been destroyed and damaged during the Syrian War; such infrastructure destruction has undoubtedly contributed to the numerous Syrians' decision to flee their country as migrants or refugees. Over one million Syrian refugees have migrated to Europe, with 530,000 settling in Germany, 110,000 in Sweden, 50,000 in Austria, and smaller numbers in other countries.[10] As this chapter will discuss, the large number of Syrians who have fled the violence in Syria and have attempted to resettle elsewhere has had an undeniable impact on the international community's approach to migration crises. In addition, as this chapter will discuss, various host countries have responded differently to the influx of Syrian refugees and migrants, by adopting different laws, policies, and executive actions.

IV NATIONAL RESPONSES: POLICY, LEGISLATION, CASES, EXECUTIVE ACTION

The vast majority of Syria's 6.7 million refugees have fled to neighboring countries and remain in the Middle East: approximately 3.6 million Syrian refugees are in Turkey; 950,000 refugees are in Lebanon; 670,000 are in Jordan; 250,000 are in Iraq; 130,000 are in Egypt.[11] In 2015, at the peak of the migrant crisis in Europe, 1.3 million Syrians had requested asylum in Europe, but the number of new asylum seekers has declined significantly. The United States has admitted 18,000 Syrian refugees between 2011 and 2016.[12] Although some Syrians have been resettled in other countries, most Syrian refugees and migrants still lack meaningful access to housing, health services, and education

---

[8] World Vision, *supra* note 6.
[9] *Id.*
[10] Phillip Connor, *The PEW Research Center, Fact Sheet*, Jan. 29, 2018, https://www .ethicsandinternationalaffairs.org/2017/rebirth-universal-jurisdiction
[11] World Vision, *supra* note 6.
[12] *Id.*

in their host countries, and most Syrians have not been resettled in developed European states or the United States. In fact, it may be argued that within Europe, the Syrian migration crisis has caused a backlash against refugees and migrants. As one commentator has noted, statelessness threatens the established nation-state system, and "[b]eing a refugee means not doing what you are told – if you did, you would probably have stayed at home to be killed."[13] In other ways, the Syrian migration crisis has caused several European Union countries to reshape their approach to receiving foreigners, from an asylum-focused approach to a resettlement-based policy. The following section will examine various countries' responses to the Syrian migration crisis.

A European Union: France, Germany, and the United Kingdom

The European Union (EU) has a complex "entry" system designed to deter unwanted migrants. In fact, since the early 1990s, as borders have disappeared within Europe and as EU citizens have obtained the free right of movement, the EU's external frontiers have become increasingly difficult to cross for various refugees and migrants. The Syrian migration crisis may have confirmed, within the EU, the necessity of such a stringent migration control system, and may contribute to the tightening of Europe's already stringent asylum-seeking protections and rights.[14]

Within the European Union, refugee and asylum procedures are streamlined through European institutions, regulations, and directives. As part of the Hague Program, the European Commission proposed the creation of the European Asylum Support Office (EASO), in order to promote cooperation among member states in asylum matters. Formal implementation of EASO started occurring in 2011, at the outset of the Syrian migration crisis. The Dublin Regulation states that the role of the EASO is to "provide solidarity measures, such as the Asylum Intervention Pool with asylum support teams, to assist those Member States which are faced with particular pressure and where applicants for international protection cannot benefit from adequate standards, in particular as regards reception and protection."[15] Other objectives of

---

[13] Trilling, *supra* note 3.

[14] As Daniel Trilling has reported, "Europe has tried to strike deals to stop the people-trafficking routes that run across the desert and through north Africa. Italy has cracked down on NGO sea rescues and paid off militias in Libya, even as evidence of torture and abuse in Libyan detention centers trickles out; the EU has explored deals with Sudan's repressive dictatorship." *Id.*

[15] Sarah Cockroft & Nicole Provax, *The European Union's Response to the Syrian Refugee Crisis: National Factors That Affect Compliance in France and Spain*, Senior Theses 198 (2017), at 11, https://scholarcommons.sc.edu/cgi/viewcontent.cgi?article=1199&context=senior_theses

the EASO include facilitation of cooperation among EU member states, collection of information from member states in order to improve implementation of the Common European Asylum System, and the creation of current and accurate reports on applicant countries of origin.[16]

Although migrants who qualify as refugees theoretically have the right to cross borders in order to seek asylum, the EU has imposed multiple barriers for those seeking asylum. In fact, the EU has closed down legal asylum routes, such as the ability to seek asylum at an overseas embassy. In addition, the EU now imposes penalties on transportation companies who allow people to travel into the EU without proper documentation. And EU authorities have signed treaties with neighboring countries so that the latter would control migration on the EU's behalf. For example, in the wake of the Syrian migration crisis, EU authorities signed an agreement with Turkey in 2016, which has significantly reduced the mobility of Syrians toward Europe.[17] Within the EU, the so-called Dublin Regulation forces asylum seekers to apply in whatever country they reach first.[18] Syrian migrants and refugees thus face tight controls when attempting to resettle within the EU: they must arrive to an EU country in order to apply for asylum (they may not seek asylum from European countries' embassies in Damascus or elsewhere), but if they travel through Turkey, they may not be able to move forward at all. In addition, because of the Dublin Regulation, Syrian refugees and migrants have to apply for asylum protection in the first EU country which they reach, which may not be the country of their preferred choice. Thus, a significant number of Syrian refugees have been forced to seek asylum in Hungary, the first EU country which they entered. This is problematic for two reasons. First, some Syrian refugees and migrants may prefer to resettle elsewhere within the EU because of better job prospects or the presence of friends and family. And, second, Hungary's President, Viktor Orbán, has increasingly turned against non-Europeans and has embraced populist values which are not accepting of Muslim refugees.[19] Other Syrian

---

[16] *Id.*

[17] Trilling, *supra* note 3.

[18] Regulation (EU) No. 604/2013 of the European Parliament and of the Council of 26 June 2013 establishing the criteria and mechanisms for determining the Member State responsible for examining an application for international protection lodged in one of the Member States by a third-country national or a stateless person (recast), Official Journal of the European Union L (180/31), June 29, 2013 ("Dublin Regulation").

[19] Orla Barry, *In Orban's Hungary, Refugees Are Unwelcome – So Are Those Who Try to Help*, PRI's The World, Feb. 11, 2019, https://www.pri.org/stories/2019-02-11/orban-s-hungary-refugees-are-unwelcome-so-are-those-who-try-help (noting that Hungary has some of the strictest immigration laws, and that refugees who live in Hungary "face regular reminders that they are

refugees have languished in filthy camps on Greek islands, ill-equipped to deal with thousands of migrants and unable to move forward.[20] Thus, Syrians attempting to enter specific EU countries have experienced difficult logistical and legal journeys and many of them have not been able to reach their preferred destinations. In addition, different EU countries have adopted varying laws and policies in order to facilitate or to prevent the resettlement of significant numbers of Syrian migrants and refugees. The following sections will briefly discuss the various paths toward asylum and resettlement that France, Germany, and the United Kingdom have adopted in the wake of the Syrian migration crisis.

1 France

Because of the Dublin Regulation, which provides that a refugee ought to seek asylum in his or her first EU country of entry, some EU member states have seen a relatively small number of Syrian asylum applications. France, one of the EU's largest and most prominent members, has not experienced a large influx of Syrian refugees and migrants. In 2015, then President François Hollande pledged to accept 30,000 Syrian refugees within the following two years.[21] However, by the following year, France had only taken in 14,000 Syrian refugees. President Hollande thus accepted an additional 1,000 refugees from Germany, in order to alleviate the pressure that Germany was facing in light of the very large number of asylum applications that it was experiencing.[22] As of today, however, it is unclear how many Syrian refugees in total France has accepted, and it is uncertain whether France will continue to accept and process additional refugee and asylum applications.

French law appears in compliance with EU law on asylum, and a refugee seeking asylum in France can rely on three different sources of law in order to do so: the 1951 Geneva Convention, which France has ratified, the French Constitution, as well as so-called subsidiary protection under French law, which grants a qualified applicant an additional form of protection.[23] Nonetheless, the asylum procedure itself in France is complex and strenuous, in particular for non-French-speaking applicants: an applicant must submit a

---

unwelcome from both governmental legislation and opinion polls") (noting also that Orbán has referred to Muslim refugees as "Muslim invaders").

[20] Trilling, *supra* note 3.
[21] Cockroft & Provax, *supra* note 15, at 12.
[22] *Id.*
[23] *Id.* at 13.

written statement as well as engage in an oral interview with French government officials before his or her application may be granted.[24] And, even if a
refugee receives asylum in France, his or her integration into French society
may be difficult. On paper, France has appeared willing to accept asylum
seekers, in light of the country's colonial past and involvement in the Middle
East. "France's shared history and role in destabilizing the Syrian region
indicates that they have a greater duty to help the Syrian people who are
fleeing this unrest."[25] However, de facto, political and societal forces within
France may render refugee integration particularly difficult. Over the past
decade, France has experienced a high rate of unemployment, which renders
the idea of accepting large numbers of refugees unappealing to many French
citizens. In addition, France has faced religious turmoil, pitting native French
citizens, most of whom identify as secular/nonreligious, against the relatively
large number of Muslim French citizens or residents. This has swayed the
public opinion against embracing an additional large number of Syrian
Muslims within French borders. "France's shared history and role in destabilizing the Syrian region indicates that they have a greater duty to help the
Syrian people who are fleeing this unrest." France may not be an attractive
destination for the Syrian refugees themselves, as several French laws ban the
free exercise of religion in public. This, combined with the rise in nationalist
and populist political movements in France, may contribute to the face that
Syrian refugees and migrants may not flee to France in large numbers any
time in the near future. "If anything, the refugees use France as a gateway
country to the United Kingdom and Germany. In addition, refugees, including Syrian refugees, are currently fleeing to countries with lower rates of
unemployment and countries with less vocal criticism of the refugee
populations."[26]

Despite appearing in compliance with EU law on asylum, France has de
facto not been a welcoming host country to Syrians. The French government
has not kept its pledge to accept a significant number of Syrian migrants and
refugees, and societal and political forces within France may be turning this
country into an inhospitable environment for Syrians. France is thus unlikely
to significantly help countries such as Turkey, Lebanon, and Jordan, which
are already hosting hundreds of thousands of Syrian migrants and refugees by
resettling some of such displaced populations.

---

[24] *Id.* at 13–14.
[25] *Id.* at 20.
[26] *Id.* at 25.

2 Germany

Unlike France, Germany has accepted larger numbers of Syrian migrants and refugees and has provided a more beneficial resettling environment. In March 2013, Germany announced that it would start a new program for admitting Syrian refugees from Lebanon. Through this program, Syrians receive a two-year temporary residence permit, which can be extended consecutively. Germany's national government has pledged to admit 20,000 Syrian refugees through this program, and fifteen German states have vowed to admit an additional 10,000 Syrians.[27] Between 2012 and 2014, Germany granted nearly 40,000 asylum applications to Syrian refugees. Germany, compared to France, has faced a significantly larger number of Syrian asylum applications and has taken in a much larger number of refugees. "A range of factors could account for the variance, including political policies and objectives, refugee friendly reputations among asylum seekers, family ties, ease of access and location, and procedural constraints."[28] The number of Syrian refugees entering Germany increased significantly in 2015, when the Austrian and German chancellors announced that migrants would be allowed to cross the border from Hungary into Austria and to continue to Germany. By the end of 2016, the total number of Syrians in Germany had reached over 600,000.[29]

In order to facilitate resettlement within Germany for such a large number of Syrians, Germany changed the manner in which it processed new arrivals. As opposed to treating the arriving Syrians as legal refugees and forcing them to undergo strenuous asylum procedures, Germany began to grant them work/ residency visas for one to three years. Thus, as opposed to tying the Syrian migrants' rights to remain within Germany to asylum procedures, Germany has been treating these cases within the framework of resettlement policies. "These humanitarian admission programs signal a change in German refugee policy."[30] The German change in policy is a direct response to the EU's request, in September 2017, to all member states to accept at least 50,000 individuals in 2018 and 2019. In fact, the largest numbers of Syrian refugees and migrants fled to neighboring countries, such as Jordan, Lebanon, and Turkey, and the EU's request for resettlement of these individuals within EU member states was an attempt to alleviate some of the pressure from housing such

---

[27] Ostrand, *supra* note 4, at 267.

[28] *Id.* at 272.

[29] *Id.; see also* DW, *Refugees in Germany: Legal Entry – Without Asylum*, Apr. 28, 2019, https://www.dw.com/en/refugees-in-germany-legal-entry-without-asylum/a-48515382

[30] See *supra* note 29.

tremendous numbers of Syrians off of Syria's neighbors.[31] In general, acceptance into a resettlement program, in Germany and elsewhere, is conditioned on the fulfillment of three criteria: a person must be deemed unable to return to his or her country of origin, and unable to build a future in the country that he or she fled to; in addition, a person must show that he or she is "especially vulnerable" – that they are not able to come to Europe on their own.

Germany may be reaping economic benefits from having accepted such a significant number of Syrians. The influx of human capital may be helping the German economy, where the population is aging and unemployment is historically low. "A combination of 'favorable labour market conditions,' language programmes and job placement initiatives are helping refugees land jobs."[32] Recent German laws, which allow asylum seekers who arrived before August 2018 to stay in Germany, if they have a steady job and speak German, may assist both Syrians as well as continue to foster the German economy, by embracing human capital.

Although Germany has accepted a large number of Syrians, through refugee and asylum procedures, and through more recent resettlement policies and programs, German attitudes toward Syrian migrants may be becoming more negative.[33] The presence of a large number of Syrians in Germany may be turning the public opinion away from empathy for those fleeing war in Syria, and it may be that Germany ceases to accept additional refugees and migrants from the Middle East. Nonetheless, it may be concluded that Germany, unlike France, has played a significant role in accepting and resettling a high number of Syrian migrants and refugees, and that such migrants and refugees perceive Germany as a hospitable environment.

In addition, German criminal laws may be changing in light of the increased presence of Syrians within German borders. Chapter 6 has already discussed changes in the imposition of individual criminal responsibility in the wake of the Syrian War. Germany has participated in this "trend" by expressing interest in prosecuting suspected Syrian war criminals within its national criminal system under the concept of universal jurisdiction.

---

[31] Ostrand, *supra* note 4, at 262 (noting that Turkey, Lebanon, Jordan, Iraq, and Egypt have already taken in the largest numbers of Syrian refugees and migrants, and that "[t]he burden placed on these countries is immense and has had adverse social and economic costs on the host communities").

[32] Siobhan Dowling, *Germany Welcomed Refugees. Now It's Reaping the Economic Benefits*, *Aljazeera*, June 20, 2019, https://www.aljazeera.com/ajimpact/germany-welcomed-refugees-reaping-economic-benefits-190617194147334.html

[33] DW, *Germans Increasingly Hostile towards Asylum-Seekers*, Apr. 25, 2019, https://www.dw.com/en/germans-increasingly-hostile-towards-asylum-seekers/a-48478777

In fact, in February 2019, German officials arrested a high-ranking Syrian official who was living in Germany, accusing him of complicity in crimes against humanity during the Syrian War.[34] This Syrian individual is being prosecuted in Germany under the principle of universal jurisdiction – a rare form of prosecution which had not been used frequently thus far in Germany or in any other countries. German prosecutors allege that universal jurisdiction can be used to bring charges against additional defendants. In December 2018, the German federal prosecutor indicated that Germany had opened close to 40 investigations into cases involving Iraqi and Syrian nationals.[35] Presumably, many such cases would be prosecuted under the concept of universal jurisdiction. In general, it may be argued that the Syrian migration may have contributed toward a renewed interest in universal jurisdiction prosecutions: according to Trial International, the number of suspects in cases which rely on universal jurisdiction increased by 18 percent in 2018, and other Syrian defendants are being investigated in Austria, France, and Sweden.[36] It may be argued that the presence of a large number of Syrians within German borders has sparked interest for German prosecutors in investigating war crimes and other grave offenses committed during the Syrian War, especially when individuals responsible for such offenses may be present in Germany. First, it is much easier for German prosecutors to collect evidence if the suspected perpetrator is in Germany, and where cases "have some connection to the domestic environment, with witnesses, perpetrators, or evidence here."[37] In light of the presence of thousands of Syrian refugees and migrants, German immigration authorities began asking them questions about their experiences during the Syrian War; this type of information was passed on to German police and special investigators, who were presumably able to use this information to issue the above-mentioned indictment.[38] And, second, cases involving Syrians are less politically charged than other universal jurisdiction prosecutions. In 2004 and 2006, European authorities attempted to bring universal jurisdiction cases against then US Defense Secretary Donald Rumsfeld, alleging that he had been complicit in the torture of Iraqis.[39] These efforts were shot down by German prosecutors because of the politically

---

[34] Cathrin Schaer, *Prosecuting Syrian War – Crimes Suspects from Berlin*, THE ATLANTIC, July 31, 2019, https://www.theatlantic.com/international/archive/2019/07/can-germany-convict-syrian-war-criminals/595054

[35] *Id.*

[36] *Id.*

[37] *Id.*

[38] *Id.*

[39] *Id.*

sensitive nature of this type of prosecution. The present universal jurisdiction prosecution of Syrian suspect(s) is vastly different and does not expose Germany to diplomatic or political backlash.

In sum, it may be argued that universal jurisdiction prosecutions of Syrian nationals for atrocity crimes in German, or other national courts is a positive development for the field of international criminal law and may constitute a Grotian moment, as this chapter will discuss below.

Unlike its neighbor, France, Germany has played a significant role in welcoming and resettling hundreds of thousands of Syrians who have fled war in their home country. And it appears that Germany has been successful in integrating such Syrians into its society and economy. The German model may be of interest to other countries in the future who may be facing the arrival of a large number of refugees or migrants from another part of the world.

3 The United Kingdom: Brexit

The United Kingdom (UK) has been a far less hospitable host to Syrian migrants and refugees. In addition, it may be argued that the arrival, or threat of arrival, of displaced individuals from the Middle East has been one of the main causes of Brexit.

Unlike Germany which resettled a large number of Syrians, the UK has accepted only 10,000 Syrian refugees.[40] Within the UK, a disproportionately large number of refugees have resettled in the north and in Scotland than in London and in the south. And almost a third of UK localities have not taken in any Syrians. According to recent statistics, some of the poorest regions in England, Yorkshire and the North East have taken three times as many refugees as the two wealthiest regions, London and the South East. Moreover, areas not generally associated with migration, such as Scotland and the Western Isles, have taken in some of the highest number of refugees.[41]

In January of 2014, the UK introduced a vulnerable persons relocation scheme for "particularly vulnerable" Syrians.[42] According to this program, admitted Syrians, including those who do not meet the refugee criteria, would be granted protected status; such status allows temporary residency for five years. "Following this period, individuals may apply for permanent settlement, known as 'indefinite leave to remain.'"[43] However, by the end of 2014, the UK

---

[40] Mark Easton & Ben Butcher, *Where Have the UK's 10,000 Syrian Refugees Gone?*, BBC, Apr. 24, 2018, https://www.bbc.com/news/uk-43826163

[41] *Id.*

[42] Ostrand, *supra* note 4, at 268.

[43] *Id.*

had granted humanitarian protection to only 143 Syrian refugees under this system – a very low number compared to the number of Syrians that both France and Germany have taken in. The UK Home Office has indicated that it would continue to help "several hundred Syrians" over a three-year period through this program.[44]

By 2015, the UK was facing increased international pressure to accept more Syrian refugees and migrants. The former UK Prime Minister, David Cameron, announced that the UK would accept a total of 20,000 Syrians by 2020, and the current UK government has debated whether to expand this target in the near future.[45] As of now, however, the UK has not resettled a significant number of Syrian refugees and migrants, and in light of its current political climate, including the ongoing Brexit negotiations, it is unlikely that it will do so in the near future.

As indicated above, it can also be argued that the Syrian migration crisis has been one of the driving forces behind the Brexit movement. Starting in 2004, the EU took in ten additional members – mostly central European states. Through the EU's free movement of labor policies, around two million people from Central and Eastern Europe migrated to Britain over the following decade. "While they integrated well into the labor market, the influx strained public services like schools, health care and transport."[46] When Germany announced in 2015 that it would open doors to unlimited new numbers of Syrian migrants and refugees, fears were sparked in the United Kingdom that such migrants and refugees would find their way across the English Channel, placing additional burdens on the British society and economy. In addition, terrorist attacks in Paris and Brussels, which had involved EU citizens as perpetrators, stoked fears that the EU policy of free movement of labor may contribute to insecurity and terrorism within the UK.[47] This provoked anti-European sentiment and may have indirectly led toward the Brexit vote. As one commentator has argued, if it had not been for Germany's decision to "allow for uncontrolled mass immigration into the heart of Europe, the pro-Brexit forces might have lost."[48] In fact, those campaigning for the Leave campaign in the United Kingdom started putting

---

[44] *Id.*

[45] BBC News, *UK Could Extend Target to Rehouse 20,000 Syrian Refugees*, Feb. 22, 2018, https://www.bbc.com/news/uk-43157002

[46] Jochen Bittner, *Is Merkel to Blame for Brexit?* N.Y. Times (Sept. 26, 2018), https://www.nytimes.com/2018/09/26/opinion/is-merkel-to-blame-for-brexit.html

[47] Council on Foreign Relations, *What Brexit Means*, July 22, 2019, https://www.cfr.org/backgrounder/what-brexit-means

[48] *Id.*

up images of fleeing Syrians, as they made their way through the Balkans, with slogans such as "Breaking Point" and "Take Back Control."[49] Support for Brexit began to pick up, resulting in the positive vote and the UK's decision to leave the EU. Many experts have argued that the Syrian migration issue was one of the several causes of Brexit. Matthew Goodwin, an expert on UK politics, has argued that "[t]he immigration issue powerfully combines anxieties over identity, economic security, and terrorism," and that the Brexit referendum was as much about immigration as it was about the British attitude vis-à-vis the EU.[50]

It remains to be seen how the UK will fare once it officially exits the EU, and whether the UK departure will serve as a model to other EU member states dissatisfied with Europe's immigration policies. It is also uncertain what future the EU faces without the UK, and whether Brexit will spark a renewed anti-immigration policy emanating from Brussels. Nonetheless, the Syrian migration's impact on Brexit and on the UK in general cannot be overlooked.

B *Turkey*

Although some EU countries, such as Germany, have accepted a relatively large number of Syrian refugees and migrants, the highest numbers thereof remain in neighboring countries, such as Jordan, Lebanon, and Turkey. This section discusses the Turkish approach to the Syrian migration, in order to assess how Turkey has coped with such a large influx of foreigners.

Turkey now hosts the largest number of Syrians: according to a World Bank report, the Turkish government has registered roughly 2.25 million Syrians through temporary protection procedures.[51] Turkey's approach to the Syrian migrant crisis has been different than those adopted by other refugee-hosting countries: Turkey has adopted a non-camp approach to hosting large Syrian populations, and in addition, the Turkish government itself has financed the resettlement efforts.[52] In contrast, many other countries have adopted a camp-based, humanitarian agencies-financed approach. The Turkish approach has

---

[49] *Id.; see also* Karla Adam & William Booth, *Immigration Worries Drove the Brexit Vote. Then Attitudes Changes*, WASHINGTON POST (Nov. 16, 2018), https://www.washingtonpost.com/world/europe/immigration-worries-drove-the-brexit-vote-then-attitudes-changed/2018/11/16/c216b6a2-bcdb-11e8-8243-f3ae9c99658a_story.html

[50] Council on Foreign Relations, *supra* note 47.

[51] World Bank Group, *Turkey's Response to the Syrian Refugee Crisis and the Road Ahead*, at 2, Dec. 2015, http://documents.worldbank.org/curated/en/583841468185391586/pdf/102184-WP-P151079-Box394822B-PUBLIC-FINAL-TurkeysResponseToSyrianRefugees-eng-12-17-15.pdf

[52] *Id.*

been praised as more beneficial for both the Syrian refugees and migrants as well as for Turkey itself. "Emerging global evidence increasingly shows that giving refugees the freedom to live outside of camp settings, providing opportunities for social and economic self-reliance, and protecting rights is more likely to result in economic benefits for host countries."[53]

In addition, the Turkish government has invested significant efforts to provide educational opportunities to Syrian migrants and refugees. The Turkish government has provided education options to Syrian children in three ways: by integrating Syrian children into the Turkish education system; by allowing community-based education (CBE) programs to run from within the Syrian community; and by facilitating Syrian children to attend temporary education centers, which are supervised by the ministry of education. These centers "have Turkish senior administration but are staffed by Syrian teachers, with education provided through a modified version of the Syrian curriculum developed by the Syrian Commission of Education under the Syrian Interim Ministry of Education."[54] The Turkish government has also provided Syrians with free access to healthcare, and has worked with the World Health Organization in order to facilitate a better public health approach by, for example, engaging in vaccination campaigns among Syrian populations.[55]

In 2013, faced with the arrival of thousands of Syrian refugees and migrants, the Turkish government passed a new Law on Foreigners and International Protection, which provided for a temporary protection regime for Syrian refugees, and detailed how such status was to be issued, and what the specific modalities for admission and registration would be.[56] Moreover, the new law outlined the rights and responsibilities of those under temporary protection, as well as outlined the coordination between various agencies involved in responding to the Syrian migration crisis.[57] The Turkish government also began to involve international organizations, civil society organizations, as well as local support groups in various efforts associated with accommodating such large numbers of Syrians within Turkish borders. For example, all Syrians with temporary protection status have been registered using biometric data; this will facilitate access by all Turkish government agencies and ministries to the information necessary in order to match individuals in need with different service providers on an expedient basis.[58]

---

[53] *Id.* at 5.
[54] *Id.* at 7.
[55] *Id.* at 9, 11.
[56] *Id.* at 3.
[57] *Id.*
[58] *Id.* at 4.

Nonetheless, the strains of hosting Syrians have been noticeable, especially in cities in the southeast of Turkey. "Tensions from Turkish communities relate to competition over jobs, rising rent prices, strains on municipal services and infrastructure, and cultural differences with SuTPs [Syrians under temporary protection]. Perception surveys show mixed attitudes – Turkish families recognize the humanitarian imperative to respond to SuTPs and show much generosity toward them; yet they are also deeply concerned about the social consequences of the presence of SuTPs in their communities."[59] Going forward, it is evident that Turkey will experience difficulty in ensuring that Syrians are fully integrated into the Turkish society, that they have meaningful job opportunities, adequate housing and other municipal services, and access to healthcare and education. Because Turkey has thus far been relatively successful in resettling a high number of Syrians, it is possible that Turkey will continue to play a significant role in the Syrian migration crisis by acting as a host country.

C United States

In addition to regional countries, such as Lebanon, Jordan, and Turkey, and the EU, some Syrian refugees and migrants have attempted to resettle in the United States. In 2016, the United States accepted approximately 12,500 Syrian refugees. In fact, President Obama's goal had been to resettle around 10,000 refugees per year. On January 27, President Donald Trump issued an executive order, suspending this refugee program and calling for a review of refugee admission procedures.[60] On March 6, 2017, President Trump issued a revised executive order which further suspended immigration from Syria and several other countries.[61] In addition to suspending immigration from Syria, the Trump administration has also set a historically low cap on refugee admissions in general, at 30,000, for fiscal year 2019.[62] These policies have de facto precluded any meaningful Syrian resettlement within the United States. In fact, while the United States allowed more than 12,000 Syrian refugees into the country in 2016, in 2018 only sixty-two Syrian refugees were admitted.

[59] *Id.* at 11.
[60] Council on Foreign Relations, *How Does the U.S. Refugee System Work?*, Oct. 10, 2018, https://www.cfr.org/backgrounder/how-does-us-refugee-system-work
[61] Sarah Pierce & Doris Meissner, *Trump Executive Order on Refugees and Travel Ban: A Brief Review*, MIGRATION POLICY, Feb. 2017, https://www.migrationpolicy.org/research/trump-executive-order-refugees-and-travel-ban-brief-review
[62] Human Rights First, *Refugee Cap Officially Set for All-Time Low 30,000*, Oct. 4, 2018, https://www.humanrightsfirst.org/press-release/refugee-cap-officially-set-all-time-low-30000

"The drop is largely the result of the Trump administration slashing the total number of refugees allowed into the country each year to 30,000, a historic low, and because of enhanced security screenings instituted for refugees from 11 countries, including Syria, that the United States consider threats to national security."[63]

It appears unlikely that the United States will, under the current administration, reverse its immigration policy and allow a larger number of Syrian refugees to come in. Moreover, it appears that the Syrian migration crisis may have been one of the driving factors in the Trump administration's decision to impose multiple travel bans on Muslim countries, including on Syria. The United States is, as of now, not playing a significant role in resettling Syrian refugees and migrants.

V INTERNATIONAL RESPONSES

It may be argued that the Syrian migration crisis has caused the international community to act, in order to alleviate the suffering of refugees and migrants, but also to better organize host countries' responses and policies. Although Syria is not the only nation in the world which has experienced a severe migration crisis, the large numbers of displaced Syrians which have moved throughout the Middle East but also within the EU has been a major driving force in persuading United Nations member states to act.

According to the United Nations, the number of worldwide refugees has reached almost twenty-six million. While most displacements tend to be caused by armed conflict, gang violence, human rights violations, and natural disasters have also contributed to increasingly forcing people out of their homes. Hundreds of thousands of refugees and migrants have attempted to cross to Europe via the Mediterranean Sea, but the vast majority of refugees (85 percent) remain in developing or middle-income countries. In light of historically high refugee and displaced persons levels worldwide, as well as in the wake of the Syrian migration crisis, the international community acted to develop a new framework in order to assist states in working together to alleviate the ongoing refugee crisis. In 2016, United Nations member states made a pledge, in the New York Declaration for Refugees and Migrants, to create a Global Compact on Refugees (GCR) and a Global Compact for Safe,

---

[63] Katie Zezima, *The U.S. Has Slashed Its Refugee Intake. Syrians Fleeing War Are Most Affected*, WASHINGTON POST, May 7, 2019, https://www.washingtonpost.com/immigration/the-us-has-slashed-its-refugee-intake-syrians-fleeing-war-are-most-affected/2019/05/07/f764e57c-678f-11e9-a1b6-b29b90efa879_story.html

Orderly and Regular Migration (GCM) by the end of 2018.[64] The purpose of these two compacts was to outline shared responsibilities among states in order to protect those who have been displaced and to ensure support for countries hosting and/or helping such refugees and migrants.

A *Global Compact on Refugees*

Based on the comprehensive refugee response framework set forth in the New York Declaration of 2016, the United Nations High Commissioner for Refugees was tasked with developing a new global compact on refugees, in consultation with states and other stakeholders. This process has entailed a series of discussions and meetings in 2017, as well as formal consultations on various drafts of the proposed document in 2018. The High Commissioner proposed a final text on the GCR in his annual report to the General Assembly in 2018; the text was adopted in December 2018.[65] "With the UN General Assembly vote in New York, an overwhelming majority of UN Member States affirmed a pact of international solidarity and cooperation for refugee protection and host community development."[66]

The GCR has been perceived as an opportunity to strengthen and streamline the international community's response to large movements of refugees. This document builds on existing international legal norms, including the 1951 Refugee Convention as well as other human rights treaties. In addition, the GCR seeks to foster state cooperation and to share responsibility among states regarding their response to refugee crisis.[67] GCR's four main objectives include: to ease pressure on host countries; to enhance refugee self-reliance; to expand access to third-country solutions; and to support conditions in countries of origin for return in safety and dignity. Significant progress can be achieved in the area of assisting displaced populations and host countries if states take action to implement the GCR.[68]

The GCR's other notable contribution is that it focuses on international cooperation among states, unlike existing treaties, such as the Refugee

---

[64] United Nations, Refugees and Migrants, Global Compact on Migration, https://refugeesmigrants.un.org/migration-compact; United Nations, Refugees and Migrants, Global Compact on Refugees, https://refugeesmigrants.un.org/refugees-compact

[65] Rescue.org, *The Global Compact on Refugees Is a Positive Step toward a Better Refugee Response*, Dec. 17, 2018, https://www.rescue.org/press-release/global-compact-refugees-positive-step-toward-better-refugee-response

[66] UN News, *Global Compact on Refugees: How Is This Different from the Migrants' Pact and How Will It Help?* Dec. 17, 2018, https://news.un.org/en/story/2018/12/1028641

[67] Id.

[68] Id.

Convention. According to the UN refugee agency's Assistant High Commissioner for Protection, Volker Turk, "The Refugee Convention focuses on rights of refugees and obligations of States, but it does not deal with international cooperation at large. And that's what the global compact seeks to address."[69] In addition, according to Turk, the GCR "responds to one of the major gaps we have faced for decades."[70]

B *Global Compact on Safe, Orderly and Regular Migration*

GCM, like the GCR, was adopted by United Nations member states in December 2018. While its purpose is similar to that of the GCR, the GCM addresses cooperation regarding migrants – individuals who do not fit the definition of a refugee.[71] As discussed above, refugees are individuals who flee their country of origin because of a fear of persecution. The refugee definition can be found in the 1951 Refugee Convention, as well as in the Statute of the United Nations High Commissioner for Refugees.[72] Migrants are not defined in any particular treaties, but most experts agree that migrants include those individuals who flee their home country for reasons other than those mentioned in the definition of a refugee

> While there is no formal legal definition of an international migrant, most experts agree that an international migrant is someone who changes his or her country of usual residence, irrespective of the reason for migration or legal status. Generally, a distinction is made between short-term or temporary migration, covering movements with a duration between three and 12 months, and long-term or permanent migration, referring to a change of country of residence for a duration of one year or more.[73]

According to the United Nations Secretary-General, António Guterres, "I'm a migrant but didn't have to risk my life on a leaky boat or pay traffickers. Safe migration cannot be limited to the global elite."[74]

In sum, in creating the GCM, United Nations member states have recognized the necessity of extending protection, through a coordinated international community's response, to displaced individuals who do not fit the definition of a refugee, but whose circumstances may be just as dire.

[69] *Id.*
[70] *Id.*
[71] *Id.*
[72] *Id.*
[73] *Id.*
[74] *Id.*

The two compacts, GCR and GCM, establish a framework for more developed and more equitable international responses to large displacement situations, involving refugees and migrants. While the compacts are not legally binding, they offer a guide to states in supporting displaced populations, by mobilizing political will within states and by providing a template for equitable responsibility-sharing. For example, in situations of large-scale displacements, the compacts provide that a host country or a country of origin can request the activation by UNHCR of a support platform, which can assist such a country's national response to the ongoing crisis.[75] In addition, the compacts, if implemented, could lead toward improved education and access to health services and other livelihood opportunities for displaced populations, because host countries, such as Uganda, Rwanda, Iran, or Lebanon would get the international support that they need from a development cooperation perspective.

According to the UN High Commissioner for Refugees, Filippo Grandi, "Decades of keeping refugees apart, consigned to camps or on the margins of society are giving way to a fundamentally different approach – including refugees in national systems, societies and economies of their host countries for the time that it is necessary, and enabling them to contribute to their new communities and to secure their own futures, pending a solution to their plight."[76]

The compacts' implementation efforts will be funded in part by the World Bank, which has already established a $2 billion financial instrument to assist low-income countries in addressing the socioeconomic impact of large refugee and migrant flows. In addition, the UNHCR and UN member states have also pledged to look toward the private sector and faith communities in order to acquire additional funding for the compacts' future implementation.[77]

It is uncertain whether the two compacts will be successfully implemented and funded, and whether they will truly assist host countries in handling large numbers of refugees and migrants. Nonetheless, the drafting and adoption of the two compacts has signaled that the international community is taking migration crises, such as the one in Syria, very seriously, and that the United Nations is willing to invest resources to confront this issue. The Syrian migration crisis has thus been a driving force in propelling international action in the realm of migration and refugee protection.

[75] *Id.*
[76] *Id.*
[77] *Id.*

VI THE SYRIAN MIGRATION CRISIS AND NEW GROTIAN MOMENTS?

The Syrian migration has produced at least three changes in which states and the international community respond to a serious influx of refugees and migrants; these changes may constitute Grotian moments. First, the migration has caused host countries to change the way in which they accept refugees and migrants, by embracing a resettlement policy, as opposed to an asylum-based approach. Second, the migration has had an impact on domestic criminal laws regarding jurisdiction by renewing interest in prosecutions based on universal jurisdiction. Last, the Syrian migration has sparked renewed interest from the international community to act and pass new guidelines in order to affront this and future migration crises. This section will briefly highlight and discuss these three Grotian moments.

As Chapter 3 has described, a Grotian moment is a time of accelerated formation of customary law, which typically occurs in the wake of a significant global event, such as a world war or another type of crisis.[78] The Syrian migration crisis may have acted as the driving force behind changes in national and international law and policy; thus, the crisis may have resulted in several Grotian moments. First, countries which have faced the influx of a large number of Syrian migrants and refugees, such as Germany and Turkey, seem to have changed the way in which they process and register arriving individuals and families. In the past, countries accepting refugees and migrants adopted asylum-based approaches to such immigration, requiring newly arrived individuals to seek asylum through onerous and at times lengthy legal procedures. Because countries such as Germany and Turkey have accepted hundreds of thousands of Syrians, the asylum approach was not tenable, as it would have resulted in a huge backlog of cases and as it would have relegated hundreds of thousands of individuals to legal limbo while they awaited the results of their asylum applications. During this time, asylum applicants may be forced to live in a refugee camp and may not have meaningful job and education and training opportunities. Germany and Turkey thus changed their approach to immigration, and adopted a resettlement policy, whereby they sought to give protected status, as opposed to asylum, to arriving Syrians. In this way, newly arrived Syrians have been able to seek housing outside of refugee camps, as well as to look for jobs and engage in other training and skills opportunities. In Germany, in particular, it appears

---

[78] *See* Chapter 3.

that Syrian migrants and refugees have been relatively well integrated into the German society, that many have learned the German language and have landed decent jobs, and that the German economy itself is reaping the benefits of this influx of labor. The Syrian migration crisis may have been the driving force in this Grotian moment: a change in host countries' immigration policies, from an asylum approach to a resettlement goal.

Second, the Syrian migration crisis may have caused another Grotian moment, by causing host countries with large numbers of migrants and refugees to engage in prosecutions of Syrian war criminals based on universal jurisdiction. As chapter six discussed, universal jurisdiction prosecutions have been rare in the past – they can be logistically difficult and expensive, and they may be politically challenging or cause diplomatic backlash. Until the present, relatively few cases had ever been prosecuted under the concept of universal jurisdiction. In the wake of the Syrian migration crisis, host countries such as Germany have found a new appreciation for the concept of universal jurisdiction. As discussed, German authorities are prosecuting at least one Syrian individual who is alleged to have committed serious crimes in Syria during the war; this individual was arrested in Germany, where he was residing. This prosecution may lead to others, and may prove to be a particularly useful model for imposing accountability on Syrian perpetrators of atrocities, who have thus far escaped the reach of all international courts.[79] Thus, the Syrian migration crisis may have contributed to this Grotian moment – a revival of universal jurisdiction prosecutions within national courts.

Third, the Syrian migration crisis may have contributed to a third Grotian moment: the international community's willingness to act, through the drafting of new international compacts, in order to alleviate refugee suffering and also in order to coordinate various host countries' responses and cooperation. Until now, refugee and migrant resettlement laws and policies have been matters of purely domestic concern, and relatively little had been done at the international level to promote and assist host country cooperation. In the wake of the Syrian migration crisis, the international community decided to act and to develop new legal documents which will both help refugees as well as promote national cooperation in terms of refugee and migrant resettlement. This Grotian moment may be of particular importance for the future, if countries which face future migration crises are able to work together in order to develop the most coordinated and efficient responses, laws, and policies,

---

[79] For a full discussion of the imposition of individual criminal responsibility for Syrian war criminals, *see* Chapter 6.

and in order to share the financial and logistical burden associated with resettling large numbers of refugees.

In sum, the Syrian migration crisis may have caused three important changes which constitute Grotian moments: a change in host countries' approach to processing and resettling large numbers of refugees and migrants; a renewed interest in universal jurisdiction prosecutions of wartime perpetrators of atrocities; and the development of new international documents on issues related to host countries' cooperation and coordination in resettlement efforts.

VII CONCLUSION

As this chapter has discussed, the Syrian migration crisis has rattled the world, and has had a particularly profound effect on the Middle East and within the EU. In the wake of this crisis, various countries have adopted different approaches to resettling Syrian migrants and refugees; country responses have varied and have resulted in the acceptance of very few Syrians, as in the United States since the Trump administration took office, or in the embrace of large numbers of Syrians, as in Germany. Moreover, the Syrian migration crisis has contributed to a renewed interest in universal jurisdiction prosecutions, and it has also prompted the international community to act, through the adoption of two new global compacts on refugees and migrants. As this chapter has argued, the Syrian migration crisis has produced at least three new Grotian moments that are likely to have long-term effects and which may shape the way that migration crises are addressed in the future.

8

International Law and the Syrian Peace Process

I INTRODUCTION

This chapter explores the novel legal framework created by the international community to structure the peace process for the resolution of the conflict in Syria.

Many observers hold the impression that peace negotiations are a purely political activity with the role of international law being limited to technical issues such as assisting with the design of mechanisms to protect human rights, or to set parameters around pathways to self-determination. In fact, nearly every peace process is circumscribed by a legal framework created by the international community within which the parties and the mediators operate. Often this framework includes both a process for negotiation as well as specified outcome objectives. These frameworks for peace negotiations, like many legal frameworks, hold variable degrees of authority depending on how and by whom they are created. Their degree of legal authority may also vary over time, and the content of the process and outcome objectives identified may be modified, evolved, and even contracted. And, as with all international law, it must intersect in an appropriate way with domestic law.

Following a brief chronological overview of the Syrian peace process, this chapter examines the initial instruments by which the international community sought to create a legal framework for the resolution of the Syrian conflict. These instruments include Arab League resolutions, declarations by key coalitions of international actors involved in seeking a resolution of the conflict, and UN General Assembly resolutions. During this discussion, the chapter sets out the key elements of the framework established by the international community that were intended to guide the negotiated resolution of the conflict.

The chapter then discusses how the UN Security Council took up the framework and sought to provide it greater coherence and legal authority through a series of UN Security Council Resolutions. In doing so the UN Security Council evolved, amended, and in some instances constrained the original framework.

The chapter briefly discusses how a sub-coalition of international actors then sought to significantly amend the process outside the framework endorsed by the UN Security Council, by replacing the peace negotiation process with a constitutional development process, and how the UN Envoy then maneuvered that process back within the initial framework.

Next, the chapter examines how the UN Envoy and the Syrian opposition party sought to implement the legal framework as it related to regime transition and the creation of a transitional governing body (TGB), and some of the challenges and questions they faced when seeking to do so.

The chapter also explores how the parties sought to bridge the outcomes envisioned by the legal framework with the requirements of domestic law, in particular how the peace process might lead to the adoption of a new constitution for Syria, but in a way that is in conformity with or legally circumvents the requirements of the current Syrian Constitution.

Finally, the chapter discusses how the international community contracted the legal framework, as it related to transitional justice, and how the parties and individual members of the international community responded.

II OVERVIEW OF PEACE PROCESS

On October 16, 2011, the Arab League – an international organization comprised at the time of twenty-two Middle Eastern and African states[1] – met to initiate talks between the Syrian government and Syrian opposition forces.[2] Calling on Assad to end the violence, the Arab League established a Syrian committee with representatives from Qatar, Egypt, Algeria, Oman, and Sudan with the goal of compelling Assad to engage in a peace process with the Syrian opposition.[3] The committee developed the Arab League Action Plan, with the agreement of Syria.

---

[1] The twenty-two states of the Arab League included: Lebanon, Iraq, Palestinian National Authority, Jordan, Egypt, Syria, Morocco, Algeria, Tunisia, Libya, Yemen, Sudan, Somalia, Qatar, Saudi Arabia, Bahrain, United Arab Emirates, Kuwait, Oman, Djibouti, Mauritania, and the Comoros.

[2] Müjge Küçükkeleş, "Arab League's Syrian Policy" (SETA Policy Brief No. 56, Foundation for Political, Economic and Social Research 2012), 6, http://www.scpss.org/libs/spaw/uploads/files/Policy/04-10-2012_SETA_Policy_Brief_No_56_Arab_Leagues_Syrian_Policy.pdf (last visited July 8, 2019).

[3] *Id.*

The Action Plan urged a cessation in the violence, the initiation of talks with the Syrian opposition, and an opening of the state to international monitors and journalists.[4] With the affirmative vote of Syria, on November 2, 2011, the Arab League adopted Resolution 7436.[5] The Syrian regime failed to initiate the prescribed actions.[6] With no signs of Syrian cooperation and the death toll continuing to rise from the regime's attacks on protesters, the Arab League suspended Syria from the league on November 12, 2011,[7] and imposed economic sanctions on the state two weeks later.[8]

While the prominent role of the Arab League in mediating the conflict encouraged states such as Russia and China, other members of the international community – including the United States and many European states – were skeptical of the ability of the Arab League on its own to create the necessary framework for a peaceful resolution of the conflict. This skepticism increased after the Arab League appointed former Sudanese military commander and suspected war criminal Mustafa al-Dabi to lead an observer mission.[9] Nonetheless, the mission ultimately reported that there was anti-regime armed resistance in Syria and that the Syrian regime used this resistance as a rationale for a brutal crackdown. The report of the monitoring mission prompted a meeting of the Arab League in Cairo on January 22, 2012. It was at this Cairo meeting that the Arab League adopted Resolution 7444, which included an updated version of the League's peace plan ("Cairo Plan").[10] The Arab League's Cairo Plan was notable in its call for Assad to peacefully transfer his power to a deputy and begin moving Syria toward a national unity government.[11] The Arab League then reached out to the UN Secretary-General and proposed a joint peace effort.

---

[4] Arab League Council, Resolution 7436 (Nov. 2, 2011), https://documents.aucegypt.edu/ SyriaReader/Documents/2-LAS%20Action%20Plan%20November%202011.pdf (last visited July 8, 2019).

[5] *Id.*; Küçükkeleş, *supra* note 2, at 8–10.

[6] Küçükkeleş, *supra* note 2, at 7.

[7] Neil MacFarquhar, *Arab League Votes to Suspend Syria over Crackdown*, N.Y. TIMES (Cairo, Nov. 12, 2011), https://www.nytimes.com/2011/11/13/world/middleeast/arab-league-votes-to-suspend-syria-over-its-crackdown-on-protesters.html (last visited July 8, 2019).

[8] Neil MacFarquhar & Nada Bakri, *Isolating Syria, Arab League Imposes Broad Sanctions*, N.Y. TIMES (Beirut, Nov. 27, 2011), https://www.nytimes.com/2011/11/28/world/middleeast/arab-league-prepares-to-vote-on-syrian-sanctions.html (last visited July 8, 2019).

[9] Küçükkeleş, *supra* note 2, at 10.

[10] "Monitoring of developments in the situation in Syria: Elements of the Arab plan to resolve the Syrian crisis," *enclosed in* Letter dated Jan. 24, 2012 from the Secretary-General addressed to the President of the Security Council, U.N. Doc. S/2012/71 (Jan. 30, 2012), https://undocs.org/en/S/2012/71 (last visited July 9, 2019).

[11] *Id.*

Supporting a political transition in Syria ran contrary to the traditional approach of the Arab League. Historically, the Arab League tended to support regime stability over political transition.[12] Yet, the Arab League signaled its willingness to work toward the removal of the Assad regime in suspending its Observer Mission on January 26, 2012, and holding meetings with the UN from January 31 through February 4, 2012.[13] At the end of these meetings, members of the Arab League joined with members of the UN Security Council to submit a Draft UN Security Council Resolution calling for Syria to comply with the League's Action Plan and begin a political transition.[14] The representatives from China and Russia vetoed the resolution.[15]

To overcome the impasse in the UN Security Council, the UN General Assembly passed an almost identical resolution (A/RES/66/253).[16] The resolution called for a political transition as well as the appointment of a UN and Arab League Joint Special Envoy who would work toward a resolution of the conflict.[17] A few days later, on February 23, 2012, the UN and Arab League Secretary-Generals jointly appointed Kofi Annan to take this role as Joint Special Envoy of the United Nations and the League of Arab States on the Syrian Crisis ("Joint Special Envoy").[18] Under this mandate, Annan produced a "Six-Point Peace Plan" aimed at galvanizing a peaceful transition process in Syria,[19] which he followed up with Geneva-based peace talks in June 2012. These talks, often referred to as the "Geneva 1 Conference," produced the Geneva Communiqué, a document that would guide the efforts toward a Syrian-led inclusive political transition for the next few years.

---

[12] Küçükkeleş, *supra* note 2, at 12.

[13] *Id.*

[14] S.C. Draft Res. 2012/77, U.N. Doc. S/2012/77 (Feb. 4, 2012) [UN Draft resolution on the situation of human rights in the Syrian Arab Republic] arts. 5, 6, https://digitallibrary.un.org/record/720648/files/S_2012_77-EN.pdf (last visited July 8, 2019).

[15] "Draft Resolution S/2012/77: Notes" (United Nations Digital Library), https://digitallibrary.un.org/record/720648?ln=en (last visited July 9, 2019).

[16] G.A. Res. 66/253, GAOR, 66th Sess., U.N. Doc. A/RES/66/253 (Feb. 21, 2012), https://undocs.org/en/A/RES/66/253 (last visited July 9, 2019).

[17] *Id.*

[18] "Kofi Annan Appointed Joint Special Envoy of United Nations, League of Arab States on Syrian Crisis," U.N. Meetings Coverage & Press Releases, U.N. Doc. SG/SM/14124 (Feb. 23, 2012), https://www.un.org/press/en/2012/sgsm14124.doc.htm (last visited July 9, 2019).

[19] "Six-Point Proposal of the Joint Special Envoy of the UN and League of Arab States," as annexed in UN Security Council, Security Council Resolution 2042 (2012) [*on authorization of the deployment of an advance team of up to 30 unarmed military observers to the Syrian Arab Republic*], 14 April 2012, S/RES/2042(2012), https://www.refworld.org/docid/4fbe14782.html (last visited June 25, 2019).

The Communiqué primarily focused on outlining plans for such a political transition, while also calling for an immediate ceasefire and the provision of humanitarian assistance.[20]

Joint Special Envoy Annan's attempts to implement both the Six-Point Peace Plan and Geneva Communiqué faced severe opposition from the Assad regime and its allies, which led Annan to resign in August 2012.[21] To replace Annan, the UN and Arab League appointed Lakhdar Brahimi to be the new Joint Special Envoy beginning September 1, 2012.[22] Over the next two years, Brahimi worked toward peace and political transition in Syria based on the action plan in the Geneva Communiqué. He led the Geneva II talks in January and February 2014, but was also frustrated by the Syrian regime's refusal to engage in productive negotiations and resigned in May 2014.[23]

On July 10, 2014, UN Secretary-General Ban Ki-moon appointed Staffan de Mistura to continue Brahimi's efforts to negotiate peace by serving as the UN Special Envoy for Syria ("UN Envoy").[24] In late summer and fall of 2015, Islamic State affiliates committed a number of terrorist attacks in Western Europe and the Middle East. These attacks, combined with the start of airstrikes by the Russian Government in September 2015 that supported the Assad regime's military efforts, catalyzed the international community to renew the efforts to secure peace in Syria. Representatives from seventeen states, the European Union, and the United Nations[25] formed the International Syria Support Group (ISSG) to discuss prospects for durable peace

---

[20] "Action Group for Syria Final Communiqué," *as annexed in* S.C. Res. 2118, SCOR, 7038th meeting, U.N. Doc. S/RES/2118 (Sept. 27, 2013) Annex II, https://www.securitycouncilreport .org/atf/cf/%7B65BFCF9B-6D27-4E9C-8CD3-CF6E4FF96FF9%7D/s_res_2118.pdf (last visited July 9, 2019).

[21] "Kofi Annan Resigns as UN–Arab League Joint Special Envoy for Syrian Crisis" (*UN News*, Aug. 2, 2012), https://news.un.org/en/story/2012/08/416872-kofi-annan-resigns-un-arab-league-joint-special-envoy-syrian-crisis (last visited July 9, 2019).

[22] "UN, Arab League Appoint Veteran Diplomat to Take over Annan's Role on Syrian Crisis" (*UN News*, Aug. 17, 2012), https://news.un.org/en/story/2012/08/417782-un-arab-league-appoint-veteran-diplomat-take-over-annans-role-syrian-crisis (last visited July 9, 2019).

[23] "Syria: UN–Arab League Envoy Brahimi Resigns" (*UN News*, May 13, 2014), https://news.un .org/en/story/2014/05/468162-syria-un-arab-league-envoy-brahimi-resigns (last visited July 9, 2019).

[24] "Secretary-General Appoints Staffan de Mistura Special Envoy for Syria, Ramzy Ezzeldin Ramzy Deputy Special Envoy for Syria," U.N. Meetings Coverage & Press Releases, U.N. Doc. SG/A1440 (July 10, 2014), https://www.un.org/press/en/2014/sga1480.doc.htm (last visited July 10, 2019).

[25] The participants at the October ISSG meeting in Vienna were: China, Egypt, the EU, France, Germany, Iran, Iraq, Italy, Jordan, Lebanon, Oman, Qatar, Russia, Saudi Arabia, Turkey, United Arab Emirates, the United Kingdom, the United Nations, and the United States.

in Syria. The ISSG met in Vienna for the first time on October 30, 2015 and then for a second time on November 14, 2015. At the conclusion of each of these meetings, the ISSG released statements (known as the Vienna Statements) that recapped the events and decisions of the respective meetings. These Vienna Statements affirmed the need for a political transition consistent with the Geneva Communiqué and sought confidence building measures that could would also help secure a ceasefire and deliver humanitarian assistance.[26] These meetings of the ISSG were instrumental in motivating the UN Security Council to pass Resolution 2254, which was to become a core pillar of the effort toward a political transition in Syria.

As the UN-led peace process continued in Geneva, the governments of Russia, Iran, and Turkey together decided to initiate a parallel process in Astana, Kazakhstan. The Astana Peace Process began January 23, 2017, shortly after a change in the US administration, and it signaled a geopolitical shift away from UN-led talks heavily supported by the US, toward talks that were primarily directed by the Russian government.[27] Substantively this entailed a shift from talks focused on the removal of Assad to talks focused on ceasefires and more limited constitutional reform. While the Astana talks claimed to be complementary to the Geneva conferences, the talks arguably aimed to supplant the UN process with discussions that were more favorable to the Assad regime. For instance, much of the language around the creation of a TGB codified in the Geneva Communiqué and UN Security Council Resolution 2254 was replaced with broad discussions of political process in Astana statements.[28]

At the conclusion of the October 2017 (seventh round) Astana talks, the Russian government declared its intent to expand the mandate of the Astana process and to host a national conference in Sochi to initiate a national dialogue process. The main Syrian opposition groups boycotted the conference, decrying its disingenuous and faulty attempt to legitimize itself as an alternative to the Geneva process. Nevertheless, the dialogue did occur from

---

[26] "Final Declaration on the Results of the Syria Talks in Vienna as Agreed by Participants" (Vienna, Oct. 30, 2015), https://eeas.europa.eu/delegations/niger/3102/final-declaration-on-the-results-of-the-syria-talks-in-vienna-as-agreed-by-participants_en (last visited July 10, 2019); "Statement of the International Syria Support Group" (Vienna, Nov. 14, 2015), https://www.un.org/undpa/en/Speeches-statements/14112015/syria (last visited July 10, 2019).

[27] Fabrice Balanche, "Will Astana Displace Geneva in the Syrian Peace Process," https://www.washingtoninstitute.org/policy-analysis/view/will-astana-displace-geneva-in-the-syrian-peace-process (last visited July 10, 2019).

[28] "Joint Statement by Iran, Russia and Turkey on the International Meeting on Syria in Astana, 21–22 December 2017" (Astana, Dec. 22, 2017), http://www.mfa.gov.tr/astanada-duzenlenen-suriye-konulu-uluslararasi-toplanti-hk-ortak-aciklama_en.en.mfa (last visited July 10, 2019).

January 29 to 30, 2018.[29] The talks culminated in the production of the Sochi Final Statement.[30] While the statement was quite deferential to the UN-led process in Geneva, the Conference falsely legitimized itself as a national dialogue and called for the establishment of a constitutional committee in a way that the Syrian opposition worried would subvert a political transition.[31] As discussed in greater detail in later sections, the Sochi Final Statement in many ways both exemplified and codified a shift from negotiations around a peace process to negotiations around a constitutional process. This shift, which was overseen and supported by UN Envoy Staffan de Mistura, would continue through de Mistura's resignation and the appointment of his successor, Geir Pedersen.[32]

III ESTABLISHING THE LEGAL FRAMEWORK

This section examines the initial instruments by which the international community sought to create the legal framework to structure the peace process for the resolution of the conflict in Syria. This framework was originally created through brief but intense Arab League engagement, which was followed by the involvement of the UN General Assembly and UN Security Council. During the course of reviewing the initial instruments, this section identifies the key elements of the framework established by the international community that were intended to guide the negotiated resolution of the conflict.

During the early years of the Syrian conflict, there were numerous statements, proclamations, and resolutions issued by various engaged international bodies. It is beyond the scope of this section to thoroughly discuss all of these international instruments that related to the many facets of the Syrian conflict. Rather, this section examines the core international instruments that established the initial legal framework for the peace process. These include the

---

[29] "Sochi Conference on Syria Opens Despite Opposition Boycott," *Radio Free Europe* (Jan. 29, 2018), https://www.rferl.org/a/syria-russia-sochi-conference-opens-without-opposition/29005414 .html (last visited July 10, 2009).

[30] Final Statement of the Congress of the Syrian National Dialogue (Sochi, Jan. 30, 2018), http:// www.mfa.gov.tr/final-statement-of-the-congress-of-the-syrian-national-dialogue_en.en.mfa (last visited July 9, 2019).

[31] "Syria Opposition Rejects Sochi Constitution Plan," *Al Jazeera News* (Jan. 30, 2018), https:// www.aljazeera.com/news/2018/01/syria-opposition-rejects-sochi-constitution-plan-180130193416723.html (last visited July 10, 2019).

[32] "Secretary-General Appoints Geir O. Pedersen of Norway Special Envoy for Syria," U.N. Meetings Coverage & Press Releases, Oct. 31, 2018, U.N. Doc. SG/A/1836-BIO/5156, https:// www.un.org/press/en/2018/sga1836.doc.htm (last visited July 23, 2019).

early resolutions and peace plans adopted by the Arab League, the UN General Assembly resolution creating a Joint Special Envoy, declarations by key coalitions of international actors involved in seeking a resolution of the conflict, the proclamation of a Six-Point Peace Plan and its endorsement by the UN Security Council, and eventually the issuance of the Geneva Communiqué.

The development of a legal framework for the peace talks began with the early efforts of the Arab League. As noted above, meeting on November 2, 2011, the League passed Resolution 7436,[33] which called for the cooperation of the Syrian regime in ending the conflict and presented an Action Plan in which the Syrian government had committed to cease its violence, release detainees, withdraw its armed forces, and grant access to international monitors.[34] The Action Plan also provided that upon significant progress in implementing the Plan, the Arab League would assist the Syrian government and the Syrian opposition in structuring a national dialogue conference designed to launch a democratic transition. Notably, the Arab League resolutions are only binding on those member states which vote for the resolutions.

As a member of the Arab League at the time, and having signed onto the November 2, 2011 agreement, the Syrian regime was legally obliged to comply with the Action Plan's dictates. Yet, the Syrian regime failed to uphold this agreement, so three months later the Arab League convened an extraordinary session in Cairo on January 22, 2012. Here, the Arab League passed Resolution 7444, which changed its tone and joined with the sentiments that had been expressed by other members of the international community in calling for Assad to step down from power.[35]

Arab League Resolution 7444 set forth the Cairo Peace Plan, which articulated the League's dismay with the "partial progress" and "insufficient" effort of the Syrian government in taking steps to end the conflict.[36] In light of this, the Cairo Peace Plan called for genuine political dialogue between the Syrian government and Syrian opposition, and it explicitly aimed at the creation of a national unity transitional government. In preambulatory clause 8, the Cairo Peace Plan calls for all parties to work toward implementing the following sequence:

---

[33] Arab League Council, Resolution 7436, *supra* note 4; Küçükkeleş, *supra* note 2, at 8–10.

[34] Arab League Council, Resolution 7436, *supra* note 4.

[35] "Monitoring of developments in the situation in Syria: Elements of the Arab plan to resolve the Syrian crisis," *enclosed in* Letter dated Jan. 24, 2012 from the Secretary-General addressed to the President of the Security Council, U.N. Doc. S/2012/71 (Jan. 30, 2012), https://undocs.org/en/S/2012/71 (last visited July 9, 2019).

[36] *Id.* at preamb. cl. 8.

(a) A government of national unity should be formed within two months of the dialogue, with the participation of the current Government and opposition under an agreed leader. Its task should be to implement the provisions of the Arab plan of action and prepare for free, multi-party parliamentary and presidential elections, in accordance with a law specifying the procedure and under Arab and international supervision;

(b) The President of the Republic should grant his Vice-President full powers for complete cooperation with the government of national unity in order to enable it to fulfil its functions in the transitional phase;

(c) Once formed, the government of national unity should declare that its aim is to establish a democratic and multi-party system in which all citizens are equal irrespective of their affiliation or sectarian or religious identity, and in which power changes hands peacefully.[37]

In calling for Assad to relinquish his executive power and cooperate with a new government of national unity, the Arab League placed a political transition at the center of its plans for Syria's post-conflict future. These explicit plans for political transition were particularly notable given the Arab League's historic tendency to support existing regimes rather than embrace new political movements.

After the extraordinary session of the Arab League in January 2012, the Arab League initiated joint meetings with the United Nations.[38] In session from January 31 to February 4, 2012, these meetings led to the production of Draft UN Security Council Resolution 2012/77 designed to enhance the legal authority and binding nature of the framework set forth in the Cairo Peace Plan. As a result, the draft resolution specifically called for Syria to comply with the League's Cairo Peace Plan and start "an inclusive Syrian-led political process conducted in an environment free from violence, fear, intimidation, and extremism, and aimed at effectively addressing the legitimate aspirations and concerns of Syria's people, without prejudging the outcome."[39] The draft resolution explicitly affirmed the process and substance of the Arab League's November Action Plan and January Cairo Peace Plan in multiple preambulatory and operative clauses. For instance, clause 7 stipulates that the UN Security Council:

Fully supports in this regard the League of Arab States' 22 January 2012 decision to facilitate a Syrian-led political transition to a democratic, plural political system, in which citizens are equal regardless of their affiliations or

---

[37] *Id.* at cl. 4.
[38] Küçükkeleş, *supra* note 2, at 12.
[39] S.C. Draft Res. 2012/77, *supra* note 14, at cl. 6.

ethnicities or beliefs, including through commencing a serious political dialogue between the Syrian government and the whole spectrum of the Syrian opposition under the League of Arab States' auspices, in accordance with the timetable set out by the League of Arab States.[40]

Somewhat surprisingly, both China and Russia vetoed the resolution, and thus it never went into effect.[41]

Given this impasse in the UN Security Council, Qatar and Saudi Arabia decided to circumvent the gridlock by presenting a very similar version of the resolution before the UN General Assembly. The UN General Assembly passed this resolution (A/RES/66/253) on February 16, 2012, with 137 in favor and 12 against and 17 abstentions.[42] A primary request of Resolution 66/253 was the appointment of a Joint Special Envoy that would work with both the UN and the Arab League toward the resolution of the conflict.[43] Accordingly, six days later, on February 23, 2012, then UN Secretary-General Ban Ki-Moon and then Arab League Secretary-General Nabil Elaraby jointly appointed Kofi Annan to be the Joint Special Envoy.[44] As Joint Special Envoy, Annan was responsible for leading the effort to secure a peaceful solution to the Syrian crisis as outlined by UN General Assembly Resolution 66/253 and the prior resolutions of the Arab League. He was charged with engaging in consultations with all stakeholders to create an inclusive, democratic, comprehensive political dialogue between the Syrian government and Syrian opposition forces.[45]

To pursue these aims, as mentioned above, Kofi Annan developed a Six-Point Peace Plan that provided six core commitments that needed to be followed to secure peace in Syria.[46] These six commitments were for the parties to (1) work with the Joint Special Envoy toward an inclusive Syrian-led political process; (2) cease all armed violence, particularly calling for an immediate end of Syrian government troop movements; (3) provide humanitarian assistance; (4) release arbitrarily detained persons; (5) respect freedom

---

[40] *Id.* at cl. 7.

[41] "Draft Resolution S/2012/77: Notes," *supra* note 15.

[42] G.A. Res. 66/253, *supra* note 16; "General Assembly Adopts Resolution Strongly Condemning 'Widespread and Systematic' Human Rights Violations by Syrian Authorities," U.N. Meetings Coverage & Press Releases, U.N. Doc. GA/11207/REV.1 (Feb. 16, 2012), https://www.un.org/press/en/2012/ga11207.doc.htm (last visited July 9, 2019).

[43] G.A. Res. 66/253, *supra* note 16, at cl 11.

[44] "Kofi Annan Appointed Joint Special Envoy of United Nations, League of Arab States on Syrian Crisis," *supra* note 18.

[45] *Id.*

[46] "Six-Point Proposal of the Joint Special Envoy of the UN and League of Arab States," *supra* note 19.

of movement for journalists; and (6) respect freedoms of association and peaceful protest.[47] The Syrian government verbally committed to the Joint Special Envoy's plan in March, yet immediately violated the ceasefire provisions.[48]

Shortly thereafter, on April 14, 2012, the UN Security Council adopted Resolution 2042 specifically for the purpose of reaffirming its support for the process created by the Joint Special Envoy, and for the substance of the Six-Point Peace Plan which was annexed to the resolution itself.[49] In the resolution's first operative clause, the UN Security Council:

> *Reaffirms* its full support for and calls for the urgent, comprehensive, and immediate implementation of all elements of the Envoy's six-point proposal (annex) aimed at bringing an immediate end to all violence and human rights violations, securing humanitarian access and facilitating a Syrian-led political transition leading to a democratic, plural political system, in which citizens are equal regardless of their affiliations, ethnicities or beliefs, including through commencing a comprehensive political dialogue between the Syrian government and the whole spectrum of the Syrian opposition.[50]

While UN Security Council Resolution 2042 has a strong focus on troop withdrawal and the cessation of armed violence, presenting the Joint Special Envoy's plan as its primary directive tied the resolution of armed violence to the resolution of the political conflict in a significant way.

To begin implementing his peace plan, Kofi Annan initiated a series of peace talks in Geneva, commonly referred to as the Geneva Talks. The first of these talks ("Geneva 1 Conference") began on June 30, 2012, with the members of the "Action Group for Syria," as the international participants were formerly called. The members of the Action Group for Syria during Geneva 1 consisted of representatives from the United Nations, the League of Arab States, the European Union, China, France, the Russian Federation, the United Kingdom, the United States, Turkey, Iraq (Chair of the Summit of the League of Arab States), Kuwait (Chair of the Council of Foreign Ministers of the League of Arab States), and Qatar (Chair of the Arab Follow-up Committee on Syria of the League of Arab States). Notably, neither the Syrian

---

[47] *Id.*
[48] "Syrian Government Accepts Annan Peace Plan," *BBC News* (Mar. 27, 2012), https://www.bbc .com/news/world-middle-east-17522398 (last visited July 23, 2019).
[49] S.C. Res. 2042, SCOR, 6751st Meeting, U.N. Doc. S/RES/2042 (Apr. 14, 2012), https://undocs .org/S/RES/2042(2012) (last visited July 9, 2019).
[50] *Id.*

government or Syrian opposition had representatives in the Action Group.[51] The talks resulted in the production of the Geneva Communiqué – a document that was later annexed to UN Security Council Resolution 2118 and would serve as a foundation for the effort toward a Syrian political transition.[52]

The Geneva Communiqué affirmed the sovereignty and territorial integrity of Syria, but also noted that the ongoing violence and human rights violations called for "the launch of a Syrian-led political process leading to a transition that meets the legitimate aspirations of the Syrian people and enables them independently and democratically to determine their own future."[53] The Action Group determined that such a process requires an immediate cease-fire, but also tied a full cessation of hostilities to a durable political resolution. The Communiqué specifies that the future political system envisioned will be "genuinely democratic and pluralistic, giving space to established and newly emerged political actors to compete fairly and equally in elections."[54]

Notably, the Communiqué specifies that Syria's transition must include the "establishment of a transitional governing body which can establish a neutral environment [. . . and] could include members of the present government and the opposition and other groups and shall be formed on the basis of mutual consent."[55] While this will be elaborated on in significant detail in a later section, it is worth noting. By introducing the idea of mutual consent into the legal framework of the peace process, the Geneva Communiqué set forth a key foundation from which political negotiations between actors with varied interests could then evolve.[56] That is, it provided a form of veto to both the Syrian government and the Syrian opposition that could secure their participation in continued negotiations.

Mutual consent provided a way toward a future Syrian government that could be "genuinely democratic and pluralistic,"[57] but could nevertheless

---

[51] Nick Meo, *Geneva Meeting Agrees "Transition Plan" to Syria Unity Government*, THE TELEGRAPH (Geneva, June 30, 2012), https://www.telegraph.co.uk/news/worldnews/middleeast/syria/9367330/Geneva-meeting-agrees-transition-plan-to-Syria-unity-government.html (last visited July 22, 2019).

[52] S.C. Res. 2118, SCOR, 7038th meeting, U.N. Doc. S/RES/2118 (Sept. 27, 2013) Annex II, http://unscr.com/en/resolutions/doc/2118 (last visited July 9, 2019).

[53] "Action Group for Syria Final Communiqué," United Nations Organization (Geneva, June 30, 2012), art. 3, https://www.un.org/News/dh/infocus/Syria/FinalCommuniqueActionGroupforSyria.pdf (last visited July 3, 2019).

[54] *Id.* at art. 6(I).

[55] *Id.* at art. 6(II).

[56] Lisa Roman & Alexander Bick, "It's Time for a New Syria Peace Process," *Foreign Policy* (Sept. 15, 2017), https://foreignpolicy.com/2017/09/15/its-time-for-a-new-syria-peace-process (last visited July 10, 2019).

[57] "Action Group for Syria Final Communiqué," *supra* note 53, at art. 6(I).

include figures from the current government as well as from the Syrian opposition. Providing that the current regime must consent to a final arrangement preserved the possibility that Assad or members of his government could remain in power, even as the United States at the time insisted that he must relinquish power.[58] This was crucial because the Russian government publicly maintained a firm commitment that it was up to the Syrian people whether or not Assad would remain.[59] This stance had caused the removal of draft language in the Communiqué that would have called for "exclud[ing] from government those whose continued presence and participation would undermine the credibility of the transition and jeopardize stability and reconciliation," a label under which Assad would likely be categorized.[60]

Although that strong vetting language was removed, the Geneva Communiqué did very directly identify the need for accountability in order to secure a durable peace. While remaining sufficiently ambiguous about Assad, the Geneva Communiqué was clear in rejecting impunity. The Communiqué stipulated:

> Accountability for acts committed during the present conflict must be addressed. There also needs to be a comprehensive package for transitional justice, including compensation or rehabilitation for victims of the present conflict, steps towards national reconciliation and forgiveness.[61]

In setting forth a place for compensation, rehabilitation, and reconciliation, the Communiqué brought pillars of transitional justice into a discussion that otherwise easily could have excluded the topic. Unfortunately, while the Geneva Communiqué encoded a strong legal principle of accountability within the central guidance for these initial negotiations, these provisions ultimately would not be included in later iterations of the legal framework.

The Geneva Communiqué represented the zenith of international engagement in establishing a framework for the peace process and specifying the broad parameters of its outcome. From that point forward the international community and the parties variously struggled to implement, preserve, or erode the core principles of the Communiqué.

The precise legal status of the Six-Point Peace Plan and its successor the Geneva Communiqué could be the subject of a lengthy inquiry, which is

---

[58] Margaret Basheer, *Geneva Communiqué: Road Map for Syria Political Transition*, VOA News (Jan. 25, 2014), https://www.voanews.com/a/geneva-Communiqué-road-map-for-syria-political-transition/1837514.html

[59] Roman & Bick, *supra* note 56.

[60] "World Powers Agree to Syria Transition Plan," *Al Jazeera* (July 1, 2012), https://www.aljazeera.com/news/middleeast/2012/06/201263017158463573.html (last visited July 10, 2019).

[61] "Action Group for Syria Final Communiqué," *supra* note 53, at art. 6(III).

beyond the scope of this chapter. The Communiqué no doubt possessed some degree of legal legitimacy and status given its origin as part of an Arab League and subsequently UN General Assembly mandated mediation effort, and the endorsement and annexing of the precursor Six-Point Peace Plan by the UN Security Council. The following section discusses how the UN Security Council then picked up the Geneva Communiqué and enhanced its legal status through direct annexation to a UN Security Council Resolution, and subsequently through an incorporation of the majority of its provisions into operative paragraphs of a resolution. In so doing, the UN Security Council also evolved and effectively amended the Communiqué.

IV SECURING AND EVOLVING THE LEGAL FRAMEWORK

This section discusses the manner in which the UN Security Council took on the role of providing greater coherence and legal authority to the framework for a negotiated settlement of the Syrian conflict. The section also discusses how in doing so the UN Security Council evolved, amended, and in some instances constrained the original framework established by the Arab League and subsequently the Joint Special Envoy.

Since the outbreak of conflict in 2011, there have been dozens of UN Security Council resolutions and Presidential Statements, and General Assembly resolutions on Syria,[62] as well as a dozen proposed resolutions that were vetoed.[63] These resolutions addressed a plethora of topics from ceasefires to counterterrorism to chemical weapons. A complete review of these resolutions is beyond the scope of this chapter. However, two resolutions in particular, UN Security Council Resolutions 2118 and 2254, sought to provide greater coherence and legal authority to the framework established to seek a negotiated resolution of the conflict.

---

[62] These resolutions and statements include: UN Security Council Resolutions 2042 (2012), 2043 (2012), 2059 (2012), 084 (2012), 2108 (2013), 2118 (2013), 2131 (2013), 2139 (2014), 2163 (2014), 2165 (2014), 2170 (2014), 2175 (2014), 2178 (2014), 2191 (2014), 2192 (201), 2199 (2015), 2209 (2015), 2235 (2015), 2249 (2015), 2254 (2015), 2258 (2015), 2268 (2016), 2314 (2016), 2319 (2016), 2328 (2016), 2332 (2016), 2336 (2016), 2361 (2017), 2379 (2017), 2393 (2017), 2394 (2017), 2401 (2018), 2426 (2018), 2449 (2018), 2450 (2018), 2477 (2019); UN General Assembly Resolutions 66/176 (2011), 66/253 A (2012), 66/253 B (2012), 67/183 (2012), 67/262 (2013), 67/282 (2013), 68/182 (2013), 68/295 (2014), 69/189 (2014), 69/304 (2015), 70/234 (2015), 70/282 (2016), 71/130 (2016), 71/203 (2016), 71/248 (2016), 72/191 (2017), 73/182 (2018); and Presidential Statements 2011/16, 2012/6, 2012/10, 2013/15, 2015/10, 2015/15.

[63] UN Security Council Resolutions that were vetoed include S/2011/612, S/2012/77, S/2012/538, S/2014/348, S/2016/84, S/2016/1026, S/2017/172, S/2017/315, S/2017/884, S/2017/962, S/2017/970, S/2018/321.

A *UN Security Council Resolution 2118*

In an early effort to provide enhanced legal authority for the Geneva Communiqué, the UN Security Council adopted Resolution 2118 on September 27, 2013. Although UN Security Council Resolution 2118 primarily focused on creating a regime to dismantle Syria's chemical weapons, the resolution also took the opportunity to endorse the Geneva Communiqué, call for its full implementation, and attach it as an annex.[64] In the preambulatory clauses of the resolution, the UN Security Council contextualized its action by:

> *Stressing* that the only solution to the current crisis in the Syrian Arab Republic is through an inclusive and Syrian-led political process based on the Geneva Communiqué of 30 June 2012, and *emphasising* the need to convene the international conference on Syria as soon as possible.[65]

While preambulatory clauses of UN resolutions are not binding, they provide critical framing for the subsequent operative clauses that sought to secure the status of the Geneva Communiqué as the framework for resolving the Syrian conflict.

Notably, in operative clause 16, the UN Security Council explicitly:

> *Endorses* fully the Geneva Communiqué of 30 June 2012 (Annex II), which sets out a number of key steps beginning with the establishment of a transitional governing body exercising full executive powers, which could include members of the present Government and the opposition and other groups and shall be formed on the basis of mutual consent.[66]

Immediately thereafter, operative clause 17 reaffirms the idea of the Geneva Communiqué as guiding the peace process as the UN Security Council:

> *Calls* for the convening, as soon as possible, of an international conference on Syria to implement the Geneva Communiqué, and *calls upon* all Syrian parties to engage seriously and constructively at the Geneva Conference on Syria, and *underscores* that they should be fully representative of the Syrian people and committed to the implementation of the Geneva Communiqué and to the achievement of stability and reconciliation.[67]

By invoking the Communiqué in the preambulatory and operative clauses as well as attaching the document as an annex, the UN Security Council used

---

[64] S.C. Res. 2118, *supra* note 52.
[65] *Id.* cl. 12.
[66] *Id.* cl. 16.
[67] *Id.* cl. 17.

Resolution 2118 to not only commit to a chemical weapons plan, but also affirm the legal framework around the peace process as one based in the Geneva Communiqué; citing both specific process and outcome elements.

Over the next few years, the international community, most notably the ISSG, seized opportunities to reaffirm the Geneva Communiqué. When the ISSG convened in Vienna in the fall of 2015 to discuss new possibilities for peace given Russian airstrikes and a number of high-profile terrorist attacks, the group acknowledged the role of the Geneva Communiqué in structuring the peace talks.[68] In particular, the ISSG's Statement on November 14, 2015, explicitly affirmed the groups support for the transitional process as laid out within the Geneva Communiqué.[69]

B *UN Security Council Resolution 2254*

The next key evolution of the legal framework for the peace process came when the UN Security Council adopted Resolution 2254, which simultaneously reaffirmed, deepened, added to, and contracted the various key elements of the Geneva Communiqué.

In the fall of 2015, the meetings of the ISSG revitalized the efforts of the UN Security Council to move forward on a path to peace. The morning of December 18, 2015, members of the ISSG – including all five Permanent Members of the UN Security Council – met at the New York Palace Hotel.[70] While there are only unofficial readouts about what transpired behind those closed doors, many observers concur that this ISSG meeting was likely crucial in resolving much of the disagreement between the major international players over future UN Security Council action on Syria. It was likely during these discussions that the final language of UN Security Council Resolution 2254 was agreed upon, paving the way for the unanimous passage of the resolution later that day.[71]

UN Security Council Resolution 2254's unanimous passage is particularly notable given that Russia and China had previously vetoed several similar

---

[68] "Final Declaration on the Results of the Syria Talks in Vienna as Agreed by Participants," and "Statement of the International Syria Support Group," *supra* note 26.

[69] "Statement of the International Syria Support Group" (Vienna, Nov. 14, 2015), https://www.un .org/sg/en/content/sg/note-correspondents/2015-11-14/note-correspondents-statement-international-syria-support (last visited July 10, 2019).

[70] Carla Stea, "Historic UN Security Council Resolution 2254 on Syria: The Backrooms of Diplomacy, US Last Minute Attempt to 'Double Cross'?" (Global Research, Dec. 23, 2015), www.globalresearch.ca/historic-un-security-council-resolution-2254-on-syria-the-backrooms-of-diplomacy-us-last-minute-attempt-to-double-cross/5497569 (last visited July 16, 2019).

[71] *Id.*

resolutions.[72] In light of this, the resolution explicitly commends the efforts of the ISSG in galvanizing its passage. Preambulatory clause 5 expresses enthusiasm for the diplomatic effort of the ISSG, and preambulatory clause 6 expresses gratitude for the ISSG's commitment in its Vienna Statements to ensuring a Syrian-led and Syrian-owned political transition.[73] In operative clause 3, the UN Security Council goes so far as to characterize the ISSG "as the central platform to facilitate the United Nation's efforts to achieve a lasting political settlement of the crisis."[74]

In addition to these references to the ISSG and their Vienna Statements, UN Security Council Resolution 2254 developed and oriented itself within the existing legal framework set up by the Geneva Communiqué. In the preambulatory paragraphs, the UN Security Council frames the resolution by

> *Reiterating* that the only sustainable solution to the current crisis in Syria is through an inclusive and Syrian-led political process that meets the legitimate aspirations of the Syrian people, with a view to full implementation of the Geneva Communiqué of 30 June 2012 as endorsed by resolution 2118 (2013), including through the establishment of an inclusive transitional governing body with full executive powers, which shall be formed on the basis of mutual consent while ensuring continuity of governmental institutions.[75]

The UN Security Council then reiterates these preambulatory endorsements in its operative clauses. In the very first operative clause, the Council "*[r]econfirms* its endorsement of the Geneva Communiqué of 30 June 2012" and "*endorses* the 'Vienna Statements' in pursuit of the full implementation of the Geneva Communiqué."[76] References to the role of the Communiqué as guiding the peace process are again made in operative clauses 2 and 5.

Moreover, UN Security Council Resolution 2254 substantively affirms the content of these elements of the legal framework in addition to affirming the documents themselves. These substantive dimensions include the convening of peace negotiations; a political transition process that includes a TGB, constitutional reform, and elections; and the implementation of confidence-building measures such as humanitarian access and release of detainees. On a number of these elements, Resolution 2254 provided greater precision than

---

[72] Denis Dyomkin et al., "U.N. Endorses Syria Peace Plan in Rare Show of Unity among Big Powers" (Reuters, Dec. 18, 2015), https://uk.reuters.com/article/us-mideast-crisis-syria-un-idUKKBN0U10J020151219 (last visited July 16, 2019).

[73] S.C. Res. 2254, SCOR, 7588th Meeting, U.N. Doc. S/RES/2254 (Dec. 18, 2018) preamb. cl. 5–7, http://unscr.com/en/resolutions/doc/2254 (last visited July 16, 2019).

[74] *Id.* at cl. 3.

[75] *Id.* at preamb. cl. 5.

[76] *Id.* at cl. 1.

the Geneva Communiqué and prior documents did. It is also noteworthy that the resolution speaks to these topics with regard to both process and outcomes. That is, most UN Security Council resolutions dictate procedures that should be followed without specifying the nature of the outcomes, such as a new constitution or a TGB, as Resolution 2254 does.

With regard to peace negotiations, Resolution 2254 builds on both Resolution 2118's call for "all Syrian parties to engage seriously and constructively at the Geneva Conference on Syria [... that] should be fully representative of the Syrian people"[77] and the Geneva Communiqué's call for parties to "engage genuinely with the Joint Special Envoy [... and] put forward effective interlocutors to work expeditiously towards a Syrian-led settlement."[78] In the preamble to Resolution 2254, the UN Security Council proclaims the goal: "to bring together the broadest possible spectrum of the opposition, chosen by Syrians, who will decide their negotiation representatives and define their negotiation positions so as to enable the political process to begin."[79]

Then, in operative clause two, the Council requests that the offices of the UN Secretary-General, especially that of the UN Envoy for Syria,

> convene representatives of the Syrian government and the opposition to engage in formal negotiations on a political transition process on an urgent basis, with a target of early January 2016 for the initiation of talks.[80]

The urgency of convening the parties is found throughout prior statements and resolutions; however, the additional details on structuring inclusive, formal negotiations through the offices of the UN comes through in UN Security Council Resolution 2254 far more than those issued prior. Resolution 2254 also more precisely articulates the timeline for negotiations. While the document preserves a degree of flexibility by identifying a "target" of early January, it is notable that it specified an exact month. The January start date is also supported by a request that the "Secretary General report back to the UN Security Council on the implementation of this resolution, including on the progress of the UN-facilitated political process, within 60 days," which meant no later than February 16, 2016.[81]

UN Security Council Resolution 2254 also buttressed the legal infrastructure around a political transition. In the preamble, the UN Security Council notes that "the only sustainable solution to the current crisis in Syria is

---

[77] S.C. Res. 2118, *supra* note 52, at cl. 17.
[78] "Action Group for Syria Final Communiqué," *supra* note 20, at Annex II, 11(d).
[79] S.C. Res. 2254, *supra* note 73, at preamb. cl. 10.
[80] *Id.* at cl. 2.
[81] *Id.* at cl. 15.

through an inclusive and Syrian-led political process that meets the legitimate aspirations of the Syrian people ... including through the establishment of an inclusive transitional governing body with full executive powers, which shall be formed on the basis of mutual consent while ensuring continuity of governmental institutions."[82] This sentiment harkens back – almost word for word – to the Geneva Communiqué's calls for "the launch of a Syrian-led political process leading to a transition that meets the legitimate aspirations of the Syrian people."[83] It also reaffirms UNSRC 2118 and the Communiqué's vision for a transitional process that includes the "establishment of a transitional governing body that can establish a neutral environment in which the transition can take place, with the transitional governing body exercising full executive powers ... formed on the basis of mutual consent."[84] In this way, Resolution 2254 largely mirrored the prior documents in discussing the creation of a TGB.

When discussing constitutional and electoral reform, however, UN Security Council Resolution 2254 draws not from the Geneva Communiqué, but rather from the language of the November 14th Vienna Statement. The UN Security Council:

> *Expresses* its support, in this regard, for a Syrian-led political process that is facilitated by the UN and, within a target of six months, establishes credible, inclusive and non-sectarian governance and sets a schedule and process for drafting a new constitution, and *further expresses its support* for free and fair elections, pursuant to the new constitution, to be held within 18 months and administered under the supervision of the United Nations, to the satisfaction of the governance and to the highest international standards of transparency and accountability, with all Syrians, including members of the diaspora, eligible to participate, as set forth in the 14 November 2015 ISSG Statement.[85]

Overall, UN Security Council Resolution 2254's call for a new constitution was more explicit than the Geneva Communiqué's call for "a review of the constitutional order."[86] The primary exception being that the Geneva Communiqué had called for ratification by "popular approval," which was left out of Resolution 2254.[87] Resolution 2254 was also more concrete than the Geneva Communiqué in providing details about the provision of free and fair

---

[82] *Id.* at preamb. cl. 5.
[83] "Action Group for Syria Final Communiqué," *supra* note 20, Annex II, art. 3.
[84] *Id.* at Annex II, art. 9(c).
[85] S.C. Res. 2254, *supra* note 73, at cl. 4.
[86] "Action Group for Syria Final Communiqué," *supra* note 20, at Annex II, art. 9(a); *see also* S.C. Res. 2118, *supra* note 52, at cl. 16.
[87] "Action Group for Syria Final Communiqué," *supra* note 20, at art. 9(c).

elections. The resolution not only established a timeline by which to set actionable steps and measure progress, but also demanded UN supervision of the elections. Holding the elections under UN guidance helps to ensure adherence to international law and prevent election fraud, increasing the likelihood that the process will genuinely be free and fair.

There were a number of provisions from the Geneva Communiqué that were omitted in UN Security Council Resolution 2254. Most significantly, Resolution 2254 did not recommit to comprehensive transitional justice, accountability, and reconciliation. Discussed in greater detail in the last section of this chapter, this omission was both evidence of and a contributor to a broader choice to sideline justice in the pursuit of peace. In a similar vein, the resolution also omitted, and consequently sidelined, efforts to secure rule of law, independence of the judiciary, and accountability of government officials. Additionally, Resolution 2254 did not call for the implementation of Joint Special Envoy Annan's Six-Point Peace Plan. Substantively, this removed calls for freedom of movement for journalists, for freedom of assembly, and for respect of the right to peacefully protest.[88]

These omissions illustrate the evolution of the legal framework from its beginning with the Arab League resolutions through the legal incorporation of the Geneva Communiqué in UN Security Council Resolution 2118 to the affirmation of the provisions that endured in UN Security Council Resolution 2254. The inclusion these provisions in Resolutions 2118 and 2254 is important for understanding the legal framework for the peace process because it is widely understood that operative clauses of UN Security Council resolutions constitute binding international obligations. While there is debate among scholars as to the enforceability of these obligations without the explicit invocation of UN Charter Chapter VII authorities, the international legal community is largely in agreement that – whether or not Chapter VI or VII is explicitly invoked – UN Security Council resolutions are legally binding under UN Charter Article 25.[89] In that way, the UN Security Council resolutions legally entrenched commitments to a transitional government, new constitution, and cessation of violence.

Subsequent to the passage of Resolution 2254, members of the UN Security Council did initially propose other draft resolutions with language that reaffirmed the legal framework around these topics as set forth by the Geneva

---

[88] S.C. Res. 2042, *supra* note 49, at Annex, arts. 5, 6.
[89] UN Charter, art. 25 (1945); Security Council Report, *Security Council Action under Chapter VII: Myths and Realities* (June 23, 2008), https://www.securitycouncilreport.org/research-reports/lookup-c-glkwlemtisg-b-4202671.php (last visited 24 July 2019).

Communiqué, Resolution 2118, and Resolution 2254.[90] These draft resolutions were vetoed, and while the vetoes were for reasons that did not focus on these reaffirmations, it may have signaled a weakening of resolve on those elements.[91] Intriguingly, of all aspects of Resolution 2254, constitutional reform is arguably the topic that became the most salient as the peace process evolved. One likely reason, which will be discussed in the next section, is the way the Russian government set up talks in parallel, or arguably competition, to the UN-led negotiations that had their focus shift significantly toward a constitutional process rather than a political transition.

V CHALLENGES TO THE LEGAL FRAMEWORK

A key element of the framework for the Syrian negotiation peace process was the initiative for a new constitution based on the principles of democracy and the rule of law.

This section discusses how a sub-coalition of international actors, led by the Russian government, sought to build upon the constitutional plank of the Geneva Communiqué in order to then significantly amend the process outside the framework endorsed by the UN Security Council. The sub-coalition aimed to redirect the process from one of a comprehensive constitutional redesign to one of constitutional reform. In doing so, the coalition sought to shift the focus from the peace negotiation process to this more limited constitutional reform process. The UN Envoy addressed this effort by maneuvering the process back within the initial framework for the peace process, but at the cost of diverting the process from a peace process to a constitutional process.

The initial framework set forth in the Geneva Communiqué noted that consultations with the Syrian people indicated strong aspirations for a future Syrian state that is "genuinely democratic and pluralistic, giving space to established and newly emerging political actors to compete fairly and equally

---

[90] S.C. Draft Res. 2016/846, SCOR, U.N. Doc. S/2016/846 (Oct. 8, 2016) cl. 9, 10, https://www.un .org/en/ga/search/view_doc.asp?symbol=S/2016/846 (last visited July 8, 2019); S.C. Draft Res. 2016/1026, SCOR, U.N. Doc. S/2016/1026 (Dec. 5, 2016) cl. 12, https://www.un.org/en/ga/ search/view_doc.asp?symbol=S/2016/1026 (last visited July 22, 2019).

[91] "Foreign Ministry Statement in Connection with Russia's Veto of the French-proposed UN Security Council Draft Resolution on Syria on October 8, 2016" (2016) Ministry of Foreign Affairs of the Russian Federation, http://special.mid.ru/en/web/guest/maps/sy/-/asset_publisher/ 9fcjSOwMERcf/content/id/2494622 (last visited July 8, 2019); "The Situation in the Middle East," SCOR, 7825th Meeting, U.N. Doc. S/PV.7825 (Dec. 5, 2016), https://www .securitycouncilreport.org/atf/cf/%7B65BFCF9B-6D27-4E9C-8CD3-CF6E4FF96FF9%7D/s_ pv_7825.pdf (last visited July 8, 2019).

in elections [... which] also means that the commitment to multiparty democracy must be a lasting one, going beyond an initial round of elections."[92] To ensure the process was fundamentally Syrian-led, however, the Communiqué also noted the importance of further popular consultations before making final judgments on the future political landscape of Syria. The Communiqué called for an inclusive national dialogue so that the Syrian people would be able to meaningfully influence the direction of their state's future.[93] These and other provisions call for a new constitution for Syria. The Communiqué describes:

> (c) On that basis, there can be a review of the constitutional order and the legal system. The result of constitutional drafting would be subject to popular approval;
>
> (d) Upon establishment of the new constitutional order, it will be necessary to prepare for and conduct free and fair multiparty elections for the new institutions and offices that have been established.[94]

These claims place a comprehensive constitutional redesign as a key element of any robust political transition for Syria. This was not only recognized by the Geneva Communiqué. As noted above, UN Security Council Resolution 2254 and the November Vienna Statement both support an inclusive, Syrian-led political process that "sets a schedule and process for drafting a new constitution, and [... for] free and fair elections, pursuant to the new constitution."[95]

Moreover, the importance of constitutional redesign as part of the political transition was also embedded in the language used by the international mediators to describe the goals of the peace process, particularly the Geneva negotiations. Most prominently, the UN Envoy Staffan de Mistura often spoke of there being four "baskets" for negotiation: "a credible non-sectarian transitional government; a future constitution; early and free parliamentary elections within 18 months; and a united war against terrorism within Syria."[96] It is notable that both the Geneva Communiqué and UN Security Council Resolution 2554 explicitly called for a constitutional redrafting process in a

---

[92] "Action Group for Syria Final Communiqué," *supra* note 20, at Annex II, art. 8.

[93] *Id.* at Annex II, art. 9 b.

[94] *Id.* at Annex II, art. 9 c, d.

[95] S.C. Res. 2254, *supra* note 73; "Statement of the International Syria Support Group," *supra* note 69.

[96] "Syrian Parties Should Join Next Round of Geneva Talks 'without Preconditions' – UN Envoy," *UN News* (Sept. 27, 2017), https://news.un.org/en/story/2017/09/567302-syrian-parties-should-join-next-round-geneva-talks-without-preconditions-un (last visited July 11, 2019).

way that embedded the drafting a new constitution within a broader process for political transformation. This characterization was not present in the Russian government-led efforts to form a constitution-drafting committee (CDC) that emerged during the Astana process.

As the Astana process was largely focused on securing a durable cessation of hostilities, it generally operated in parallel to, but not in competition with, the Geneva process. At the seventh Astana conference, however, Russian representatives announced that the Russian government would host a national conference in Sochi with a more targeted focus on constitution drafting. Although the Syrian opposition boycotted the talks, the Russian government moved forward with the conference in January 2018, which it named the Congress of the Syrian National Dialogue.[97] The conference culminated in the production of the Sochi Final Statement, which proclaimed that the attending parties had "agreed to form a constitutional committee comprising the Government of the Syrian Arab Republic delegation along with widely-represented opposition delegation for drafting of a constitutional reform as a contribution to the political settlement under the UN auspices in accordance with UN Security Council Resolution 2254."[98]

Although the Sochi Final Statement expresses adherence to the prescriptions of Resolution 2254, the broad language leaves interpretative ambiguity. It is possible to interpret the language as denoting that the creation of a constitutional committee will be aligned with Resolution 2254 as opposed to denoting that the entirety of the political settlement will adhere with Resolution 2254. The distinction matters because the constitutional *reform* that is indicated in the Sochi Statement is a significant step back from the drafting of a *new constitution* as part of a political transition that is indicated in Resolution 2254.

The Sochi Final Statement also called for a shift in the sequencing of the peace process. Prioritizing the constitutional process was out of sequence with the steps outlined in Resolution 2254, which called for the establishment of a TGB prior to the drafting of a new constitution. The sequencing is of particular significance for the Syrian opposition because beginning a constitutional process before replacing the current regime with a neutral interim one makes it much more likely that the regime will merely co-opt the constitutional process to create the veneer of renewed legitimacy rather than allow the process to bring about meaningful democratic change.

---

[97] "Sochi Conference on Syria Opens Despite Opposition Boycott," *supra* note 29.
[98] Final Statement of the Congress of the Syrian National Dialogue, *supra* note 30.

In a similar vein, the Sochi Final Statement worried the Syrian opposition because the Sochi negotiations – which the Syrian opposition boycotted – were named as the "Congress of the Syrian National Dialogue." The Syrian opposition feared that in framing the Sochi talks as a national dialogue, the leadership could frame the talks as satisfying the Geneva Communiqué's requirement of a national dialogue – even though the Sochi talks were not a genuinely inclusive, meaningful dialogue process. Alleviating some of these fears, however, was the Sochi Final Statement's deferral to the UN-led Geneva process for decisions on many of the specific issues around forming a Constitutional Committee. The Sochi Final Statement noted:

> Final agreement is to be reached in the UN-led Geneva process on the mandate and terms of reference, powers, rules of procedure, and selection criteria for the composition of the Constitutional Committee. We appeal to the United Nations Secretary-General to assign the Special Envoy for Syria for the assistance of the Constitutional Committee work in Geneva.[99]

Given this deference to the Geneva process, as well as the Syrian opposition's immediate rejection of the Sochi proposal,[100] UN Envoy Staffan de Mistura sought to reshape the interest in forming a CDC galvanized by the Sochi Statement to an interest in creating a UN-led process for establishing the membership and mandate of a CDC. De Mistura had been heavily involved in the plans formulated at Sochi, and he tried to use his position as UN Envoy to bridge the parallel processes of Astana, Sochi, and Geneva, as well as coalesce support around the narrower focus of starting a constitutional drafting process.[101]

Yet, the formation of a CDC was not a simple undertaking. De Mistura initially suggested that the Syrian government, Syrian opposition, and the UN collectively form a CDC by each appointing fifty delegates. However, the regime opposed the idea of the UN selecting "neutral," potentially non-Syrian, delegates. Each delegation was also encouraged to include an appropriate representation of women, civil society, and marginalized groups, yet the initial members proposed failed to provide the desired diversity in delegates.[102] The severe disagreement between the parties made it quite difficult to agree on delegates and approve procedures, and Staffan de Mistura ultimately resigned from his post at the end of December 2018 before he could fully

---

[99] *Id.*
[100] "Syria Opposition Rejects Sochi Constitution Plan," *supra* note 31.
[101] Nicholas Norberg, "A Primer on Syria's Constitutional Committee," *Lawfare* (Dec. 22, 2018), https://www.lawfareblog.com/primer-syrias-constitutional-committee (last visited July 10, 2019).
[102] *Id.*

form a CDC.[103] When Geir Pedersen took over as UN Envoy for Syria in January 2019, Pedersen resumed Mistura's efforts to establish a CDC and continued talks to confirm the final members of the committee.[104]

As will be discussed below, shifting the negotiations from a political process into a constitutional process would not only amend the legal framework, but would bring the negotiations within the purview of Syrian domestic constitutional law, and thus potentially limiting the available outcomes that could be settled upon. It would also more squarely require the agreement to comply with the process rules established in the Syrian Constitution, and limit the ability of the parties to rely on the status of the peace agreement as a means for circumventing the restrictive requirements of the Syrian Constitution.

VI IMPLEMENTING THE LEGAL FRAMEWORK

This section now turns to the question of how the UN Envoy and the Syrian opposition party sought to implement the outcomes identified in the legal framework, and some of the challenges and questions they faced when seeking to do so. By way of example this section examines the outcome of regime transition and the creation of a Transitional Governing Body (TGB).

The crux of the legal framework for the democratic transformation in Syria envisioned by the international community, and by the Syrian opposition, was the creation of a TGB. The idea of a TGB was enshrined in the Geneva Communiqué, which provided for:

> The establishment of a transitional governing body which can establish a neutral environment in which the transition can take place. That means that the transitional governing body would exercise full executive powers. It could include members of the present government and the opposition and other groups and shall be formed on the basis of mutual consent.[105]

The TGB was envisioned at a time when it was generally believed by the international community that there would be a fairly rapid transition in Syria, and it would be necessary to have in place a process for transition so as to avoid

---

[103] "Briefing to the Security Council by Staffan de Mistura, United Nations Special Envoy for Syria," *United Nations Office at Geneva* (Dec. 20, 2018), https://www.unog.ch/unog/website/news_media.nsf/(httpNewsByYear_en)/ED8EC889oDC3BBA3C125836Aoo334F17 (last visited July 11, 2019).

[104] Elya Altynsarina, "12th Round of Astana Process Peace Talks Advances Work to Launch Constitutional Committee" (2019) Astana Times, https://astanatimes.com/2019/04/12th-round-of-astana-process-peace-talks-advances-work-to-launch-constitutional-committee (last visited July 10, 2019).

[105] "Action Group for Syria Final Communiqué," *supra* note 20, Annex II, 9(a).

state collapse. The TGB was also seen as a necessary component in ensuring a democratic transition in Syria, which, at the time, was perceived as essential to removing or minimizing the key drivers of conflict.

The momentum for a transition was so powerful during the summer of 2011 that it prompted President Obama to famously declare that "the time has come for President Assad to step aside."[106] Over time as the likelihood of a quick transition diminished, the TGB became entrenched as a core functional demand of the Syrian opposition and for a considerable amount of time remained at the center of the Geneva negotiation process. As noted above, as late as 2015, the UN Security Council, in Resolution 2254, reaffirmed its commitment that the "only sustainable solution" to the Syrian conflict is an inclusive, Syrian-led political process that includes "the establishment of an inclusive transitional governing body with full executive powers, which shall be formed on the basis of mutual consent while ensuring continuity of governmental institutions."[107]

The concept of a TGB entails a governance body that can provide a neutral environment by exercising full executive power during the interim period of a political transition. The body would be formed by the mutual consent of both the Syrian government and Syrian opposition, likely including members of both parties.

Despite its codification in the legal framework for the peace process, the Syrian regime rejected any discussion of a TGB, mainly because it would require Assad to relinquish a significant amount of executive power and provide the Syrian opposition with authority and some control over Syrian government institutions.[108] Nonetheless, the UN and the Syrian opposition engaged in extensive consultations on the nature of a TGB should it come to pass. A review of these negotiations is relevant given that is not unusual for a peace process in the interim to consist substantially of a negotiation with one of the parties, and especially if there is a sense that at the end there might be an imposed peace under Chapter VII, or a major change in circumstances that then bring certain issues, such as the TGB to the fore.

---

[106] Macon Phillips, "President Obama: 'The future of Syria must be determined by its people, but President Bashar al-Assad is standing in their way'" (White House Archives, Aug. 18, 2011), https://obamawhitehouse.archives.gov/blog/2011/08/18/president-obama-future-syria-must-be-determined-its-people-president-bashar-al-assad (last visited July 17, 2019).

[107] S.C. Res. 2254, *supra* note 73, at preamb. cl. 5.

[108] Associated Press, "Syria's Assad Rejects 'Transitional Body' Demanded by Opposition," *CBC/Radio-Canada* (Mar. 30, 2016), https://www.cbc.ca/news/world/syria-assad-rejects-transitional-body-1.3512154 (last visited July 17, 2019).

Creating a TGB sounds fairly straightforward, though it does raise a number of legal and practical considerations, as well as timing and sequencing considerations in relation to an overall peace process.

As the international community attempted to restart the Geneva peace talks in the late summer and fall of 2016, the Syrian opposition – led by the High Negotiations Commission – put forth a detailed plan for a TGB in its proposal for an "Executive Framework for a Political Solution Based on the Geneva Communiqué" ("HNC Executive Framework").[109] The HNC Executive Framework outlined a political transition that would occur in three phases: (1) a six-month negotiation process under a temporary truce during which confidence-building measures would be implemented, (2) a year-and-a-half transitional period following the signing of a formal agreement, which would feature a TGB with the executive power to begin implementing a new constitutional framework, launch a national dialogue, and secure a comprehensive ceasefire, and (3) a final transition period that would last through the implementation of the outcomes of the national dialogue and the revisions called for by the constitutional process.[110]

In outlining the second stage, the HNC Executive Framework provides significant detail as to the opposition's aspirations for a TGB. The Syrian opposition sought to make clear that the primary priority of the transitional period is "the formation of a Transitional Governing Body necessitating the departure of Bashar al-Assad and his clique."[111] In assuming both executive and legislative power, the TGB, in the view of the opposition, was intended to serve as an accountable and transparent interim authority that would not begin ruling Syria, but rather go about "securing the necessary conditions to enable [Syrians] to express their free will in determining the future of their country."[112]

One of the first conundrums faced by the UN Envoy and the parties was the extent of governing powers and responsibilities that the TGB would possess. Was it to be a "light" entity with a degree of oversight of the existing institutions, or was it to assume control and authority over the vast majority of powers held by the current government? Whereas a light oversight body might be insufficient to actually prompt and entrench a democratic transition, it

[109] High Negotiations Commission for the Syrian Revolution and Opposition Forces, "Executive Framework for a Political Solution Based on the Geneva Communiqué (2012)" (Sept. 2016), http://www.nuhanovicfoundation.org/user/file/2016,_hnc,_executive_framework_for_a_political_solution_based_on_geneva_communiqu%C3%A9.pdf (last visited July 17, 2019).
[110] *Id.* at 3–5.
[111] *Id.* at 16.
[112] *Id.*

would be quite difficult to set up an interim body with full authority that could successfully oversee a complex and highly personalized regime designed over decades to serve the interests of a specific family. Attempting to do so might result in significant governance gaps.

To determine the nature of the governance that would be exercised by the TGB, the UN Envoy and the Syrian opposition debated which tasks and functions should be included in governance, and how best to ensure the political transition process proceeded in accordance with UN Security Council Resolution 2254. On one hand, the TGB could be established as an oversight body that provides broad policy guidance and has some limited veto authority. Alternatively, the TGB could possess more direct implementation authority if it was ceded many of the executive powers currently held by the president.[113]

The question of the authority of the TGB is also tied to the continuity of existing institutions, including the legislature, the judiciary, and municipal governing structures. With the creation of a TGB, Syria's legislature (the People's Council of Syria) could be completely dissolved – either with new members appointed by the TGB or its legislative authority assumed by the TGB – or the People's Council could remain largely intact with only a few members replaced. In countries where previously passive parliaments were left intact during the transition, they then became highly active – with the goal of thwarting a transition that would undermine their prerogatives. Similarly, a TGB could undertake a substantial restructuring and reform of the judicial branch in order to meet international standards, which could take years, or replace particular judicial actors suspected of corruption or other crimes. With respect to municipal governance, a TGB could retain centralized control of many administrative responsibilities, devolve a significant portion of these responsibilities to governorates or provinces, or establish new joint councils to co-manage these responsibilities. The UN and the opposition found it exceptionally difficult to balance the need for a complete transformation of a system built around authoritarian repression into one which promoted democratic rule and durable peace, with the risks that too much reform too quickly could destabilize the fragile state structure.

Similarly, the TGB might find that as a result of its own initiative, or as the consequence of provisions within a peace agreement, it would need to relate to newly created or modified institutions. For instance, it was contemplated as part of the peace process that representatives from the fourteen governorates

---

[113] Syrian Arab Republic's Constitution of 2012, arts. 96–116, https://www.constituteproject.org/constitution/Syria_2012.pdf (last visited July 17, 2019).

would be temporarily appointed to replace the People's Council, in which case the TGB would need to navigate a new relationship between its executive power and this new legislative authority, and would need rules for doing so. Alternatively, if a peace agreement called for the creation of a constituent assembly, the TBG might be responsible for forming or overseeing such an assembly. Additionally, while the TGB might have oversight power over other institutions, there need also to be checks on the TGB's power. This could come from the Supreme Constitutional Court, the Supreme Judicial Council, or a newly created temporary/transitional judicial oversight body. Efforts to ensure accountability would also be necessary and might prompt the creation of a monitoring commission – either created by the TGB or possibly by the international community – that would work to secure the rule of law, ensure the effective implementation of final agreements, arbitrate disputes that arise, and involve the international community in continued financial support during the post-conflict period.

In addition to debating the powers of a TGB, a primary question addressed during the initial rounds of negotiation was how members of the TGB might be selected. The Geneva Communiqué provided that this would be done through mutual consent. This requirement, while perceived as necessary, was highly contentious, and the UN and opposition spent as much time on this issue as on nearly any other issue. Representatives could be appointed by the parties; for example, some by the Syrian opposition, some by the Syrian regime, and some by a neutral third party such as the UN or ISSG, with the parties consenting not to contest the members appointed by the other parties. Alternatively, all the members could be appointed by a neutral, mutually agreed upon third party. Or each party would be entitled to veto any member proposed by another party, possibly with a limit on the number of times they could exercise this veto. Similarly a party could propose a list of candidates two or three times the number of available seats, and then the other party selects acceptable members from that list. The ways in which "mutual consent" could be implemented appeared to be limitless.

The UN and the Syrian opposition were deeply worried about ensuring a non-sectarian character for the TGB and sought ways to ensure that under whichever method was adopted, the representatives would not be selected based on their identity, but rather that they would be selected, on the basis of merit, and with a view to promoting diversity in the geopolitical interests of the representatives. In a partial effort to accomplish this objective, the HNC Executive Framework proposed by the opposition sought to create criteria that would exclude any individuals that were affiliated with terrorist groups or suspected by the Commission of inquiry for Syria of having committed war crimes or crimes against humanity.[114] The HNC Executive Framework also proposed that 30 percent of the TGB's representatives were to be women.[115]

Key to the functioning of a TGB would be how it might be structured as well as its own internal rules of procedure and decision making. The body could function as a small executive council or as a larger executive and legislative committee. An entity with a smaller number of representatives was preferred as it was perceived as being more efficient for decision making during the interim period, though it might do so at the expense of diversity and inclusion. Given the implicit and explicit power of the chairperson, especially in the context of a transition from an authoritarian regime, there was substantial and lively debate as to the powers associated with that position. Some argued that the chairperson's responsibilities would encompass the whole spectrum from setting the agenda of the TGB to serving as the diplomatic head of state. In this context, the process for electing the chairperson was highly contentious, with a preference for a supermajority, though this could delay the selection of a chairperson, and stall the operation of the TGB, thus permitting the institutions of the regime to continue on with limited oversight. There was also consideration of a rotating chairperson, such that every member of the TGB would have the opportunity to lead the body, essentially reducing the role to a ceremonial one, and leaving the TGB with weak leadership.

In addition to the procedures for deciding the chair, there would need to be set procedures for decision making. These rules of procedure would determine whether the TCB operated by majority, or supermajority on all or some questions, and if there would be a special right of veto by certain members on specific issues (such as decision to declare a state of emergency, determinations over extensions of the transition period, or judgments that affect certain sectors of Syrian society). The crux of the issue here is whether the parties anticipated that the regime members would represent the interests of the Assad regime, and would continue to accomplish their objectives through a manipulation of the TGB process forced upon them by the peace process, or whether they would represent the interests of "moderates" who were involved in some form of regime transition as part of the path toward resolving the conflict. Similarly, there was the question of whether the opposition would continue to represent the initial democratic oriented opposition, or the increasingly militarized opposition. The parties found it nearly impossible to

---

[114] High Negotiations Commission for the Syrian Revolution and Opposition Forces, *supra* note 109, at 19.

[115] *Id.*

decide upon a set of international rules of procedure without entirely knowing the full nature of the parties that would be signing the agreement, and by that time it might be too late to create effective rules for efficient operation. In this case, parties in other conflicts have tended to reach out to the international community to operate as a good faith overseer.

Given that the purpose of the TGB would not only be to implement not only an agreement, but also to ensure compliance with the Geneva Communiqué and UN Security Council Resolution 2254, it became necessary to consider how one might enshrine these international obligations into the domestic operation of the TGB, and what degree of international oversight or assistance might be necessary. The significant involvement already of the ISSG suggested that it would serve as a viable option for the provision of international support and oversight. The parameters of such engagement would naturally be set forth in the political settlement, and then likely ratified by a UN Security Council resolution.

Finally, the architects of plans for the TGB considered that given the widespread atrocities and violence against civilians it would be necessary to determine to what degree the TGB would exercise authority over the security services. In particular, the opposition was interested in the authority to replace key leadership positions such as the minister of defense and chief of staff of the armed forces with members of the TGB. The Syrian opposition also expressed significant interest in the ability of the TGB to create oversight mechanisms, including a joint military council.[116] The opposition was conflicted, however, on the question of whether the chair of the TGB would serve as the new commander-in-chief. This was viewed favorably if it was assured the opposition would control the chair, but with great apprehension if the parties settled on a rotating chair, or if the regime were to be able to secure the chair. The UN and the opposition also discussed the question of whether it might be best to dissolve the intelligence and security service bodies in their entirety, but this may prompt a high degree of instability, as was the case with Iraq and de-Ba'athification. The oversight–dissolution–reform debate was never fully resolved, foreshadowing the great difficulty in implementing a framework providing for inclusive and democratic management of a transitional process.

While the international community can create a legal framework establishing both a process and outcomes for a peace negotiation, it has a very limited ability to set forth the specific details of the desired outcomes. Those details must be negotiated by the mediator and the parties, and are often

---

[116] *Id.* at 19–20.

extremely complex in terms of how they relate to one another, and the impact that they will have on the ability of the parties to effect a stable transition and a durable peace.

VII RESOLVING CONFLICTS BETWEEN THE LEGAL FRAMEWORK AND DOMESTIC LAW

The section explores how the parties sought to bridge the outcomes envisioned by the legal framework with the requirements of domestic law. In particular, it discusses how the peace process could lead to the adoption of a new constitution for Syria in a way that either is in conformity with or legally circumvents the requirements set by the 2012 Syrian Constitution.

The effort to create a new or amended constitution is a common legal conundrum arising in peace negotiations. While many aspects of the peace negotiation process are governed by international law, with only the faintest role for domestic law, constitutional modification is nearly always squarely governed by domestic law in parallel to international law.

In the case of Syria, Article 150 of the 2012 Syrian Constitution specifically requires that a new constitution as well as any amendments to the existing Constitution would need to be both passed by three-quarters of parliament and approved by the president.[117] This presents an interesting legal dilemma in which the legal authority to bring into being a TGB and possibly extinguish the current parliament seems to reside with a vote of the current parliament. Yet, the entire multi-year peace process then hinges on a vote of the very parliament the process seeks to eliminate or sideline. Moreover, accepting and using the amendment and adoption procedures of the 2012 Constitution was seen as risking a legitimization of the structure that many Syrians, and in particular the opposition, found illegitimate. It also arguably contradicted the provisions laid out in UN Security Council Resolution 2254 and the Geneva Communiqué that explicitly call for a constitution-drafting process as part of a political transition.

A number of approaches were formulated during the negotiations to overcome this conundrum. Some were grounded in international law more than others. For example, one political maneuver – which would rely on the domestic constitution more than international law – would be for President Assad to invoke Article 114 of the 2012 Syrian Constitution allowing him to take "quick action" in response to grave threats facing the state. International

---

[117] Syrian Arab Republic Constitution of 2012, *supra* note 113, art. 150.

pressure could hypothetically convince Assad to issue such an Article 144 emergency decree that would immediately recognize new procedures for constitutional reform and rewriting, most likely as laid out in a comprehensive peace agreement or a similar but more limited interim agreement. He could also use Article 114 to amend Article 150 of the Constitution, which that lays out the current procedures for amendment or replacement. Alternatively, he could use Article 115 (granting the president the power to create special bodies) to authorize the rules of procedure for a CDC.[118]

The remaining options formulated during negotiations relied more heavily on international law. First, there is an argument that the 2012 Syrian Constitution's amendment procedures fundamentally contradict the Geneva Communiqué and UN Security Council Resolution 2254, which implicitly supersede or suspend the existing constitutional arrangement. This argument is amplified by the sentiment that post-conflict constitutions, as well as post-conflict amendments to preexisting constitutions, are not generally bound by preexisting ratification or amendment procedures. For instance, the Dayton Peace Accords presented a new constitution without operating within or being constrained by the prior Bosnian Constitution.[119] This was also the case with the South African Interim Constitution and with the Comprehensive Political Settlement of the Cambodia Conflict of 1991.[120]

Second, it is also possible that a foundational document for a CDC could stipulate a new ratification or amendment adoption process to replace the illegitimate procedure reflected in the current 2012 Syrian Constitution. The foundational document for a drafting committee could come in many forms, ranging from a negotiated proposal signed onto by the parties to a unilateral declaration by the UN. The content of the foundational document could also vary widely, depending on whether it dictated ratification directly through the drafting committee, through public referendum, or another entity. In laying out one of these processes for constitutional drafting and approval, the foundational document could provide an alternate source of legal authority to override the current amendment procedures laid out in by Article 150 of the existing constitution.

---

[118] *Id.* at art. 114, 115, 150.

[119] Dayton Peace Agreement (Dec. 14, 1995), https://www.osce.org/bih/126173 (last visited July 11, 2019).

[120] South African Interim Constitution (1993), http://www.justice.gov.za/legislation/acts/1993-200 .pdf (last visited July 11, 2019); Agreement on a Comprehensive Political Settlement of the Cambodia Conflict ("Paris Agreement") (1991), https://peacemaker.un.org/sites/peacemaker .un.org/files/KH_911023_FrameworkComprehensivePoliticalSettlementCambodia.pdf (last visited July 11, 2019).

If each party accedes to the agreement, the document could be viewed as a peace agreement between the two parties, thereby likely rising to the legal threshold of a treaty and crystallizing its legal status under international law. Comparative state practice indicates that the international community generally recognizes peace agreements signed between states and non-state actor after internal conflict as legally binding. Notably, the 2012 Syrian Constitution does not require that the state take affirmative steps – such as enacting new legislation – to formally incorporate the provisions of treaties into the domestic system prior to their taking effect. In this way, elevating the foundational document to the level of international treaty might circumvent the conflict with domestic law.

As a peace agreement, the document would be viewed as more legally binding by the parties than would be a unilateral declaration of the UN Envoy. However, if the parties did not form such an agreement, then there is prior state practice to suggest that the UN could issue a unilateral directive for a new constitutional process. For instance, in East Timor, the UN Security Council acted under its Chapter VII authority to establish an interim administration.[121] The Special Representative authorized by this UN Security Council resolution was then able to issue Regulation 2001/2, which elucidated the terms of membership and drafting procedures for the constitution-drafting body.[122]

The potentially constraining factor of domestic law on the legal framework for a peace negotiation may be one reason why the Russian government sought to shift the peace process into a constitutional process. In so doing, it would not only amend the legal framework, but also create additional complications or restraints on the ability of the Syrian opposition to negotiate key elements of the Geneva Communiqué, such as the creation of a TGB.

VIII CONTRACTING THE LEGAL FRAMEWORK

This section discusses how the international community contracted the legal framework, as it related to transitional justice, and how the parties and individual members of the international community responded in an effort to maintain a role for accountability and transitional justice in the peace process.

Although, the Geneva Communiqué included a call for comprehensive transitional justice, this element of the framework was diluted, and eventually

---

[121] S.C. Res. 1272, SCOR, 4057th Meeting, U.N. Doc. S/RES/1272, http://unscr.com/en/resolutions/doc/1272 (last visited July 11, 2019).
[122] UNTAET, Regulation No. 2001/2, U.N. Doc. UNTAET/REG/2001/2 (Mar. 16, 2001).

vetoed by subsequent efforts aimed at reinforcing the overall framework. While the Syrian opposition raised questions of justice multiple times in its proposals, the Syrian regime routinely rejected attempts to introduce genuine accountability into any formal settlement. Even the UN mediators, however, were reluctant to issue strong calls for justice or introduce mechanisms for stopping impunity. This state of affairs prompted the UN General Assembly to step forward and create the Commission of Inquiry, and subsequently the International, Impartial and Independent Mechanism (IIIM).

In 2012, the Geneva Communiqué established a commitment to an outcome of accountability as well as to a comprehensive process for transitional justice as a necessary precursor to national reconciliation. The Communiqué was unambiguous in its view that accountability and transitional justice were key elements of the legal framework governing the resolution of the Syrian conflict. As noted in prior section, the Geneva Communiqué called for a "comprehensive package for transitional justice, including compensation or rehabilitation for victims of the present conflict, steps towards national reconciliation and forgiveness."[123]

The Syrian opposition sought to build upon the commitment of the Communiqué by raising the issue of accountability and transitional justice throughout a number of the various iterations of negotiations and including commitments to justice in many of its core public statements. For instance, when the main Syrian opposition group issued their HNC Executive Framework in 2016, they included a number of provisions addressing transitional justice. First, the High Negotiations Commission reaffirmed the Communiqué's commitment to transitional justice and national reconciliation, proclaiming:

> Immediate measures shall be taken to promote transitional justice and national reconciliation. A transitional justice, accountability, and reconciliation program will be defined in the agreement in accordance with international norms and standards and the Geneva Communiqué.[124]

The HNC Executive Framework then expanded upon the Communiqué's commitment by calling for a transitional justice committee that would create particular mechanisms and institute systemic reforms to advance those goals, noting in particular:

---

[123] "Action Group for Syria Final Communiqué," *supra* note 20, at Annex II, art. 6(III).
[124] High Negotiations Commission for the Syrian Revolution and Opposition Forces, *supra* note 109, at 14.

The transitional justice committee shall work in accordance with international transitional justice standards; and therefore it must consider and propose mechanisms to ensure accountability, reparation for the victims (materially and morally), achieve institutional reform, propose mechanisms to investigate violations and crimes, and keep records related to human rights violations.[125]

To supplement these domestic efforts, the HNC Executive Framework also called for ratification of the Rome Statute to open up the possibility for prosecutions at the International Criminal Court. The High Negotiations Commission commits to "[w]ork to accede and ratify the Rome Statute of the International Criminal Court to ensure the non-recurrence of human rights violations."[126] The Syrian opposition also signaled this jurisdiction could be retroactive and cover crimes from the early stages of the revolution.

In addition, the Syrian opposition emphasized domestic accountability for atrocity crimes, as well as the need for the lustration and vetting of those suspected of committing atrocity crimes. Specifically, the HNC Executive Framework provided that:

Individuals who were involved in grave violations of human rights and war crimes against the Syrian people, including military and security officials, shall be held accountable by virtue of law. They shall be replaced by figures who have not been involved in any violations without resorting to a complete eradication policy or uncalculated reactions. This shall be based on integrity, merit, and adherence to the law.[127]

Unsurprisingly, however, these officials – who were largely part of the current Syrian regime – were less than enthused by the prospect of being removed from power and held responsible for their behavior during the conflict. Across the various rounds of the negotiations the government of Syria was adamantly opposed to the inclusion of justice mechanisms, trying to pivot the conversation away from securing an end to impunity toward securing an end to the violence.

Unfortunately, the UN Security Council did not match the enthusiasm of the Syrian opposition for accountability and transitional justice as key elements of the legal framework for resolving the Syrian conflict. As noted above, the Geneva Communiqué was annexed to UN Security Council Resolution 2118. Yet, when in 2014 the French government proposed a UN Security

---

[125] *Id.* at 23.
[126] *Id.*
[127] *Id.* at 25.

Council draft resolution (S/2014/348) that condemned the human rights violations perpetrated by Syrian authorities and referred those violations to the International Criminal Court,[128] this resolution was vetoed by the representatives from Russia and China.[129]

Subsequently in 2015 when the UN Security Council adopted Resolution 2254, it explicitly referenced a number of provisions of the Communiqué relating to the TGB, constitution, and an inclusive peace process, but it made no reference to the provision for accountability and transitional justice.

In order to open up other avenues for the pursuit of justice alongside the continued negotiations for peace, the UN created two bodies that were charged with investigating and analyzing evidence of atrocity crimes in Syria. First, on August 22, 2011, the Human Rights Council passed Resolution S-17/1 creating a Commission of Inquiry.[130] The resolution called for:

> an independent international commission of inquiry, to be appointed by the President of the Human Rights Council, to investigate all alleged violations of international human rights law since March 2011 in the Syrian Arab Republic, to establish the facts and circumstances that may amount to such violations and of the crimes perpetrated and, where possible, to identify those responsible with a view to ensuring that perpetrators of violations, including those that may constitute crimes against humanity, are held accountable.

Since initially creating the body in August 2011, the Human Rights Council extended the Commission's mandate multiple times.[131] The Commission of Inquiry published over twenty reports detailing an array of human rights violations committed in Syria based on thousands of interviews with victims and witnesses inside and outside of Syria.[132] Unfortunately, the Commission was limited in scope and not authorized to take prosecutorial action based on the results of its investigations.

---

[128] S.C. Draft Res. 2014/348, SCOR, U.N. Doc. S/2014/348 (May 22, 2014), https://www.un.org/en/ ga/search/view_doc.asp?symbol=S/2014/348 (last visited July 8, 2019).

[129] "Referral of Syria to International Criminal Court Fails as Negative Votes Prevent Security Council from Adopting Draft Resolution" (2014) United Nations, https://www.un.org/press/en/ 2014/sc11407.doc.htm (last visited July 8, 2019).

[130] G.A. Res. S-17/1, GAOR, 17th Special Session, U.N. Doc. S-17/1, cl. 13, https://www.ohchr.org/ Documents/HRBodies/HRCouncil/CoISyria/ResS17_1.pdf

[131] United Nations Human Rights Council, "Independent International Commission of Inquiry on the Syrian Arab Republic" (OHCHR.org, 2019), https://www.ohchr.org/EN/HRBodies/ HRC/IICISyria/Pages/AboutCoI.aspx (last visited July 18, 2019).

[132] *Id.*

Frustrated by repeated vetoes and threats of vetoes in the UN Security Council, and disappointed by the limitations of the Commission of Inquiry, the UN General Assembly passed Resolution 71/248 on December 21, 2016 to create an IIIM to Assist in the Investigation and Prosecution of Persons Responsible for the Most Serious Crimes under International Law Committed in the Syrian Arab Republic since March 2011."[133] In establishing the entity, the General Assembly not only emphasized the "need to ensure accountability for crimes involving violations of international law," but also linked the achievement of credible and comprehensive accountability to reconciliation and sustainable peace and thus to any viable political resolution of the conflict.[134] The IIIM was established to work in cooperation with the Commission of Inquiry to:

> collect, consolidate, preserve and analyze evidence of violations of international humanitarian law and human rights violations and abuses and to prepare files in order to facilitate and expedite fair and independent criminal proceedings, in accordance with international law standards, in national, regional or international courts or tribunals that have or may in the future have jurisdiction over these crimes, in accordance with international law.[135]

As with the Commission of Inquiry, the IIIM is not empowered to prosecute or adjudicate cases. Rather, it serves as a mechanism for the collection and analysis of materials documenting violations of international law, so that evidence is fully prepared for a future date in which proceedings can occur in courts (whether national or international).[136]

The contraction of the legal framework for the negotiation process to exclude accountability and transitional justice was not determinative of the role of justice, as other actors, including the General Assembly were able to exercise powers within their jurisdiction to create mechanisms to preserve at least some role for accountability. And, as discussed in a related chapter, individual states have sought to utilize universal jurisdiction as a means for holding individuals accountable for atrocity crimes, and a number of nongovernmental organizations as well as regime defectors have undertaken substantial documentation efforts to preserve the historical record, and to preserve evidence for potential prosecutions.

---

[133] G.A. Res. 71/248, GAOR, 71st Session, U.N. Doc. A/RES/71/248, https://undocs.org/en/A/RES/71/248 (last visited July 18, 2019).

[134] *Id*, at cl. 1–2.

[135] *Id.* at cl. 4.

[136] International, Impartial and Independent Mechanism, "Mandate" (IIIM.UN.org), https://iiim.un.org/mandate (last visited July 18, 2019).

IX CONCLUSION

Those seeking to understand the role played by peace negotiations in bringing about a resolution of a conflict often focus exclusively on the political dimensions of the conflict and the negotiations themselves. The role of the legal framework is often overlooked or minimized, or seen purely through the lens of the technical aspects relating to the design of mechanism for the implementation of the agreement. As discussed in this chapter, most peace processes, and in particular the Syrian peace process operate within a legal framework created by the international community, and to some degree by the parties themselves. This framework may include both a process for negotiation, as well as specified outcome objectives (though it is rarer to identify specific outcomes). In the case of Syria, the framework was established through a series of declarations and resolutions by the Arab League, various evolved coalitions of interested and empowered states, the UN General Assembly, and the Security Council. With each iteration of the framework, it achieved enhanced legal authority and greater clarity, as well as being amended, modified, or contracted.

The manner in which the Arab League, followed by the General Assembly and then Security Council established the legal framework will likely set the model or template for how the international community creates future legal frameworks. Despite the rather chaotic approach to the actual negotiations, the international community has, in hindsight, been fairly deliberate and persistent in its articulation of a legal framework for the peace process, and in a way that has preserved that process in the face of numerous threats to derail it. The practice of initially annexing the framework, whether it be the initial Six Point-Peace Plan, or the Geneva Communiqué, followed in subsequent resolutions by including specific excerpts in operative language, will likely become a trend for ensuring specificity and continuity in the legal framework.

It is also notable that when the UN Security Council sought to amend or modify the legal framework it did so through textual changes to the language that it incorporated into the operative paragraphs of its resolutions. When it sought to contract elements of the framework, it did so either through a blunt veto of a resolution seeking to bring into operation a specific element, such as referring the case to the International Criminal Court, or it declined to incorporate those elements into the operative paragraphs of a resolution.

Finally, the efforts of the UN Security Council in the context of Syria represent a continuation and augmentation of the willingness of the Council to specify outcomes such as the requirement to launch a process for constitutional reform and hold subsequent elections. Notably, the willingness to specify a transitional government body, which implied regime change, is a fairly dramatic and forward-leaning outcome, and one which while tempered in the nuance of how the provision is drafted, remained at the core legal framework for the resolution of the conflict throughout the many UN Security Council reaffirmations.

9

Conclusion

Historically, crystallization of new rules of customary international law was viewed as a protracted process that took decades, if not centuries, to complete. But, sometimes, during periods of sweeping geopolitical change, customary international law can ripen quite rapidly. Often those periods correspond with major wars. Named in honor of Hugo Grotius, whose masterpiece *De Jure Belli ac Pacis* helped usher in the modern system of international law at the end of the Eighty Years' War, "Grotian moments" are transformative developments that generate the unique conditions for accelerated formation of customary international law. Has this book proved that the Syrian conflict was a Grotian moment? And, if so, what will the legacy of Syria be?

To provide historical perspective for that assessment, Chapter 3 examined how World War II and the postwar Nuremberg trials rapidly launched new paradigms of human rights law and international criminal law. Nuremberg, we believe, represents the prototypical Grotian moment. Before Nuremberg, what a state did to its own citizens was its own business, and individuals were not accountable under international law. The Tribunal's formation was in response to the most heinous atrocity in the history of humankind – the extermination of six million Jews and several million other "undesirables" by the Nazi regime. From an orthodox view of customary international law formation, the amount of state practice was quite limited, consisting only of the negotiation of the Nuremberg Charter by four states, its accession by nineteen others, the judgment of the Tribunal, and a General Assembly resolution endorsing its principles. Moreover, the time period from the end of the war to the General Assembly endorsement of the Nuremberg Principles was a mere year, a drop in the bucket compared to the amount of time it ordinarily takes to crystallize customary international law. Yet, despite the limited state practice and minimal time, the ICJ, European Court of Human Rights, and four international criminal tribunals have confirmed that the

Nuremberg Charter and judgment immediately ripened into customary international law. The Grotian moment concept rationalizes this outcome. Nuremberg reflected a novel solution to unprecedented atrocity in the context of history's most devastating war. It is this context of fundamental change and great need for a timely response that explains how Nuremberg could so quickly and universally be accepted as customary international law.

How does Syria compare? As documented in Chapter 2, Syria represents one of the most intense and lengthy conflicts in modern times, with a large number of foreign states (including four of the five Permanent Members of the Security Council) involved in both the fighting and the international efforts at attaining peace and accountability. The Syrian conflict has witnessed the rise and fall of the largest, richest, and best-equipped terrorist organization in history. It has seen the widespread use of chemical weapons by a government for the first time since World War I. And it has seen the greatest migration of refugees since World War II. With all that, it should come as no surprise that the Syrian conflict has served as a laboratory for the generation of so many new principles and norms in such a short time.

This book has explored five areas of customary international law that were transformed or are in the process of being transformed by the Syrian conflict. In each, we see a similar pattern: a context of human suffering on a vast scale meriting an international response; paralysis within the UN Security Council; the bold leadership of individual or a small group of states acting as custom pioneers; the clear articulation of a new legal principle by the custom pioneers; and the rapid acceptance of the new legal principle by a large number of other states – all within a short period of time.

As described in Chapter 4, starting in September 2014 the United States and several of its allies began to bomb ISIS targets in Syria without Syria's permission. Syria protested that international law, as reflected in the International Court of Justice's opinions in the 2004 *Wall* and 2005 *Congo* cases, permitted use of force against non-state actors only when they were under the effective control of the territorial state. Acting as a custom pioneer, the United States had been arguing for the past decade that states had a right to attack non-state actors when the territorial state is unable or unwilling to suppress the threat they pose. According to the United States, al-Qaeda and ISIS represented a new kind of threat, in which a non-state actor possesses many of the attributes of a state: massive wealth, sophisticated training and organization, and access to destructive weaponry. To respond to the fundamental change and momentous threat presented by these uber-terrorist groups operating in Syria, the law of self-defense had to change. After the United States and its allies conducted more than 5,500 air strikes on ISIS targets in Syria, the Security Council confirmed this new interpretation when it unanimously adopted Resolution 2249 on November 20, 2015, which stated that use of force against ISIS in Syria without Syria's authorization is permissible based on self-defense. The coalition attacks led to the near-complete demise of ISIS. The case study of use of force against ISIS demonstrated one of the central facets of the Grotian moment theory, namely that when a rule of customary international law is emerging and there is still some doubt as to its status, a unanimous non-binding resolution of the General Assembly or Security Council can consolidate the custom and remove doubts which might have existed.

As Chapter 5 details, Syria had history on its side as it protested when the United States, France, and the United Kingdom invoked the principle of humanitarian intervention to justify their air strikes against three government chemical weapons facilities in Syria on April 14, 2018. Every past use of force for humanitarian intervention without Security Council authorization had been rejected as unlawful by the international community, including the popular 1999 NATO bombing of Serbia to protect the Kosovar Albanian people which had been labeled "unlawful but legitimate." One of the reasons for that assessment was that the US and UK described the 1999 NATO bombing campaign as "sui generis" and not intended to constitute precedent. The April 2018 air strikes on Syria were different. The participating countries asserted the legality of the air strikes and embraced a common justification – humanitarian intervention to prevent the regime's continued use of chemical weapons against civilians – rather than cite only factual considerations that render use of force morally defensible. For customary international law to rapidly crystallize during a Grotian moment, norm pioneers must be clear in their articulation of the new rule, its contours, and application. Asserting that a situation is exceptional might preserve future flexibility, but it also makes it easier for the precedent to be abused by other countries since its contours are left purposely vague. This time, by telling the Security Council that it was acting "lock step" and "in complete agreement" with the United Kingdom, the United States associated itself with the clearly annunciated legal principle set forth by the United Kingdom. The international community's support was vast, with only Russia and a handful of other states opposed.

Recalling Chapter 3's description of the formation of customary international law as a process of claim and response, what effect will Russia's rejoinder to the April 2018 air strikes have on the acceptance of this new international legal principle? There are three reasons why Russia's objection will not likely prove significant. First, Russia, itself, had asserted a right of humanitarian intervention in an attempt to justify its invasion of South Ossetia, Georgia in 2008. Second, Russia's main argument was that the United

States, United Kingdom, and France had acted improvidently since Syria's responsibility for use of chemical weapons had not been proved. Third, in assessing Russia's actions with respect to the Syrian conflict, one must keep in mind that the Assad regime allows Russia to keep its only naval base outside the former Soviet Union at the Syrian Mediterranean port of Tartus. And, for that reason, Russia will seemingly do everything in its power to keep Assad (or other pro-Russian regime leaders) in power.

This brings us to one of the most unusual aspects of the Syrian crisis, namely Russia's willingness to use its veto in the Security Council to block resolution after resolution designed to foster regime change, stop atrocities, prevent use of chemical weapons, and hold perpetrators accountable. As discussed in Chapter 6, as a result of perceived Russian abuse of the veto, a large number of countries were emboldened to bypass the Security Council as a decision-making body in an effort to achieve accountability for grave atrocities in Syria. The creation of the IIIM by the General Assembly with a mandate to procure evidence to be used in criminal prosecutions was not only unprecedented, it represented a major power shift from the Security Council to the General Assembly. The only comparable action of this nature occurred in 1950 when the UN General Assembly adopted the Uniting for Peace Resolution, which resolves that "if the Security Council, because of lack of unanimity of the permanent members, fails to exercise its primary responsibility to act as required to maintain international peace and security ... the General Assembly shall consider the matter immediately with the view to making recommendations to Members ... in order to restore international peace and security."[1] How far this power shift leads remains to be seen.

Chapter 6 also tells the story of how the massive number of Syrians fleeing the violence and atrocities in Syria had a pivotal impact on the international community's approach to international criminal justice. Before the Syrian conflict, the global enforcer mode of universal jurisdiction was on the wane. Under this type of jurisdiction, investigations, indictments, and requests for extradition may be initiated for certain international crimes even when the act occurred abroad, the perpetrator and victims are not nationals of the prosecuting state, and the perpetrator is not located within the prosecuting state's territory when criminal processes are launched. In the early years of the new millennium, under pressure from the United States, countries such as Belgium and Spain had curtailed their universal jurisdiction laws, leading noted jurist Antonio Cassese to observe in 2003 that universal jurisdiction is on

---

[1]   U.N. G.A. Res. 377 (1970).

"on its last legs, if not already in its death throes."[2] But Germany's adoption of the structural investigation model using a global enforcer approach to universal jurisdiction to investigate and prosecute Syrian perpetrators, and the United States support of the German effort, may presage a resurgence in this far-reaching type of universal jurisdiction.

The millions of Syrian refugees have had other impacts as well. Chapter 7 describes how countries that have faced the influx of a large number of Syrian migrants and refugees, such as Germany and Turkey, have fundamentally changed the way in which they process and register arriving individuals and families. In the past, countries accepting refugees and migrants adopted asylum-based approaches to such immigration, by requiring newly arrived individuals to seek asylum through onerous and at times lengthy legal procedures. Because countries such as Germany and Turkey have accepted hundreds of thousands of Syrians in a short period of time, the asylum approach was not practicable, as it would have resulted in a huge backlog of cases and as it would have relegated hundreds of thousands of individuals to legal limbo while they awaited the results of their asylum applications. During this time, asylum applicants may be forced to live in a refugee camp and may not have meaningful job and education and training opportunities. Germany and Turkey thus changed their approach to immigration, and adopted a novel resettlement policy, whereby they sought to give protected status, as opposed to asylum, to arriving Syrians. In this way, newly arrived Syrians have been able to seek housing outside of refugee camps, as well as to look for jobs and engage in other training and skills opportunities. In Germany, in particular, it appears that Syrian migrants and refugees have been relatively well integrated into the German society, that many have learned the German language and have landed decent jobs, and that the German economy itself is reaping the benefits of this influx of labor. The German approach was codified in two non-binding but influential international instruments adopted in December 2018 – the Global Compact on Refugees and the Global Compact for Safe, Orderly and Regular Migration. The Syrian migration crisis was the driving force in this Grotian moment: a sweeping change in host countries' immigration policies, from an asylum approach to a resettlement policy.

Finally, Chapter 8 examined how the international community's efforts at peace negotiations to end the Syrian conflict will likely serve as a model for how the international community approaches peace negotiations across the globe. In the Syrian context, a framework for the process and an enumeration

[2] Antonio Cassese, *Is the Bell Tolling for Universality? A Plea for a Sensible Notion of Universal Jurisdiction*, 1 J. Int'l Crim. Just. 589 (2003).

of outcome objectives were established through a series of declarations and resolutions by the Arab League, coalitions of interested states, the UN General Assembly, and the Security Council. Despite major political and geopolitical changes during the conflict, the approach has moved the peace process steadily forward in the face of numerous threats to derail it. While we have not yet seen a conclusion to these efforts, the novel practice of initially annexing the framework and stipulating the outcome objectives in subsequent resolutions will likely become a trend for ensuring specificity and continuity in future efforts to negotiate peace.

We believe the generation of new rules of customary international law arising out of the Syrian conflict that we have described in this book corroborate the Grotian moment concept. But in closing, we would like to address four questions that we have encountered at conferences where we have presented our findings.

The first is whether the case studies are perhaps more evolutionary than we characterize them? For example, the argument that states can use force against independent non-state actors was used by the United States for over a decade to justify its Predator Drone strikes against al-Qaeda throughout the Middle East before its attacks on ISIS in Syria. And the argument for unauthorized humanitarian intervention had been percolating long before the US–France–UK air strikes on the Syrian chemical weapons facilities. As such, does the Grotian moment concept really just represent the tipping point that every rule of customary international law encounters as it ripens? To some extent that is true, but what makes a Grotian moment extraordinary is the context of fundamental change behind the tipping point.

The second question is whether it is too early to tell whether the changes we describe are really new rules of international law? In recognition of this difficulty, Chapter 3 warns that during times of international flux, it may be easy to spot a turning point that is not really there. Stefan Andersson's book about how the Vietnam War changed international law was published fifty years after the war, enabling the author to reassess some of the conclusions of the noted authors who tackled the subject in the 1970s as the war was just concluding. We will certainly have a clearer picture of the contributions of the Syrian conflict to international law with the benefit of a decade or two of hindsight. But we believe the evidence is sufficient to conclude that the Syrian conflict has brought about some significant changes in international law, though the full implications remain to be seen.

The third question is how do we differentiate the Grotian moment concept from the much-criticized concept of so-called instant custom? Grotian moments, such as the Syrian conflict, represent instances of rapid, as opposed to instantaneous, formation of customary international law. In addition to non-binding General Assembly or Security Council resolutions, some underpinning of state practice is necessary, whether it precedes the resolution consistent with Professor McDougal's "claim and response" approach,[3] or follows the resolution as envisioned in Professor D'Amato's "articulation and act" approach.[4]

And the final question is whether the Grotian moment concept is potentially destabilizing? Despite the distinction between instant custom and the phenomenon of Grotian moments, some states and commentators are apprehensive about a concept that rationalizes rapid formation of customary international law. For them, international law is best created exclusively through treaties, as to which states can opt out by non-action, simply by declining to ratify the instrument. So long as customary norms take many decades to ripen into law, customary international law does not seem threatening. It is another matter if customary law can form within just a few years and is deemed binding on states that have not affirmatively manifested their persistent objection. In such case, they may abhor a concept of law formation that appears more revolutionary than evolutionary.

But such apprehension is unwarranted. For, this book does not advocate something new and dangerous, but rather provides doctrinal grounding for, and historic corroboration of, a phenomenon that has existed since at least World War II. The five case studies involving the international law changes triggered by the Syrian conflict demonstrate continuing international recognition that customary international law must have the capacity in unique circumstances to respond to rapidly evolving developments by producing rules in a timely and adequate manner.

---

[3] M. S. McDougal & N. A. Schlei, *The Hydrogen Bomb Tests in Perspective: Lawful Measures for Security*, 64 YALE L.J. 648 (1955).

[4] ANTHONY A. D'AMATO, CONCEPT OF CUSTOM IN INTERNATIONAL LAW 88 (1971).

The Chautauqua Blueprint for a Statute for a Syrian Extraordinary Tribunal to Prosecute Atrocity Crimes

On August 27, 2013, several chief prosecutors of the various international criminal tribunals, convened at the Chautauqua Institution, and called for accountability for atrocity crimes committed in Syria.

In furtherance of the Seventh Chautauqua Declaration, this "blueprint" or "discussion draft" for a "Statute for a Syrian Extraordinary Tribunal to Prosecute Atrocity Crimes" has been prepared by a group of international experts as a starting point to help inform continuing discussions on an accountability mechanism that is fair and effective under the distinct circumstances of Syria. It reflects insights gained from a series of meetings and workshops over the past two years led by the Public International Law & Policy Group (PILPG), including several meetings organized by the Syria Justice and Accountability Centre, which brought together Syrian lawyers, jurists, and civil society leaders with international experts to discuss transitional justice in Syria. It also reflects comments received from a drafting committee whose members include several former international tribunal chief prosecutors, international tribunal judges, and leading practitioners and academic experts in the field of international criminal law.

Over the course of the several meetings in the United States and Turkey, participants discussed the structure, mandate, and functioning of a potential future extraordinary tribunal to prosecute atrocity crimes in Syria, based on international and global best practices. There was strong sentiment that the Tribunal should be domestic, but with international elements. The participants identified characteristics of the Syrian domestic criminal justice system that could be integrated into the structure and procedure of an extraordinary tribunal to ensure that such a justice mechanism is uniquely tailored to Syria.

The purpose of a Syrian extraordinary tribunal would be to prosecute those most responsible for atrocity crimes committed in Syria by all sides of the conflict when the political situation permits, presumably following a change in government. It would be complementary to the ordinary criminal and military courts of Syria, which would prosecute lower-level perpetrators, and to an international tribunal if one were to be established or given jurisdiction to prosecute the highest-level perpetrators. Several of the provisions are in brackets with alternative proposals, followed by commentary in the footnotes and an annexed report explaining the context and advantages and disadvantages of the bracketed alternatives.

The expert drafting committee believes the time is ripe for this discussion draft. It can help the Syrian opposition demonstrate its commitment to the rule of law, ensure that accountability plays an appropriate role in peace negotiations, put Syrian officials and military commanders on all sides on notice of potential criminal liability, and lay the groundwork for justice rather than revenge in the immediate aftermath of transition.

Co-Chairs of the Drafting Committee:

> M. Cherif Bassiouni, Emeritus Professor of Law at DePaul University, and former chairman, Drafting Committee, United Nations Diplomatic Conference on the Establishment of an International Criminal Court;
>
> David Crane, Professor, Syracuse University College of Law, and former Chief Prosecutor of the Special Court for Sierra Leone;
>
> Michael Scharf, Associate Dean, Case Western Reserve University School of Law, managing director of the PILPG, and former Attorney-Adviser for United Nations Affairs, US Department of State.

Committee Members:

> Sir Desmond de Silva, QC, former Chief Prosecutor of the Special Court for Sierra Leone;
>
> Mark Ellis, executive director of the International Bar Association;
>
> Justice Richard Goldstone, former Justice of the Constitutional Court of South Africa, and former Chief Prosecutor of the International Criminal Tribunals for the former Yugoslavia and Rwanda;
>
> Larry Johnson, adjunct professor at Columbia Law School, former UN Assistant Secretary-General for Legal Affairs who drafted the statutes for the Yugoslavia Tribunal, the Cambodia Tribunal, and the Special Tribunal for Lebanon;
>
> Gregory Noone, director of the Fairmont State University National Security and Intelligence Program and Assistant Professor of Political Science and Law, and former head of the International Law Branch in the International and Operational Law Division at the Pentagon;

Michael Newton, professor, Vanderbilt University Law School, and former Deputy to the Ambassador at Large for War Crimes Issues, US Department of State;

William Schabas, professor, Middlesex University Faculty of Law, and former member of the International Truth Commission for Sierra Leone; and

Paul Williams, president of the PILPG, and Rebecca Grazier Professor of Law and International Relations, American University.

Contributors:

David Scheffer, director of the Center for International Human Rights at Northwestern University School of Law, UN Special Expert on United Nations Assistance to the Khmer Rouge Trials, and former US Ambassador at Large for War Crimes Issues; and

Judge Patricia Wald, former judge of the International Criminal Tribunal for the former Yugoslavia and Chief Judge of the US Court of Appeals for the District of Columbia Circuit.

DRAFT STATUTE FOR A SYRIAN [EXTRAORDINARY][SPECIAL] TRIBUNAL TO PROSECUTE ATROCITY CRIMES[1]

Section One: Establishment, Organization, and Competence of the Tribunal

Part One: Establishment and Competence of the Tribunal
Article 1

(a) A Tribunal is hereby established and shall be known as the [Syrian Extraordinary Tribunal to Prosecute Atrocity Crimes] [Syrian Special Tribunal to Prosecute Atrocity Crimes] (hereinafter "the Tribunal").[2]

---

[1] "Statute" means Tribunal charter, rather than a law establishing the Tribunal. This Statute could be approved by a decree by the transitional government, or by enacting a transitional justice law. Timing will be an important consideration in the transitional phase and the government will have an interest in implementing transitional justice as soon as possible to facilitate post-conflict healing and transition.

[2] The word "Extraordinary" may be better than "Special" because of sensitivities related to the establishment of "special courts" under the Assad government. On the other hand, those who are familiar with the mixed record and criticisms of the "Extraordinary Chambers in the Courts of Cambodia" have suggested avoiding the word "Extraordinary" in the name of the Syrian Tribunal. "Atrocity crimes" are those international crimes recognized in the Statute of the International Criminal Court, namely war crimes, crimes against humanity, and genocide.

(b) The competencies of the Tribunal and of the bodies complementing its work shall be according to the provisions of this Statute.

(c) The Tribunal will bring to trial those [most responsible][3] [who bear the greatest responsibility][4]

Article 2 The Tribunal shall be fully independent from the existing courts, though it is authorized to utilize the Syrian constabulary.

Article 3 The Tribunal shall have its seat in Damascus [and may conduct proceedings elsewhere in Syria].

Part Two: Organization of the Tribunal
Article 4 The Tribunal shall consist of the following organs:

1. The judiciary, consisting of the following:
   i. [One or more trial chambers;] [Three or more trial chambers;][5]
   ii. A Cassation Chamber, which shall have the jurisdiction to review decisions of the Trial Chambers, headed by the Tribunal's President; and
   iii. A panel of Investigative Judges, headed by a Chief Investigative Judge.
2. A Prosecutions Office headed by a Chief Prosecutor;
3. A Defense Office, headed by the Head of the Defense Office;
4. An Office of Victims' Counsel;
5. A Registry, which shall be responsible for the Tribunal's administrative, public outreach, and security services, headed by the Registrar.

---

[3] Pursuant to the jurisprudence of the SCSL and ECCC, "those most responsible" would probably include about 100 high-level defendants. "Those who bear the greatest responsibility" may be a slightly higher threshold, focusing on about fifty of the highest-level defendants.

[4] A new Syrian government may also choose to accept the jurisdiction of the International Criminal Court (ICC) over the situation arising in Syria after March 15, 2011, in which case the ICC could exercise jurisdiction over individuals accused of war crimes, crimes against humanity, and genocide in cases in which domestic courts are unable or unwilling to prosecute, such as if high-level accused perpetrators are present in a third country which is not willing to extradite them to Syria for prosecution. The ICC traditionally takes jurisdiction over only a handful of highest-level defendants, so there would still be a need for the Syria Tribunal to prosecute the next level of culpable civilian and military leaders.

[5] It is hard to predict in advance precisely what will be needed regarding the number of trial chambers. Some of the experts have opined that it will be much easier to undertake and support a single trial chamber. Each trial would likely involve a dozen defendants charged with related crimes.

Article 5 – The Trial Chambers

(a) The Trial Chambers shall be composed of [independent judges]. [independent judges and one reserve judge per chamber].[6]
(b) Each Trial Chamber shall be an Extraordinary Chamber composed of three professional judges.
(c) [Of the three judges two (including the President of the Trial Chamber) shall be Syrian and one shall be a foreign judge]. [All of the judges in the Trial Chambers shall be Syrian][7]
(d) The Court shall permit foreign judges as international observers.
(e) The president shall appoint one or more legal advisers who may be non-Syrians to assist the Trial Chamber judges.

Article 6 – The Cassation Chamber

(a) The Cassation Chamber shall serve as both appellate chamber and court of final instance. It shall also serve as the Cassation Commission in relation to administrative matters set forth in this Statute.
(b) The Cassation Chamber shall be composed of five members.[8]
(c) [Three of the five Cassation Chamber Judges (including the President) shall be Syrian and two shall be foreign judges]. [All of the judges in the Cassation Chambers shall be Syrian][9]
(d) No member of any Trial Chamber can simultaneously be a member of the Cassation Chamber or a Tribunal Investigative Judge.

---

[6] Ever since presiding judge Richard May died in the middle of the ICTY's Milošević trial, some of the international criminal tribunals have adopted the practice of having a reserve judge sit with the other judges in case one of them is removed, becomes too ill to participate, or dies during the trial proceedings. This ensures that the trial can continue with a full bench without the delay of appointing a replacement judge.

[7] Participants at the working group meetings expressed a preference for a judiciary comprised solely of Syrian judges, though some were open to the idea of having a foreign judge on each panel. The benefit of having a foreign judge on each panel is that it would guard against impropriety and enhance the appearance of fairness. Working alongside their domestic counterparts, international judges would greatly contribute to the administration of justice, offering a broader perspective on international criminal law and thus ensuring credibility for the new court. International judges can provide a significant skillset, as they can offer experience in complex international criminal matters.

[8] The existing Cassation Court in Syria is made up of five judges, as is the Appeals Chambers of each of the international criminal tribunals.

[9] Participants at the working group meeting expressed a preference for a Cassation Chamber comprised solely of Syrian judges. Others felt that if foreign judges were used, they should be from Arab nations or should at least have Arabic language fluency, as Arabic would be the official language of the Tribunal.

Part Three: Appointment and Termination of Judges and Prosecutors
Article 7 – Appointment of Judges and Prosecutors

(a) Judges and prosecutors shall have high moral character, a spirit of impartiality and integrity, [fluency in the Arabic language,][10] and experience, particularly in criminal law.

(b) Judges and prosecutors shall be independent in the performance of their functions, and shall not accept or seek any instructions from any government or any other source.

(c) The Tribunal's Syrian judges and Public Prosecutors shall be nominated by a Judicial Council.

   The Judicial Council shall be comprised of [nine] members [elected from among the judges and public prosecutors in Syria] [elected from among the members of the Syrian bar] and shall be under the supervision of the Cassation Commission.[11]

(d) [The Tribunal's Judges and Prosecutors shall be appointed from among the currently practicing judges and prosecutors in Syria.][12] [The Tribunal's Judges and Prosecutors shall be appointed from among the members of the Syrian bar.]

(e) The Judicial Council shall nominate all international judges to the Tribunal from a list of names recommended by the [UN Secretary-General][Secretary-General of the Arab League].[13]

Article 8 – End of Term

(a) The term of service of a judge, prosecutor, or other officer of the Tribunal shall be terminated only pursuant to the provisions of this Article for one of the following reasons:

   1. If he is convicted of a felony that is not a political felony nor an accusation fabricated against him;

---

[10] If foreign judges are used, it may be necessary to allow non-Arabic-speaking judges to participate, but this will require that all proceedings be simultaneously interpreted into a language the judge speaks fluently.

[11] Use of a "Judicial Council" is intended to help insulate the selection of the Tribunal's judges and prosecutors from political interference. One of the experts opined that political pressure will be pervasive with or without such a selection mechanism.

[12] Some participants and participating experts voiced concern about whether there is a sufficient pool of qualified, unbiased judges in the existing Syrian judiciary. The second option would therefore open the pool to practicing Syrian attorneys.

[13] If the Tribunal includes international judges, there will need to be a mechanism for obtaining names of qualified international judges. Nominations could be made by the UN Secretary-General or the Secretary-General of the Arab League.

2. If he presents false or misleading information about his credentials;

3. If he fails to perform his duties without a legitimate reason; or

4. If he requests to end his service with the Tribunal.

(b) Decisions regarding termination of a judge, prosecutor, or officer of the Tribunal shall be made by a vote of at least four members of the Cassation Commission. If the situation involves a member of the Cassation Commission, that person shall not participate in the termination proceedings and the decision shall be made by a vote of at least three members of the Cassation Chamber.

Part Four: Presidency of the Tribunal
Article 9

(a) The President of the Tribunal shall:

1. Chair the proceedings of the Cassation Commission.

2. Name the [presiding and alternate] judges of the Trial Chambers.

3. Name substitute judges to the Trial Chambers in case of absence.

4. Appoint, upon a majority vote of the Cassation Commission, the Tribunal's Registrar, Chief Prosecutor, Head of the Defense Office [, and head Victims' Counsel.][14]

(b) The President of the Tribunal shall have the right to appoint foreign experts in international and criminal law to assist the Investigative Judges, Trial Chambers, and the Cassation Chamber.[15]

Part Five: Investigative Judges of the Tribunal
Article 10

(a) The Tribunal's Investigative Judges shall undertake the investigation of those accused of crimes stipulated in this Statute.[16]

(b) A sufficient number of Investigative Judges shall be appointed.

(c) The Investigative Judges shall choose the Chief Investigative Judge and his deputy from among them.

(d) The Chief Investigative Judge shall refer cases to Tribunal investigative judges individually.

---

[14] As explained below, though some international tribunals employ Victim's Counsel, the experts recommend against the appointment of Victim's Counsel for this tribunal.

[15] Involving international experts in this role may help to improve the capacity of the Investigative Judges, Trial Chamber, and the Cassation Chamber, and enhance the appearance of fairness.

[16] The Syrian domestic criminal system utilizes investigative judges.

(e) Each of the Investigative Judges' Offices shall be composed of a Judge for investigation and qualified staff as may be required for the work of an investigative judge.

(f) Each Investigative Judge shall have the right to gather evidence from whatever source he deems appropriate and to question all relevant parties directly.

(g) Each Investigative Judge shall act independently as a separate entity from the Tribunal. He shall not be under nor receive requests or orders from any government departments, or from any other party.

(h) The decisions of the Investigative Judge can be appealed in cassation before the Cassation Commission within [fifteen days] after the notification or deemed notification of the decision in accordance with the Statute.

(i) [The Chief Investigative Judge, with the consent of the President of the Tribunal, may appoint foreign nationals to assist the Investigative Judges with respect to cases covered by this Statute.]

Section Two: Other Departments of the Tribunal

Part One: Prosecutions Office
Article 11

(a) The Prosecutions Office shall be responsible for the prosecution of persons responsible for crimes within the jurisdiction of the Tribunal.

(b) Each Public Prosecutor shall act with complete independence and is considered as a separate entity from the Tribunal. He shall not be under nor receive instructions from any government department or from any other party.

(c) A sufficient number of Public Prosecutors shall be appointed.

(d) The President of the Tribunal shall select a Chief Prosecutor and a Deputy from among the Public Prosecutors.

(e) Each office of a Public Prosecutor shall be composed of a Prosecutor and other qualified staff.

(f) The Chief Prosecutor shall assign individual cases to a Prosecutor to try in court.

(g) The Chief Public Prosecutor, in consultation with the President of the Tribunal, shall have the right to appoint foreign nationals to act as experts assisting the prosecutors concerning the preparation and prosecution of cases covered by this Statute. Foreign advisers shall be persons of high moral character and integrity. It would be preferable that such foreign experts have worked in a prosecutorial capacity in his or her respective country or in an international war crimes tribunal.

Part Two: Defense Office
Article 12

(a) [Every defendant shall be represented by defense counsel, either retained or appointed, and may not advocate on his own behalf in front of the Tribunal.] [Every defendant shall have the right to self-representation or to be represented by defense counsel, either retained or appointed.][17]

(b) The Defense Office shall protect the rights of the defense, provide support and assistance to defense counsel and to the persons entitled to legal assistance, including, where appropriate, legal research, collection of evidence and advice, and appearing before the Chamber in respect of specific issues.

(c) The President of the Tribunal shall appoint an independent Head of the Defense Office, who shall be responsible for the appointment of the Office staff and the drawing up of a list of Public Defenders for defendants that do not retain their own counsel at their own expense.

(d) A sufficient number of Public Defenders shall be appointed.

(e) The Head of the Defense Office, in consultation with the President of the Tribunal, shall have the right to appoint foreign nationals to act as experts assisting the Defense Office concerning the preparation and trial of cases covered by this Statute. Foreign advisers shall be persons of high moral character and integrity. It would be preferable that such foreign experts have worked in a prosecutorial or defense capacity in his or her respective country or in an International War Crimes Tribunal.

Part Three: Victims' Counsel
Article 13
The purpose of the Victims' Counsel is to: [participate in criminal proceedings against those responsible for crimes within the jurisdiction of the

---

[17] Requiring that the defendant be represented by counsel may reduce the opportunity for grandstanding and disruptive conduct on the part of the accused, as in the Milosevic trial, for example. Although Article 14 of the ICCPR provides that there is a right to be represented by counsel, or to represent oneself, many countries in the world require defendants in serious and complex cases to be represented by counsel, and this has not been viewed as inconsistent with the ICCPR. The international tribunals permit self-representation as a conditional right, and appoint stand-by counsel to step in when the right is abused or when the defendant's health disrupts the trial.

Tribunal by supporting the prosecution; and] assist Victims in seeking [reparations]/[damages]/[collective and moral reparations], as provided in the Rules of Procedure.][18]

Part Four: Registry

Article 14 – Structure and Responsibilities

(a) The Tribunal shall have [an international Registrar and a Syrian Deputy Registrar] [a Syrian Registrar and an international Deputy Registrar] [a Syrian Registrar and Deputy Registrar][19] selected by the President, with the concurrence of a majority of the Cassation Commission.

(b) The Registrar and its staff shall be responsible for the administration and servicing of the Tribunal, including providing, in consultation with the Office of the Prosecutor, measures to protect the safety, physical and psychological well-being, dignity, and privacy of victims and witnesses.

Article 15 – Tribunal's Budget

(a) The expenses and salaries of the Tribunal shall be as follows:

[1. The expenses and salaries of the Tribunal, including Judges, Prosecutors, Defense Counsel, [Victims' Counsel], and Staff shall be borne by Arab States with whom long-term financing agreements have been negotiated].

---

[18] This entire Article is in brackets because the Statutes of the ICTY, ICTR, and SCSL do not provide for a "Victims' Counsel," while the Statutes of the ECCC, STL, and ICC do. Further, the role of Victims' Counsel has been evolving in those international tribunals, as the tribunals seek to balance the rights of the victims and the need for an orderly, efficient, and fair trial. The trend has been to curtail the role of Victims' Counsel, especially in cases where there are thousands of victims. Allowing victims and their counsel to participate in trials may present a myriad of logistical and legal challenges for this new court. This is particularly true in an extremely volatile and dangerous environment as exists, and will continue to exist, in Syria. The focus for the new court should be on ensuring that victims have a meaningful and constructive way to address the court in the post-trial stage of the proceedings and obtain restitution when feasible. Further, defendants will potentially be deprived of the right to an expeditious trial when victims participate. The cases heard by the new court will be extraordinarily complex, necessitating lengthy trials. Victim participation lengthens the trials even further, often presenting repetitious questioning of witnesses and additional filings for the court to address and decide upon, and for the defense to spend time refuting. Regarding equality of arms, victim participation and the ability of victims "to lead and challenge evidence" can create procedural disadvantage for the defense. When victims have the ability to lead evidence, allocation of the burden of proof becomes murky and defendants have a greater burden to contend with all of the additional information presented against them by victim participants. Although Syria has civil party participation in its courts, for the reasons stated above, the experts believe that a different approach may be more desirable for this Tribunal.

[19] The options of having either an international Registrar or an international Deputy Registrar are intended to bolster the independence of the Registry and inject international expertise.

[1. The expenses and salaries of the Tribunal, including Judges, Prosecutors, Defense Counsel, [Victims' Counsel], and Staff shall be borne 50 percent from international donors and 50 percent from the Syrian government.][20]

[1. The expenses and salaries of the Tribunal, including Judges, Prosecutors, Defense Counsel, [Victims' Counsel] and Staff shall be borne by the Syrian national budget. The Tribunal may receive additional assistance for their expenses from other voluntary funds contributed by foreign governments, international institutions, non-governmental organizations, and other persons wishing to provide financial assistance to the Tribunal.]

2. The expenses of any international [advisers]/[judges] shall be borne by [voluntary funds contributed by foreign governments, international institutions, non-governmental organizations, and other persons wishing to assist the proceedings].

3. [The defense counsel may receive fees for representing an indigent defendant as determined by the Registrar.][21]

(b) The Tribunal's Registrar shall have control over allocation and disbursement of the Tribunal's funds, subject to an annual budget approved by [an Oversight Board made up of an international chair and representatives from the Syrian Bar, Parliament, and Civil Society] [the Tribunal's Cassation Commission.][22]

---

[20] This option is modeled upon the funding provision of the Special Tribunal for Lebanon.

[21] Other Tribunals do not provide funding for retained counsel where the Defendant has sufficient money to pay for the defense. Where the Defendant is "indigent" (i.e., lacks sufficient funds for his defense), a Public Defender and two assistants would be appointed to represent the defendant, paid for by the Tribunal. A general review of the defendant's financial means should be sufficient to ensure that the accused has met the basic requirements for being classified as indigent. Thus, in the interest of justice there should be a presumption of indigence unless there is compelling evidence to suggest otherwise. This approach would mirror jurisdictions where legal aid is an automatic entitlement in criminal cases. Based on the experience of international and mixed courts, Syria should ensure significant flexibility in determining how a defendant's indigence should be calculated. This will be important since the vast majority of defendants will likely be indigent. The Tribunal will also be able to decide how best to structure the legal support teams for defendants.

[22] International experts have advocated for an oversight committee to ensure that the people of Syria are comfortable that justice is being served without concern of corruption/back room deals/political pressure. It may also help if the Registrar is an international with registry experience. The point for an international registrar and neutral oversight board is to instill a confidence with the people of Syria and to outside donors that the effort is above board and that monies are being spent efficiently and with accountability. To ensure complete neutrality, the Chairman of the oversight committee could be an international appointed by the UN Secretary General with the concurrence of the Syrians.

Article 16 – Public Outreach and Information Unit

(a) Within the Registry, the Tribunal shall have a Public Outreach and Information Unit to provide information on the Tribunal itself, its jurisdiction, functions, and powers.

(b) The Public Outreach Unit would also inform and explain the Tribunal's proceedings and its decisions as cases proceed.

(c) The Public Outreach and Information Unit will have a Director, who will be selected by the Registrar of the Tribunal. The Director of the Public Outreach and Information Unit shall select a Spokesperson, who will act as the Tribunal's liaison with the media and the public.[23]

Section Three: Jurisdiction and Crimes

Part One

Article 17 – Jurisdiction of the Tribunal

(a) The Tribunal shall have personal jurisdiction over [any individuals accused of atrocity crimes within Syria.][24] [any individuals who bear the greatest responsibility for atrocity crimes within Syria.][25] [any Syrian nationals or residents of Syria accused of atrocity crimes within Syria][26] [any Syrian nationals or residents of Syria who bear the greatest responsibility for atrocity crimes within Syria][27]

---

[23] Such a liaison may help to ensure a consistent "face" for the Tribunal and a uniform message concerning its proceedings and judgments.

[24] This option would enable the Tribunal to prosecute non-Syrians who either acted in Syria or whose actions abroad had an effect in Syria. While some participants favored this option, others felt that it could have a devastating impact on neighboring countries – Lebanon being the most fragile. They also pointed out that prosecution of non-Syrians in this particular conflict will be seen political.

[25] The wording of the jurisdiction of the Tribunal can have serious practical implications for the proceedings before it. For example, the Statute for the Extraordinary Chambers in the Courts of Cambodia (ECCC) gave the ECCC jurisdiction over "senior leaders of Democratic Kampuchea and those who were most responsible for the crimes and serious violations of Cambodian penal law, international humanitarian law and custom, and international conventions recognized by Cambodia." The ECCC interpreted its jurisdiction in a restrictive manner. The limitation can be for the prosecutor's discretion by mentioning it only in Article 1(c). By placing it here it would become a jurisdictional element for the judges to determine.

[26] This option confines the Tribunal's jurisdiction to Syrian nationals or residents, and paired with Article 1(c) would place the "greatest responsibility" determination within the Prosecutor's discretion.

[27] This option also confines the Tribunal's jurisdiction to Syrian nationals or residents but would require the judges to determine that the defendant met the "greatest responsibility" threshold.

(b) the Tribunal shall have subject matter jurisdiction over atrocity crimes, defined as the crime of genocide, crimes against humanity, and war crimes [as well as the following crimes under Syrian law: [list].][28]

(c) The Tribunal shall have temporal jurisdiction for atrocity crimes committed in Syria [since March 15, 2011] [since 1970, including in particular incidents of special concern such as the February 1980 Tamdor Prison Massacre, the February 1982 massacre at Hama, and the civil war that began in March 2011.][29]

(d) In interpreting the crimes within its jurisdiction, theories of liability, evidentiary matters, and standards for sentencing, the Tribunal may have resort to existing international jurisprudence.

Part Two: Definitions of Crimes[30]
Article 18 – The Crime of Genocide[31]

(a) For the purposes of this Statute and in accordance with the Convention on the Prevention and Punishment of the Crime of Genocide, dated September 9, 1948, which Syria acceded to on June 25, 1955, "genocide" means any of the following acts committed with intent to destroy, in whole or in part, a national, ethnic, racial, or religious group, as such:
   1. killing members of the group;
   2. causing serious bodily or mental harm to members of the group;

---

[28] While the Statutes of some Tribunals include serious domestic crimes (including corruption and wasting natural resources) as well as international crimes, the participants in the workshops favored limiting the Tribunal's subject matter jurisdiction to international crimes.

[29] Most of the participants in the workshops favored limiting the Tribunal's temporal jurisdiction to crimes committed since March 15, 2011. Some felt that 1980s atrocities should also be covered, while others felt that it would be extremely difficult to prosecute these older cases. The experts on the Drafting Committee strongly felt that the temporal jurisdiction should begin with the neutral date of March 15, 2011, and that the Statute avoid naming situations, as that may be seen as injecting bias.

[30] The crimes in this Statute are defined as they are in the Rome Statute establishing the ICC. The crimes in the Rome Statute are further defined in an instrument known as the "Elements of Crimes," on which the Syrian Delegation joined consensus in Rome. According to Article 15 of the International Covenant on Civil and Political Rights, a treaty that Syria has ratified, international crimes are lawfully punishable even where there is no domestic law criminalizing them at the time of their commission. International crimes, including those defined in the Rome Statute, are not subject to the prohibition on ex post facto application of criminal law.

[31] There has been little to suggest that genocide has been committed during the Syrian conflict, but workshop participants felt it was important to include the crime so as not to prejudge the characterization of crimes and to serve a deterrent function.

3. deliberately inflicting on the group conditions of life calculated to bring about its physical destruction in whole or in part;
4. imposing measures intended to prevent births within the group; and
5. forcibly transferring children of the group to another group.

(b) The following acts shall be punishable:
1. genocide;
2. conspiracy to commit genocide;
3. direct and public incitement to commit genocide;
4. attempt to commit genocide; and
5. complicity in genocide.

Article 19 – Crimes against Humanity

(a) For the purposes of this Statute, "crimes against humanity" means any of the following acts when committed as part of a widespread or systematic attack directed against any civilian population, with knowledge of the attack:
1. Murder;
2. Extermination;
3. Enslavement;
4. Deportation or forcible transfer of population;
5. Imprisonment or other severe deprivation of physical liberty in violation of fundamental norms of international law;
6. Torture;
7. Rape, sexual slavery, enforced prostitution, forced pregnancy, or any other form of sexual violence of comparable gravity;
8. Persecution against any identifiable group or collectivity on political, racial, national, ethnic, cultural, religious, gender or other grounds that are universally recognized as impermissible under international law, in connection with any act referred to in this paragraph or any crime within the jurisdiction of the Tribunal;
9. Enforced disappearance of persons; and
10. Other inhumane acts of a similar character intentionally causing great suffering, or serious injury to body or to mental or physical health.

(b) For the purposes of paragraph (a):
1. "Attack directed against any civilian population" means a course of conduct involving the multiple commission of acts referred to in the above paragraph against any civilian population, pursuant to or in furtherance of a state or organizational policy to commit such attack;

2. "Extermination" includes the intentional infliction of conditions of life, such as the deprivation of access to food and medicine, calculated to bring about the destruction of part of a population;

3. "Enslavement" means the exercise of any or all of the powers attaching to the right of ownership over a person and includes the exercise of such power in the course of trafficking in persons, in particular women and children;

4. "Deportation or forcible transfer of population" means forced displacement of the persons concerned by expulsion or other coercive acts from the area in which they are lawfully present, without grounds permitted under international law;

5. "Torture" means the intentional infliction of severe pain or suffering, whether physical or mental, upon a person in the custody or under the control of the accused; except that torture shall not include pain or suffering arising only from, inherent in or incidental to lawful sanctions;

6. "Persecution" means the intentional and severe deprivation of fundamental rights contrary to international law by reason of the identity of the group or collectivity; and

7. "Enforced disappearance of persons" means the arrest, detention or abduction of persons by, or with the authorization, support or acquiescence of, the State or a political organization, followed by a refusal to acknowledge that deprivation of freedom or to give information on the fate or whereabouts of those persons, with the intention of removing them from the protection of the law for a prolonged period of time.

Article 20 – War Crimes

(a) For the purposes of this Statute, "war crimes" means: Grave breaches of the Geneva Conventions of 12 August 1949, namely, any of the following acts against persons or property protected under the provisions of the relevant Geneva Convention:

1. Willful killing;

2. Torture or inhuman treatment, including biological experiments;

3. Willfully causing great suffering, or serious injury to body or health;

4. Extensive destruction and appropriation of property, not justified by military necessity and carried out unlawfully and wantonly;

5. Willfully denying the right of a fair trial to a prisoner of war or other protected person;

6. Compelling a prisoner of war or other protected person to serve in the forces of a hostile power;
7. Unlawful confinement;
8. Unlawful deportation or transfer; and
9. Taking of hostages.

(b) Other serious violations of the laws and customs applicable in international armed conflict, within the established framework of international law, namely, any of the following acts:

1. Intentionally directing attacks against the civilian population as such or against individual civilians not taking direct part in hostilities;
2. Intentionally directing attacks against civilian objects, that is, objects which are not military objectives;
3. Intentionally directing attacks against personnel, installations, material, units or vehicles involved in a peacekeeping mission in accordance with the Charter of the United Nations or in a humanitarian assistance mission, as long as they are entitled to the protection given to civilians or civilian objects under the international law of armed conflict;
4. Intentionally launching an attack in the knowledge that such attack will cause incidental loss of life or injury to civilians or damage to civilian objects which would be clearly excessive in relation to the concrete and direct overall military advantage anticipated;
5. Intentionally launching an attack in the knowledge that such attack will cause widespread, long-term, and severe damage to the natural environment which would be clearly excessive in relation to the concrete and direct overall military advantage anticipated;
6. Attacking or bombarding, by whatever means, towns, villages, dwellings or buildings which are undefended and which are not military objectives;
7. Killing or wounding a combatant who, having laid down his arms or having no longer means of defense, has surrendered at discretion;
8. Making improper use of a flag of truce, of the flag or of the military insignia and uniform of the enemy or of the United Nations, as well as of the distinctive emblems of the Geneva Conventions, resulting in death or serious personal injury;
9. The transfer, directly or indirectly, by the government of Syria or any of its instrumentalities of parts of its own civilian population into any territory it occupies, or the deportation or transfer of all or parts of the population of the occupied territory within or outside this territory;
10. Intentionally directing attacks against buildings that are dedicated to religion, education, art, science, or charitable purposes, historic

monuments, hospitals, and places where the sick and wounded are collected, provided they are not military objectives;

11. Subjecting persons of another nation to physical mutilation or to medical or scientific experiments of any kind that are neither justified by the medical, dental or hospital treatment of the person concerned nor carried out in his or her interest, and which cause death to or seriously endanger the health of such person or persons;

12. Killing or wounding treacherously individuals belonging to the hostile nation or army;

13. Declaring that no quarter will be given;

14. Destroying or seizing the property of an adverse party unless such destruction or seizure be imperatively demanded by the necessities of war;

15. Declaring abolished, suspended, or inadmissible in a court of law, or otherwise depriving, the rights and actions of the nationals of the adverse party;

16. Compelling the nationals of the hostile party to take part in the operations of war directed against their own country, even if they were in the belligerent's service before the commencement of the war;

17. Pillaging a town or place, even when taken by assault;

18. Employing poison or poisoned weapons;

19. Employing asphyxiating, poisonous, or other gases, and all analogous liquids, materials, or devices;

20. Employing bullets which expand or flatten easily in the human body, such as bullets with a hard envelope which does not entirely cover the core or is pierced with incisions;

21. Committing outrages upon personal dignity, in particular humiliating and degrading treatment;

22. Committing rape, sexual slavery, enforced prostitution, forced pregnancy, or any other form of sexual violence of comparable gravity;

23. Utilizing the presence of a civilian or other protected person to render certain points, areas, or military forces immune from military operations;

24. Intentionally directing attacks against buildings, material, medical units and transport, and personnel using the distinctive emblems of the Geneva Conventions in conformity with international law;

25. Intentionally using starvation of civilians as a method of warfare by depriving them of objects indispensable to their survival, including willfully impeding relief supplies as provided for under international law; and

26. Conscripting or enlisting children under the age of fifteen years into the national armed forces or using them to participate actively in hostilities.

(c) In the case of an armed conflict, any of the following acts committed against persons taking no active part in the hostilities, including members of armed forces who have laid down their arms and those placed hors de combat by sickness, wounds, detention or any other cause:

1. Violence to life and person, in particular murder of all kinds, mutilation, cruel treatment, and torture;
2. Committing outrages upon personal dignity, in particular humiliating and degrading treatment;
3. Taking of hostages; and
4. The passing of sentences and the carrying out of executions without previous judgment pronounced by a regularly constituted court, affording all judicial guarantees which are generally recognized as indispensable.

(d) Serious violations of the laws and customs of war applicable in armed conflict not of an international character, within the established framework of international law, namely, any of the following acts:

1. Intentionally directing attacks against the civilian population as such or against individual civilians not taking direct part in hostilities;
2. Intentionally directing attacks against buildings, material, medical units and transport, and personnel using the distinctive emblems of the Geneva Conventions in conformity with international law;
3. Intentionally directing attacks against personnel, installations, material, units, or vehicles involved in a peacekeeping mission in accordance with the Charter of the United Nations or in a humanitarian assistance mission, as long as they are entitled to the protection given to civilians or civilian objects under the international law of armed conflict;
4. Intentionally directing attacks against buildings that are dedicated to religion, education, art, science, or charitable purposes, historic monuments, hospitals, and places where the sick and wounded are collected, provided they are not military objectives;
5. Pillaging a town or place, even when taken by assault;
6. Committing rape, sexual slavery, enforced prostitution, forced pregnancy, or any other form of sexual violence of comparable gravity;
7. Conscripting or enlisting children under the age of fifteen years into armed forces or groups or using them to participate actively in hostilities;
8. Ordering the displacement of the civilian population for reasons related to the conflict, unless the security of the civilians involved or imperative military reasons so demand;

9. Killing or wounding treacherously a combatant adversary;
10. Declaring that no quarter will be given;
11. Subjecting persons who are in the power of another party to the conflict to physical mutilation or to medical or scientific experiments of any kind that are neither justified by the medical, dental or hospital treatment of the person concerned nor carried out in his or her interest, and which cause death to or seriously endanger the health of such person or persons; and
12. Destroying or seizing the property of an adversary, unless such destruction or seizure be imperatively demanded by the necessities of the conflict.

Section Four: General Principals of Criminal Law

Part One: Criminal Responsibility
Article 21 – Individual Criminal Responsibility

(a) A person who commits a crime within the jurisdiction of this Tribunal shall be individually responsible and liable for punishment in accordance with this Statute.
(b) In accordance with this Statute a person shall be criminally responsible and liable for punishment for a crime within the jurisdiction of the Tribunal if that person:
   1. Commits such a crime, whether as an individual, jointly with another or through another person, regardless of whether this person is criminally responsible or not;
   2. Orders, solicits, or induces the commission of such a crime, which in fact occurs or is attempted;
   3. Aids, abets, or otherwise assists in the commission or attempted commission of such a crime, including providing the means for its commission;[32]
   4. In any other way that contributes to the commission or attempted commission of such a crime by a group of persons acting with a

---

[32] This provision is worded slightly differently from the provision in the Statutes of the International Tribunals, which provide: "For the purpose of facilitating the commission of such a crime, aids, abets or otherwise assists in its commission or its attempted commission, including providing the means for its commission." This revision avoids the problem that has surfaced in recent ICTY cases, that have interpreted "for the purpose of facilitating the commission of such a crime" as a substantial restriction.

common purpose. Such contribution must be intentional and must either:

  (i) be made with the aim of furthering the criminal activity or criminal purpose of the group, and where such activity or purpose involves the commission of a crime within the jurisdiction of the Tribunal; or

  (ii) have knowledge of the intention of the group to commit the crime;

5. In respect to the crime of genocide, directly and publicly incites others to commit genocide;

6. Attempts to commit such a crime by commencing to execute an action with the intent to commit such crime, but the crime did not occur because of circumstances independent of the person's intentions. However, it is considered a pardonable excuse if a person exerts effort that otherwise prevents the execution or completion of the crime. He shall not be liable for punishment under this Statue for the attempt to commit that crime if that person completely and voluntarily gave up the criminal purpose.

(c) In addition to other grounds of criminal responsibility under this Statute, a military commander or civilian superior shall be criminally responsible for crimes within the jurisdiction of the Tribunal committed by subordinates under his or her effective authority/command and control, where (i) the commander or superior either knew or, owing to the circumstances at the time, should have known that the subordinates were committing or about to commit such crimes; and (ii) the forces commander or superior failed to take all necessary and reasonable measures within his or her power to prevent or repress their commission or to submit the matter to competent authorities for investigation and prosecution.

(d) The official position of any accused person, whether as president, prime minister, member of the cabinet, command, government, or military shall not relieve such person of criminal responsibility nor mitigate punishment. Notwithstanding any prior decree or law, no person is entitled to any immunity to avert responsibility for the crimes stipulated in this Statue.

Article 22 – Grounds for Excluding Criminal Responsibility
A person shall not be criminally responsible if, at the time of that person's conduct:

1. The person suffers from a mental disease or defect that destroys that person's capacity to appreciate the unlawfulness or nature of his or her

conduct, or capacity to control his or her conduct to conform to the requirements of law;

2. The person is in a state of intoxication that destroys that person's capacity to appreciate the unlawfulness or nature of his or her conduct, or capacity to control his or her conduct to conform to the requirements of law, unless the person has become voluntarily intoxicated under such circumstances that the person knew, or disregarded the risk, that, as a result of the intoxication, he or she was likely to engage in conduct constituting a crime within the jurisdiction of the Tribunal;

3. The person acts reasonably to defend himself or herself or another person or, in the case of war crimes, property which is essential for the survival of the person or another person or property which is essential for accomplishing a military mission, against an imminent and unlawful use of force in a manner proportionate to the degree of danger to the person or the other person or property protected. The fact that the person was involved in a defensive operation conducted by forces shall not in itself constitute a ground for excluding criminal responsibility under this subparagraph;

4. The conduct which is alleged to constitute a crime within the jurisdiction of the Tribunal has been caused by duress resulting from a threat of imminent death or of continuing or imminent serious bodily harm against that person or another person, and the person acts necessarily and reasonably to avoid this threat, provided that the person does not intend to cause a greater harm than the one sought to be avoided. Such a threat may either be: (i) Made by other persons; or (ii) Constituted by other circumstances beyond that person's control.

5. The Tribunal shall determine the applicability of the grounds for excluding criminal responsibility provided for in this Statute to the case before it.

Part Two: Legal Burden of Proof
Article 23
The legal burden of proof that will be applied by the Tribunal will be "beyond a reasonable doubt."[33]

---

[33] This provision is intended to address the criticism that the burden of proof to the satisfaction of the court or proof to a moral certainty used in many inquisitorial systems is less rigorous than the burden of proof beyond a reasonable doubt that is used in all international criminal tribunals. While the Syrian domestic criminal procedure is an inquisitorial one, a burden of proof that is unambiguously that of "beyond a reasonable doubt" should be stipulated in the Statute.

Section Seven: Rules of Procedure and Evidence

Article 24

(a) [The Tribunal shall apply the Rules of Procedure stipulated in the attached annex.] [The President of the Tribunal, with the concurrence of a majority of the Tribunal's Investigative, Trial Chamber, and Cassation Chamber judges, shall promulgate the rules of Procedure for the Tribunal. In doing so, the President shall be guided by best practices of international, hybrid, and internationalized tribunals and the need for efficient and fair administration of justice.][34]

(b) Proposals for amendment of the Rules may be made by a Judge, the Chief Prosecutor, the Head of the Defense Office, or the Registrar. The President of the Tribunal, with the concurrence of a two-thirds majority of the Tribunal's Investigative, Trial Chamber, and Cassation Chamber judges, shall adopt amendments to the Rules of Procedure for the Tribunal. An amendment shall, unless otherwise indicated, enter into force immediately. The Registrar shall publish the amendment by appropriate means.

Section Eight: Trial Proceedings

Article 25 The Tribunal shall ensure that trials are fair and expeditious and are conducted in accordance with existing procedures in force, with full respect for the rights of the accused and for the protection of victims and witnesses.

Article 26 – Trials in Absentia[35]

1. The Tribunal may conduct trial proceedings in the absence of the accused, if he or she:

(a) has expressly and in writing waived his or her right to be present;

(b) has not been handed over to the Tribunal by the State authorities concerned;

---

[34] The Rules of Procedure can either be adopted by the Tribunal itself or appended to the Tribunal's Statute. Several of the participating experts favored including draft rules with the Statute, arguing that it would add substantial delay to delegate that responsibility to the judges after they have been appointed.

[35] This provision is modeled on that contained in the Statute of the Special Tribunal for Lebanon. Since there is a high likelihood that high-level regime leaders will flee the country, trials in absentia may be necessary to bring some measure of justice. This section makes clear that the Tribunal reserves the right to prosecute perpetrators whose surrender to the custody of the Tribunal has been blocked by another state in violation of applicable legal obligations.

(c) has absconded or otherwise cannot be found and all reasonable steps have been taken to secure his or her appearance before the Tribunal and to inform him or her of the charges against him or her.

2. When hearings are conducted in the absence of the accused, the Tribunal shall ensure that:
   (a) the accused has been notified, or served with the indictment, or notice has otherwise been given of the indictment through publication in the media or communication to the State of residence or nationality;
   (b) the accused has designated a defense counsel of his or her own choosing or, if the accused cannot afford counsel, by a Public Defender;
   (c) whenever the accused refuses or fails to appoint a defense counsel, a Public Defender is assigned by the Defense Office of the Tribunal with a view to ensuring full representation of the interests and rights of the accused.

3. In case of conviction in absentia, the accused, if he or she had not designated a defense counsel of his or her choosing, shall have the right to be retried in his or her presence before the Extraordinary Tribunal, unless he or she accepts the judgment.

Section Nine: Rights of the Accused

Article 27

(a) All persons shall be equal before the Tribunal.

(b) The accused is presumed innocent until proven guilty before the Tribunal in accordance with this Statute.

(c) The accused shall be entitled to a public hearing pursuant to the provisions of this Statue and the Rules made hereunder.

(d) In the determination of any charge against the accused pursuant to this Statue, the accused shall be entitled to a fair hearing conducted impartially and to the following minimum guarantees:
   1. To be informed promptly of the detail, nature, cause, and content of the charge against him;
   2. To have adequate time and facilities to prepare his defense and to communicate freely with counsel of his own choosing in confidence, provided they are members of the Syrian bar;
   3. To be tried without undue delay;

4. To be tried in his presence, and procure legal counsel of his choosing. If the defendant cannot afford legal counsel, he will be appointed a Public Defender;

5. Through his counsel to call defense witnesses and the right to examine said witnesses and prosecution witnesses and to present evidence that enforces his defense pursuant to this Statue;[36]

6. Not to be compelled to testify against himself or to confess guilt, and to remain silent, without such silence being a consideration in the determination of guilt or innocence.

(e) The accused must be represented by legal counsel who are members of the Syrian Bar and may not represent himself or herself before the Tribunal.

(f) Trials shall be public and open to representatives of foreign States, of the media and of national and international nongovernment organizations unless in exceptional circumstances the Tribunal decides to close the proceedings for good cause in accordance with existing procedures in force where publicity would prejudice the interests of justice.

(g) The Tribunal shall provide for the protection of victims and witnesses. Such protection measures shall include, but not be limited to, the conduct of in camera proceedings and the protection of the victim's identity.

Section Ten: Penalties

Article 28

(a) The penalties that shall be imposed by the Tribunal shall be [imprisonment]/[imprisonment or death].

(b) The penalty for any crimes in this Statute shall be determined by the Trial Chamber taking into account such factors as the gravity of the crime, the individual circumstances of the convicted person and relevant international and foreign precedents.

---

[36] This provision is similar to that of the Iraqi High Tribunal. Other Tribunals allow defendants to represent themselves, but this has led to disruptions, delays, and incitement to violence. The death penalty is one of the most contentious issues. While Syrian participants at the workshops have overwhelmingly favored the inclusion of capital punishment for this Tribunal, international experts have opined during the meetings that the death penalty will mean that the Tribunal will not be able to obtain assistance from the EU and UN, will lead to persistent criticism from human rights organizations, and will prevent countries from extraditing accused persons back to Syria.

(c) In addition to imprisonment, the Trial Chamber may order the confisca-
tion and forfeiture of personal property, money, and real property acquired
unlawfully or by criminal conduct [without prejudice to the rights of bona
fide third parties.]

Section Twelve: Enforcement of Sentences

Article 29

(a) Imprisonment shall be served in prisons in Syria that meet international
standards.
(b) No authority, including the President, may grant a pardon or mitigate the
punishment issued by the Tribunal.

ANNEX
Discussion of Questions Related to an Extraordinary Tribunal for Syrian Atrocity Crimes

This annex summarizes the discussion of twenty-two issues covered during
PILPG-led meetings that brought together Syrian lawyers, jurists, and civil
society leaders with international experts to discuss transitional justice in Syria
when the political situation permits, presumably following a change in government or leadership. This summary provides further context to the pros and
cons of the various options that are set forth in the Draft Tribunal Statute and
covers other issues that may be addressed in the Tribunal's Rules.

1. Should a special tribunal for atrocity crimes be separate and independent
   from the Syrian court system or a special chamber that is part of the Syrian
   courts?
The large majority of participants favored a separate tribunal given the lack of
faith in the fairness and independence of the existing Syrian courts. For the
same reasons, the participants felt the Tribunal should have its own Appeal
Chamber (in Syria this is known as a "Cassation Camber") rather than send
appeals to the existing Syrian Courts of Appeal.
2. Is there sensitivity to the name selected for the special tribunal?
Many of the international tribunals use the word "Special" in their title (eg,
Special Court for Sierra Leone, Special Tribunal for Lebanon). Some participants pointed out that calling a Syrian Tribunal a "Special Tribunal" might be

a bad idea since the regime used "Special Courts" to punish political crimes and enemies of the regime. The term "Extraordinary Tribunal" (as used in Cambodia) was viewed as preferable for this reason. Other participants said that the name selected wouldn't make much difference, and that in Arabic "Special" and "Extraordinary" would likely be translated using the same Arabic word.

3. Where should the Tribunal be located?

Nearly all of the participants felt strongly that the Tribunal should be located in Syria. There was debate about whether it should sit only in Damascus or also elsewhere in Syria.

4. What should be the subject matter jurisdiction of the Tribunal?

The Tribunal could be given jurisdiction over atrocity crimes (war crimes, genocide, crimes against humanity – including arbitrary detention and mis-treatment of prisoners) and/or domestic crimes (murder, corruption, wasting natural resources, the crime of revocation of the Kurds citizenship, etc.). The large majority of participants favored confining the Tribunal's jurisdiction to international crimes because too many people committed the domestic crimes (without authorization from above) for those crimes to be the object of a special Tribunal. Interestingly, some of the participants felt it was import-ant for the Tribunal to be able to prosecute genocide, believing that genocides had been committed in Syria even after the specific definition of the crime was explained to them. Finally, there was discussion of the international crimes exception to the "no crime, no punishment" principle (enshrined in Article 15 of the ICCPR), which provides that international crimes can be prosecuted in domestic courts even if the country did not criminalize such crimes at the time they were committed. This is an important principle for Syria because the Assad Regime ratified the Geneva Conventions and Geno-cide Convention, but did not domesticate those Conventions by enacting domestic laws.

5. What should be the personal jurisdiction of the Tribunal?

The Tribunal would be either a complement or an alternative to the establish-ment of an international tribunal or referral of the situation to the Inter-national Criminal Court. The participants agreed that the Tribunal should not prosecute all perpetrators, but only the leaders and most heinous offend-ers. Lower level offenders would be prosecuted by ordinary domestic courts. Other Tribunals such as the Special Court for Sierra Leone and the Cambo-dian Tribunal limit personal jurisdiction to "Those most responsible" or "Those with greatest responsibility." The former would be about 100 high ranking figures. The latter would be a smaller group, perhaps 50. There was also discussion about whether the gravity threshold for personal jurisdiction should be for the prosecutor to determine in his discretion or for the court to decide, meaning it is an issue that the defense could raise. There was recognition that the Tribunal should be able to prosecute the most serious offenders on all sides of the conflict, not just the Assad Regime. Finally, there was a discussion about how to ensure that the immunities issued by the Assad Regime (including for members of the military) do not apply to the Tribunal. In this regard, it may be necessary for the Tribunal Statute to be passed as a law, not just an Executive Decree.

6. What should be the temporal jurisdiction of the Tribunal?

All participants agreed that the Tribunal should be able to prosecute atrocity crimes since March 15, 2011 (that is, the start of the civil war). Some participants felt that particularly heinous crimes committed during the 1980s should also be prosecutable, while others felt that it would be extremely challenging to do so given the difficulties of proof for crimes committed thirty years in the past.

7. What should the structure of the Tribunal look like?

The participants stressed that the Tribunal should look like something that Syrians are familiar with. There would need to be Investigative judges, three-person trial chambers, and five-person appeals chambers. The participants discussed the need to have alternate judges for lengthy trials to ensure that the trial does not have to be terminated if something happens to a judge. Although Syrian courts have pre-trial chambers, many participants felt that would not be necessary for the Special Tribunal. If the Tribunal were to have three Trial Chambers (nine judges and three alternate judges), one Appeal Chamber (five judges and one alternate judge), and five investigative judges, that would mean a total of twenty-three judges would be needed at a minimum.

8. Should there be international judges?

The participants recognized that having one international judge on each trial and the appeals chamber would enhance the appearance of fairness and could increase the quality of the judicial opinions, but there was no consensus that the Statute should require international judges. Some participants felt that the same outcome could be ensured by having international advisers to each chamber.

9. How should judges be selected?

The participants suggested several mechanisms to enhance the fairness and independence of the judges, such as having the Syrian Bar select them, having a Committee of elders select them, or creating a Judicial Council to select them. The participants opined that Judges who served on the regime's Special Tribunals should not be permitted to apply for a position on this Tribunal, but simply being a judge during the Assad Regime should not disqualify a person.

10. How should judges be replaced?

The greatest criticism of the Iraqi High Tribunal was with respect to a provision that allowed the President of the country to replace a judge for any reason at any time. The President ended up replacing both trial chamber and appeals chamber judges in the middle of the Saddam trial in a way that made it look like the trial was not independent or fair. The participants discussed mechanisms for ensuring that judge removal and replacement does not undermine the Tribunal's independence, including having the decision made by a super-majority of the Cassation Chamber.

11. Should there be dissenting opinions?

Although international tribunals follow the practice of issuing dissenting opinions, that is not done in Syrian courts. Some of the participants felt that it would be better to follow the Syrian practice on this matter, so as not to raise questions about the soundness of the trial chamber judgments. Others felt that dissenting opinions at the Trial Chamber level are useful to framing issues for appeal.

12. What should be the relation between the Tribunal and Truth Commissions?

The participants did not believe people who confess before a Truth Commission should have amnesty or other immunity from prosecution by the Special Tribunal. However, several participants felt that a person's confession before a Truth Commission should not be able to be used as evidence against that person before the Tribunal.

13. What should Victim Participation and Compensation look like?

Like other civil law countries, Syria has a tradition of having "parties civil" (victim's counsel) participate in criminal judicial proceedings as sort of a second prosecutor. Some of the international tribunals (the Cambodia Tribunal, the Lebanon Tribunal, and the ICC) also employ Victims Counsel for this purpose. But these tribunals have struggled with conflicts between Victims Participation and efficient trials in cases where the numbers of victims are in the thousands. Some participants favored a limited form of Victims Participation for the Tribunal. Other participants felt that there should be a separate mechanism for victim reparations outside of the Tribunal, and therefore there would be less need for Victim Participation at the Tribunal.

14. Should the Tribunal allow Trials in Absentia?

The Nuremberg Tribunal allowed trials in absentia. The Yugoslavia Tribunal employed a "Rule 61" proceeding which was like a trial in absentia. The ICC requires the presence of the accused for a case to commence. The Lebanon Tribunal allows trials in absentia. Many of the participants felt that, since there was a likelihood that some of the worst perpetrators would escape to other countries, that the Tribunal should be able to try them in absentia. Consistent with Syrian law, if the person was later brought to custody in Syria, he would be entitled to a new trial.

15. Should the Tribunal allow self-representation?

The several international tribunals allow defendants to represent themselves if they wish to do so, unless such self-representation becomes "persistently disruptive." The Iraqi High Tribunal permitted Saddam and the other defendants to act as co-counsel to their retained lawyers, asking questions during cross examination of witnesses. This is also the practice in ordinary Syrian courts. Many countries do not permit defendants in serious criminal cases to represent themselves, and instead require that they either use retained counsel or public defenders. There was a lengthy discussion about how self-representation can wreck the trial. A suggestion that some favored was that all defendants be represented by Syrian lawyers at all times, and that the defendants not be permitted to cross-examine witnesses themselves, except through written questions posed to the judges.

16. Should the Tribunal allow lawyers from outside Syria?

Saddam Hussein and his co-defendants were represented by a team of celebrity defense counsel, including several former Attorney Generals and Ministers of Justice from several countries. Unfortunately, these high-profile defense counsels were not particularly good trial attorneys and had an agenda other than obtaining an acquittal based on the evidence. The participants felt that only Syrian-certified lawyers should be allowed to appear before the Tribunal. In addition, the participants agreed that there should be a Defense Office, from which public defenders would be appointed to represent defendants that can't afford or do not elect to retain their own counsel. Following the model of the international tribunals, there should also be stand-by public defenders, ready to step in if retained counsel boycotts the trial or is removed for misconduct.

17. How should the Rules of Procedure be written?

The Yugoslavia Tribunal judges wrote the Rules of Procedure for the Tribunal after they were selected. The Rwanda Tribunal and the Special Court for Sierra Leone largely used the Yugoslavia Tribunal Rules with some modifications approved by the judges. The ICC Elements of Crimes and Rules of Procedure were drafted by the Assembly of State Parties rather than the Court's judges. The participants felt that the Special Tribunal would need its own Rules, separate from those of the ordinary Syrian courts, and that such rules should reflect international best practices to the extent practicable, but should also be designed with an expeditious trial in mind. There was no consensus as to whether the judges should be entrusted with drafting the Rules or whether the Rules should be appended to the Statute of the Tribunal. As a sub issue, the participants pointed out that like Lebanon, the Syrian system recognizes a type of co-perpetrator liability similar to Joint Criminal Enterprise liability, which is employed by the ICTY, ICTR, ECCC, and SCSL. As another sub issue, the participants said that the Prosecutor should be able to appeal an acquittal, and that the appeal should not be limited to errors of law. There was debate about whether the Cassation Chamber would in the event of a successful appeal by either the prosecutor or defense issue a revised judgment or be required to remand the case for further proceedings by the Trial Chamber.

18. What burden of proof should the Tribunal employ?

Like most civil law countries, the Syrian courts employ a standard of proof in criminal trials that translates into "proof to the satisfaction of the judges" or "proof to a moral certainty." Human rights NGOs criticized the Iraqi High Tribunal for not explicitly employing the standard of proof employed in common law countries and the international tribunals, namely "proof beyond a reasonable doubt." The participants opined that in effect the two standards are the same, and that it would not be a problem using the words "beyond reasonable doubt" in the Tribunal's Statute or Rules.

19. Should there be a death penalty?

This was one of the most contentious issues of the meetings and workshops. The participants recognized, based on the Iraqi High Tribunal experience, that insisting on the death penalty would mean that the UN, European countries, and others would refuse to assist and/or fund the Tribunal, and that human rights organizations would be highly critical of the Tribunal if it employed the death penalty. On the other hand, many of the participants believed that the Syrian people would insist that high level offenders of atrocity crimes should be subject to the death penalty.

20. Should the Tribunal televise its trials?

There was debate about whether the Tribunal should televise trials gavel to gavel or rather release trial highlights edited by the Tribunal's Outreach Office. All of the international tribunals utilize gavel-to-gavel television (and internet) coverage, with a twenty-minute delay to protect witness identities from being made public. The participants felt the Syrian people would want to see as much of the proceedings as possible, but they recognized that gavel-to-gavel TV coverage can encourage trial participants to act inappropriately. There was no consensus on this issue. The participants did all agree that there should be a Public Outreach Unit and Tribunal Spokesperson to explain the rulings on a day to day basis to the viewing public.

21. How can trial participants be kept safe?

One of the biggest problems in the Saddam trial was that three defense counsel and several witnesses were assassinated during the trial. The participants agreed that security measures must be in place to ensure the safety of witnesses, defense counsel, prosecutors, and judges. At the same time, they felt that the trial should be public, and that judges' identities should not be hidden.

22. How should the Tribunal be funded?

The participants recognized that if the government controls all its funding, the Tribunal will not be able to be independent. One proposal to ensure the Tribunal's independence is for funding to come 50 percent from the Syria government and 50 percent from international donors. Another approach would be to have the expenses and salaries of the Tribunal come from the Syrian government, while the Tribunal could receive additional assistance from voluntary funds contributed by foreign governments and entities wishing to assist the proceedings. Yet another proposal was for the Tribunal to receive funds for its Syrian judges, prosecutors, officers, and staff from the Syrian government, while foreign sources provided funds for international advisers and judges. It was also proposed that the Tribunal's Registrar should have control over allocation and disbursement of the Tribunal's funds, subject to an annual budget approved by either an Oversight Board (chaired by an international appointed by the Secretary-General of the UN with the concurrence of the Syrian government) or the Tribunal's Cassation Chamber.

Index

accountability paradigms. *See* international accountability paradigms

Afghanistan
Taliban government in, 40–41. *See also* al-Qaeda
use of force in, after 9/11 attacks, 40–41

air strikes against Syria, for chemical weapons use. *See* chemical weapons

al-Abadi, Haidar, 32

al-Assad, Bashar, 4–5, 108. *See also* chemical weapons; peace process; Syria conflict
Arab Spring protests under, 5–6
Syria conflict under, 10–11

al-Assad, Hafez, 4

al-Assad, Rifaat, 108

al-Atasi, Nur al-Din, 4

al-Awlaki, Anwar, 48

al-Baghdadi, Abu Bakr, 16, 55

Albright, Madeleine, 73–74, 77

al-Dabi, Mustafa, 135

al-Harithi, Ali Aaed Senyan, 45

al-Jarba, Ahmed, 12

al-Khatib, Moaz, 12

al-Maliki, Nouri, 30

al-Moallem, Walid, 12

al-Qaeda. *See also* Bush Doctrine
ISIS compared to, 31
in Syria conflict, 5–7
International al-Qaeda, 9
US attacks against al-Qaeda, 9
use of force by, 37–38

Alston, Philip, 42–43

Amin, Idi, 65

Andersson, Stefan, 178

Annan, Kofi, 70, 136–137, 142–143. *See also* Geneva Communiqué
Geneva Talks and, 143–144

anticipatory self-defense, 43–49
under customary international law, 36–37

AOGs. *See* armed opposition groups

Arab League, 134–137, 139–142
Action Plan by, 134–135
Cairo Peace Plan, 140–142

Arab Spring
in Syria, 5–6
Syria conflict and, 9–10

armed opposition groups (AOGs), 6

Ashburton (Lord), 36–37

Astana Peace Process, 138–139

asylum, for refugees
through Common European Asylum System, 114–115
EASO, 114–115
through protected status, 113–116

Ban Ki-Moon, 137–138, 142

Belgium, universal jurisdiction in, 103–105

Bellinger, John, 87

bin Laden, Osama, 37–38, 48. *See also* al-Qaeda

Blair, Tony, 67–68, 73–74

Brahimi, Lakhdar, 137

Brexit negotiations, Syrian refugee crisis and, 122–123

Bush, George H. W., 104

Bush, George W., 4–5

Bush Doctrine, self-defense under, 41–48
anticipatory self-defense, 43–49
as Grotian moment, 48–54
historic provenance of, 41–42

213

Bush Doctrine, self-defense under (cont.)
  international application of, justification for,
    47–48
  under *jus ad bellum* principle, 46–47
  under *jus in bello* principle, 46–47
  neutrality under, 42
    Hague Convention rules and, 42–43
  during Obama administration, 45–47
  preventive self-defense, 44–48
    through drone technology use, 45–46
  response to terrorism under, 42–48

Cairo Peace Plan, 140–142
Cambodia Tribunal, 21
  JCE liability, 21–23
Cameron, David, 122
Cassese, Antonio, 73
Castro, Fidel, 104
chemical weapons, air strikes against use of, in
    Syria, 60–63
  Chinese criticism of, 88
  as Grotian moment, 80–86
  incidents of, in Syria 193
  international response to, 83–86
  legal rationale for, articulation of, 80–83
  by multinational forces, 62–63
  during Obama administration, 60–61
  OPCW, 85
  Russia and, 60–61
  during Trump administration, 61–62
  under UN Charter, 71, 77, 80, 88–89
  UN Security Council resolutions against, 81,
    85–86
  United Kingdom and, 59, 81–83
  by United States, 59–61, 80–82
Cheney, Dick, 104
China, on air strikes against Syria, for chemical
    weapons use, 88
Common European Asylum System, 114–115
Congress of the Syrian National Dialogue, 155
continental shelf concept, 21, 26–27
  Law of the Sea Convention, 27
Convention on the Continental Shelf, 2
Convention on the Rights of the Child, 16
Cowles, Willard, 97–100
crimes against humanity. *See* war crimes and
    crimes against humanity
customary international law
  anticipatory self-defense under, 36–37
  continental shelf concept in, 21, 26–27
  development of, 19–21

international factors in, 1–2
  timeframes for, 2
Grotian moments in, 2, 26–28
humanitarian interventions under, 73–74
international constitutional moments, 2
  United Nations Charter, 2
in *Max Planck Encyclopedia of Public
    International Law*, 26
new rules of, 1
Pinkerton rule in, 22

Daesh, 7. *See also* Islamic State of Iraq and
    Syria; Islamic State of Iraq and the
    Levant
  International Daesh, 9
De Jure Belli ac Pacis (Grotius), 2, 173
Declaration on Outer Space (UNGA), 27
Demjanjuk, John, 99–100
drone technology, use of force through, 45–46
Dunford, Joseph, 62–63

EASO. *See* European Asylum Support Office
East Timor, humanitarian interventions in, 64
Eichmann, Adolph, 99–100
Elaraby, Nabil, 142
EU. *See* European Union
European Asylum Support Office (EASO),
    114–115
European Court of Human Rights, 25
European Union (EU)
  asylum structures in
    Common European Asylum System,
      114–115
    under Dublin Regulation, 115
    EASO, 114–115
  migration crisis in, after Syria conflict,
    114–125
  in Syria conflict, 9
Evans, Gareth, 78

Falk, Richard, 3
Fallon, Michael, 61
Fleischer, Ari, 41
France
  refugees in, from Syria conflict, 116–117
  in Syria, 4
Free Syrian Army (FSA), 7

GCM. *See* Global Compact for Safe, Orderly
    and Regular Migration
GCR. *See* Global Compact on Refugees

Geneva Communiqué, 139–170. *See also*
   peace process
Geneva Talks, in Syrian peace process, 143–144
German War Crimes Unit, 106–108
Germany
   refugees in, from Syria conflict, 91, 118–121
      universal jurisdiction applications, 120–121
   universal jurisdiction in, 106–108
      refugee cases under, 120–121
Global Compact for Safe, Orderly and Regular
   Migration (GCM), 126–127
Global Compact on Refugees (GCR), 126–128
"global enforcer" approach, to universal
   jurisdiction, 97, 103–108
   in Belgium, 103–105
   German War Crimes Unit, 106–108
   revival of, 106–108
   in Spain, 105–106
Goldstone, Richard, 69
Grandi, Filippo, 129
Grotian moments, 55–57, 173
   air strikes against Syria as, for chemical
      weapons use, 80–86
   Bush Doctrine as, 48–54
   continental shelf concept, 21, 26–27
   in customary international law, 2, 26–28
   as destabilizing forces, 179
   "instant custom" as distinct from, 178–179
   Kosovo crisis, 72–78
   9/11 attacks as, 48–54
   Nuremberg trials, 21–26
      European Court of Human Rights and, 25
      international law influenced by, 23
      UNGA and, 24, 26–28
   outer space law, formation of, 27
   Syrian migration crisis as, 130–132
      through institutional structures,
         development of, 130–131
      through international compacts, 131–132.
         See also Global Compact for Safe,
         Orderly and Regular Migration; Global
         Compact on Refugees
   theoretical approach to, analysis of, 178
   Yugoslavia Tribunal, 27–28
Grotius, Hugo, 2, 173
Guterres, Antonio, 128

Hague Convention, neutrality rules of, 42–43
Haley, Nikki, 61
Hariri, Rafiq, 4–5
Hassan, Jamil, 91, 107–108

Hezbollah, 8
Hijab, Riad, 11
Holder, Eric, 46–47
Hollande, François, 116
human rights law, civilian murder under, 17
humanitarian interventions
   authorization of, 71–72
   under customary international law, 73–74
   in East Timor, 64
   historical development of, 63–80
      Peace of Westphalia as influence on, 63–64
      UN Security Council resolutions in, 64–65
   just war theory principles and, 71
   in Kosovo, 64
      as Grotian moment, 72–78
      international reaction to, 72–78
      by NATO, 65–69
      Operation Allied Force, 66–69
      Russian response to, 68–69
      UN Security Council resolutions on, 66–67
   in Libya, 64
   under responsibility to protect doctrine,
      70–72, 75–78
      ICISS report and, 70–73
      UN Security Council authorization and,
         77–78
   in Rwanda, 64
   in Somalia, 64
   in South Africa, 64
   in Southern Rhodesia, 64
   through UN Security Council resolutions
      historical record for, 64–65
      for Kosovo crisis, 66–67
      responsibility to protect doctrine and,
         77–78
Hussein, Saddam, 30–31, 65, 75, 104

IAEA. *See* International Atomic Energy Agency
Ibn al Khattab, Omar, 47
ICC. *See* International Criminal Court
ICISS report. *See* International Commission
   on Intervention and State Sovereignty
   Report
ICJ. *See* International Court of Justice
IIIM. *See* International, Impartial and
   Independent Mechanism to Assist in
   the Investigation and Prosecution of
   Those Responsible for the Most
   Serious Crimes under International
   Law Committed in the Syrian Arab
   Republic

"instant custom," Grotian moment as distinct from, 178–179
Inter-American Treaty of Reciprocal Resistance, 39
International, Impartial and Independent Mechanism to Assist in the Investigation and Prosecution of Those Responsible for the Most Serious Crimes under International Law Committed in the Syrian Arab Republic (IIIM), 91–96
  authority of, 93–96
  establishment of, 92–93
  purpose of, 96
  in Syrian peace process, 170
  UNGA and, 92–93
international accountability paradigms.
    See also universal jurisdiction
  during civil war in Syria, 90–91
  IIIM, 91–96
    authority of, 93–96
    establishment of, 92–93
    purpose of, 96
    in Syrian peace process, 170
    UNGA and, 92–93
International al-Qaeda, 9
International Atomic Energy Agency (IAEA), 4–5
International Commission on Intervention and State Sovereignty (ICISS) Report, 70–73
International Committee of the Red Cross, 16–17, 47
international constitutional moments, 2
  United Nations Charter as, 2
International Court of Justice (ICJ), use of force rulings by, 35–36, 50–51
International Covenant on Civil and Political Rights (ICCPR), 16
International Criminal Court (ICC), Syria conflict in, 91–92
international human rights law
  international humanitarian law compared to, 17
  principle of proportionality in, 17
international humanitarian law
  codification of, 16
  international human rights law compared to, 17
  non-derogable rights under, 17–18
  principle of proportionality in, 17

Syria conflict under, 16–18
after Yugoslavia Tribunal, 27–28
international law. *See also* customary international law
  in *Max Planck Encyclopedia of Public International Law*, 26
  nulem crimin sine lege principle, 22–23
  Nuremberg trials as influence on, 23
  use of force under, for self-defense against non-state actors, 32, 34–35, 57–58
International Syria Support Group (ISSG), 137–138, 148–149
international tribunals. *See specific tribunals*
Iran, in Syria conflict, 8
Iraq
  ISIS in, 31
  use of force in, as self-defense against non-state actors, 29–30
ISIL. *See* Islamic State of Iraq and the Levant
Islamic State of Iraq and Syria (ISIS)
  al-Qaeda compared to, 31
  development of, 30
  Hussein and, 30–31
  international war on
    historical context for, 30–33
    US involvement in, 31–33
  in Iraq, 31
  in Syria conflict, 6–7, 30–31
  UN Security Council Resolution 2249 and, 54–55
  use of force against, 29, 54–55, 78–85
Islamic State of Iraq and the Levant (ISIL)
  in Syria conflict, 6–7
  US use of force against, 33–34
Israel, use of force by, as self-defense against non-state actors, 50
ISSG. *See* International Syria Support Group

joint criminal enterprise (JCE) liability, 21–23
Jordan, in Syria conflict, 8
jus ad bellum (lawfulness of resort to force) principles, 46–47, 71
jus in bello (lawfulness of means) principles, 46–47
  principle of proportionality, 46–47
just war theory, 71

Koh, Harold, 45–47, 87–88
Koplow, David, 55
Kosovo crisis, as humanitarian intervention, 64
 as Grotian moment, 72–78
 international reaction to, 72–78
 by NATO, 65–69
 Operation Allied Force, 66–69
 Russian response to, 68–69
 UN Security Council resolutions on, 66–67

Lavrov, Sergei, 62
Law and the Indo-China War (Moore), 3
Law of the Sea Convention, 27
Law on Foreigners and International Protection, Turkey (2013), 124
lawfulness of means principle. *See jus in bello* principle
lawfulness of resort to force principle. *See jus ad bellum* principle
Learmont, Jams, 33
Libya, humanitarian interventions in, 64

McDougal, Myers, 19
McKenzie, Kenneth, 62–63
Mahmoud, Abdel Salam, 108
Maleh, Haitham, 12
Mamluk, Ali, 108
Marchi-Uhel, Catherine, 96
Martinez, Jenny, 2
Matheson, Michael, 74
Max Planck Encyclopedia of Public International Law, 26
Mendelson, Maurice, 20–21
migrants
 definition of, 111, 128
 refugees compared to, 111
 from Syria conflict
  in France, 116–117
  in Germany, 91, 118–121
  throughout Middle East region, 119
  in Turkey, 123–125
  in UK, 121–123
  in United States, 125–126
migration crisis, after Syria conflict, 112–126
 in EU nations, 114–125. *See also specific nations*
 as Grotian moment, 130–132
  through institutional structures, development of, 130–131
  through international compacts, 131–132

  through universal jurisdiction, application of, 131
 international responses to, 126–129. *See also* refugees
  GCM, 126–129
  GCR, 126–128
 national responses to, 113–126. *See also* refugees
Milošević, Slobodan, 66
Mistura, Staffan de, 137–139, 154–157
Moore, John Morton, 3
Muslim Brotherhood, 4

Nanda, Ved, 73
NATO. *See* North Atlantic Treaty Organization
neutrality, under Bush Doctrine, 42
 Hague Convention rules and, 42–43
9/11 attacks, in United States. *See also* Bush Doctrine
 as Grotian moment, 48–54
 NATO response to, 39
 OAS response to, 39
 use of force as response to
  after attacks, as self-defense against non-state actors, 37–54
  before attacks, 34–37
"no safe haven" approach, to universal jurisdiction, 97
non-derogable rights, under international humanitarian law, 17–18, *see also jus cogens norm*,
North Atlantic Treaty Organization (NATO), 39
 Kosovo crisis and, 65–69
nulem crimin sine lege principle, 22–23
Nuremberg and Vietnam (Taylor), 3
Nuremberg trials, 21–26
 European Court of Human Rights and, 25
 international law influenced by, 23
 UNGA and, 24, 97–101

OAS. *See* Organization of American States
Obama, Barack, 13
 air strikes against Syria, for chemical weapons use, 60–61
 Bush Doctrine during, 45–47
OPCW. *See* Organization of the Prohibition of Chemical Weapons
Operation Allied Force, 66–69
Operation Olive Branch, 8, 14

Orbán, Viktor, 115
Organization of American States (OAS), 39
Organization of the Prohibition of Chemical
    Weapons (OPCW), 85
outer space law, formation of, 27

Panetta, Leon, 45
Peace of Westphalia, 2
    humanitarian interventions as influence on,
        63–64
peace process, for Syrian conflict, 134–139
    Arab League in, 134–137, 139–142
        Action Plan by, 134–135
        Cairo Peace Plan, 140–142
    Astana Peace Process and, 138–139
    Congress of the Syrian National Dialogue
        and, 155
    Geneva Talks in, 143–144
    Geneva I 136–137
    Geneva II 137
    IIIM in, 170
    ISSG in, 137–138, 148–149
    legal framework for, 139–170. *See also*
        specific topics
        challenges to, 153–157
        contracting of, 166–170
        domestic law in conflict with, 134–164
        establishment of, 139–146
        evolution of, 146–153
        implementation of, 157–164
        security of, 146–153
    mutual consent in, 144–145
    Sochi Final Statement in, 155–156
    Syrian Constitution (2012), development of,
        134–164
        Article 114, 164–165
        Article 115, 165
        Article 144, 164–165
        Article 150, 164
    Syrian opposition in, 155–157, 167
        on domestic accountability for atrocity
            crimes, 168
        TGB and, 157–164
    UN Security Council resolutions, 146–153,
        171–172
        Resolution 2042, 143
        Resolution 2118, 147–148, 168–169
        Resolution 2254, 148–153, 155–156, 160, 169
Pedersen, Geir, 139, 157
People's Protection Units (YPG), 7
Permanent Court of International Justice, 83–84

Pershing, John, 53
Pinochet, Augusto, 105
piracy, under universal jurisdiction, 97–99
    barbarism as element of, 98
    in *United States v. Smith*, 98–99
Powell, Colin, 104
preventive self-defense, 44–48
    through drone technology use, 45–46
Princeton Principles, for universal jurisdiction,
    102–103
proportionality, principle of, 17

Qatar, in Syria conflict, 8

Rafsanjani, Hashemi, 104
Refugee Convention (1951), 111–112, 128
refugees
    definition of, 111, 128
    migrants compared to, 111
    protected status of, 111–112
        as asylum seekers, 113–116
            through Common European Asylum
                System, 114–115
            under Dublin Regulation, 115
            through EASO, 114–115
    from Syria conflict, 5
        demographics of, 113–114
        in France, 116–117
        in Germany, 91, 118–121
        international responses to, 126–129
        throughout Middle East region, 119
        national responses to, 113–126. *See also*
            specific nations
        in Turkey, 123–125
        in UK, 121–123
        in United States, 125–126
responsibility to protect doctrine, 70–72, 75–78
    ICISS report and, 70–73
    UN Security Council authorization and, 77–78
Reyes, Raul, 30, 48
Robertson, George, 67
Rumsfeld, Donald, 120–121
Russia
    on air strikes against Syria, response to, 60–61
    Kosovo crisis and, response to, 68–69
    in Syria conflict, 6, 8
        as military intervention, 10
Rwanda, humanitarian interventions in, 64

Sabra, George, 12
Saudi Arabia, in Syria conflict, 8

Scharf, Michael, 21–22
Schwarzkopf, Norman, 104
SDF. *See* Syrian Democratic Forces
self-defense. *See* use of force
Sharon, Ariel, 104
Simma, Bruno, 68
Sochi Final Statement, in peace process, 155–156
Socialist Baath Party, 4
Soderberg, Nancy, 77–78
Somalia, humanitarian interventions in, 64
South Africa, humanitarian interventions in, 64
Southern Rhodesia, humanitarian
  interventions in, 64
Spain, universal jurisdiction in, 105–106
Special Tribunal for Lebanon (STL), 49–50
Statute of the International Criminal Court
  (1998), 28
STL. *See* Special Tribunal for Lebanon
Syria. *See also* chemical weapons; peace process
  Arab Spring protests in, 5–6
  civil war in, 10
    international accountability paradigms
      during, 90–91
    Constitution of 2012, 134–164
      Article 114, 164–165
      Article 115, 165
      Article 144, 164–165
      Article 150, 164
    under French rule, 4
    independence protests in, 4–5
    Muslim Brotherhood, 4
    Ottoman rule of, 4
    Socialist Baath Party in, 4
    in United Arab Republic, 4
    use of force in, as self-defense against non-
      state actors
      by Turkey, 57–58
      by United States, 29–30, 51–54
Syria conflict. *See also* al-Assad, Bashar;
    refugees; *specific topics*
  al-Qaeda in, 5–7
    International al-Qaeda, 9
    US attacks against, 25.60AOGs, 6
  Daesh, 7. *See also* Islamic State of Iraq and
    Syria; Islamic State of Iraq and the
    Levant
    International Daesh, 9
  domestic actors in, 7
    al-Qaeda in, 5–7
    FSA, 7, 16–17
    ISIS/ISIL as, 6–7, 30–31

SDF, 7
YPG, 7
foreign paramilitary organizations in, 8–9
  Hezbollah, 8
government involvement in, 7
in International Criminal Court, 91–92
under international humanitarian law, 16–18
local parties in, 7
migration as result of. *See* migration crisis;
  refugees
migration crisis after, 112–126
non-state (foreign) actors in, 5–6, 8–9
  EU states, 9
  Iran, 8
  Jordan, 8
  Qatar, 8
  Russia, 6, 8
  Saudi Arabia, 8
  Turkey, 8
  United States, 9
  UK, 9
origins of, 4–7
peace process for, 6
refugees as result of. *See* migration crisis;
  refugees
regional instability as result of, 6–7
Russian involvement in, 6, 8
  as military intervention, 10
timeline for, 9–16
  al-Assad, B., and, 10–11
  Arab Spring protests, 9–10
  civil war in, 10
  rise and expansion of ISIS, 10
  Russian military intervention, 10
Turkey in, 8
  in Operation Olive Branch, 8, 14
Syrian Constitution (2012), 134–164
  Article 114, 164–165
  Article 115, 165
  Article 144, 164–165
  Article 150, 164
Syrian Democratic Forces (SDF), 7
Syrian National Council, 12
Syrian opposition, in peace process, 155–157,
    167
  on domestic accountability for atrocity
    crimes, 168
  TGB and, 157–164

Taliban government, in Afghanistan, 40–41
Taylor, Telford, 3

terrorism
  Bush Doctrine as response to, 42–48
  international definitions of, 34–49
  after Special Tribunal for Lebanon (STL),
    49–50
TGB. *See* transitional governing body
Torture Convention, 16, 18
  universal jurisdiction under, 105–106
Trahan, Jennifer, 95
transitional governing body (TGB), in Syria,
  157–164
Trilling, Daniel, 114
Truman, Harry, 21, 26–27
Truman Proclamation, 21, 26–27. *See also*
  continental shelf concept
Trump, Donald, 16
  air strikes against Syria, for chemical
    weapons use, 61–62
  refugee policy under, 125–126
Turk, Volker, 128
Turkey
  refugees in, from Syria conflict, 123–125
    institutional structural development for, 124
    under Law on Foreigners and
      International Protection, 124
    protection mechanisms for, 124
  in Syria conflict, 8
    Operation Olive Branch, 8, 14
  use of force by, into Syria, 57–58

UK. *See* United Kingdom
UN. *See* United Nations
UN Charter. *See* United Nations
UN Security Council. *See* United Nations
UNGA. *See* United Nations
United Arab Republic, 4
United Kingdom (UK)
  air strikes against Syria by, for chemical
    weapons use, 59, 81–83
  refugees in, from Syria conflict, 121–123
    Brexit negotiations influenced by, 122–123
  in Syria conflict, military intervention by, 9
United Nations (UN)
  General Assembly (UNGA)
    Declaration on Outer Space, 27
    Nuremberg trials affirmed by, 24, 97–101
  Security Council resolutions. *See also* peace
    process
    against chemical weapons use, in Syria,
      81, 85–86

    for humanitarian interventions, 64–67,
      77–78
  in Syrian peace process. *See* peace process
  UN Charter, 2
    air strikes against Syria under, 71, 77, 80,
      88–89
United States (US). *See also* Bush Doctrine;
  9/11 attacks
  air strikes against Syria by, for chemical
    weapons use, 59–61, 80–82
  ISIS and, military intervention against,
    31–33
  refugees in, from Syria conflict, 125–126
    during Trump administration, 125–126
  in Syria conflict, 9
  use of force by, as self-defense against non-
    state actors, 34
    in Iraq, 29–30
    against ISIL, 33–34
    in Syria, 29–30, 51–54
United States v. Smith, 98–99
universal jurisdiction, 96–108. *See also* war
  crimes and crimes against humanity
  abuse of, 106
  definition and scope of, 96–103
  "global enforcer" approach, 97, 103–108
    in Belgium, 103–105
    German War Crimes Unit, 106–108
    revival of, 106–108
    in Spain, 105–106
  gravity of crimes in, 97
  "no safe haven" approach, 97
  piracy crimes under, 97–99
    barbarism as element of, 98
    in *United States v. Smith*, 98–99
  place of crimes in, 97
  Princeton Principles for, 102–103
  under Torture Convention, 105–106
US. *See* United States
use of force, in self-defense against non-state
  actors, 33–54
  humanitarian abuses in, 65
  International Court of Justice rulings on,
    35–36, 50–51
  under international law, 32, 34–35, 57–58
  in Iraq, 29–30
  against ISIS and, 29, 54–55, 78–85. *See also*
    Syria
  by Israel, rejection of, 50
  on land, 52–53

after 9/11 attacks, 37–48. *See also* Bush
    Doctrine
  in Afghanistan, 40–41
  Grotian moment as result of, 48–54
  international response to, 39–41
  by al-Qaeda, 37–38
before 9/11 attacks, 34–37
  anticipatory self-defense, under customary
    international law, 36–37
  state attribution, 35–36
in Syria
  by Turkey, 57–58
  by United States, 29–30, 51–54
for terrorism
  international definitions of, 34–49
  after Special Tribunal for Lebanon
    (STL), 49–50
  by Turkey, into Syria, 57–58
under UN Charter, 30, 34–35
  early examples of, 37
US arguments for, 34. *See also* Bush
    Doctrine; 9/11 attacks
  in Iraq, 29–30
  against ISIL, 33–34
  in Syria, 29–30, 51–54

Van Schaack, Beth, 107–108
The Vietnam War and International Law
  (Falk), 3
Villa, Francisco (Pancho), 37, 53

war crimes and crimes against humanity
  by Demjanjuk, 99–100
  by Eichmann, 99–100
  international application of, 101–102
  Nuremberg trials for, 21–26
    European Court of Human Rights and, 25
    international law influenced by, 23
    UNGA and, 24, 97–101
    during World War II, 99–101. *See also*
      Demjanjuk, John; Eichmann, Adolph
Webster, Daniel, 36–37
Weller, Mark, 54
Wenaweser, Christian, 92–93
Whiting, Alex, 92

Yaron, Amos, 104
YPG. *See* People's Protection Units
Yugoslavia Tribunal, 27–28
Yuridia, Abuldaye, 104
Yazidis 136–137

CPSIA information can be obtained
at www.ICGtesting.com
Printed in the USA
LVHW031652160320
650195LV00001B/1